SOMETHING *from* NOTHING

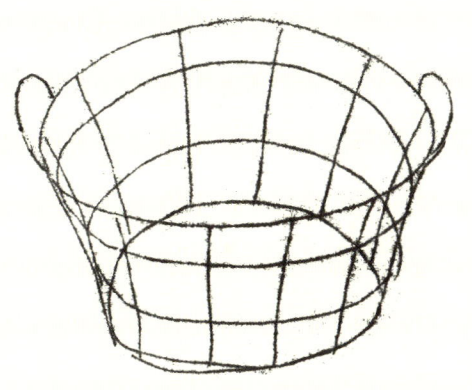

SOMETHING *from* NOTHING

by ALISON ROMAN

Photographs by
CHRIS BERNABEO

Something from Nothing first published by
CLARKSON POTTER/PUBLISHERS

This edition published in 2025 by
Quadrille, Penguin Random House UK,
One Embassy Gardens, 8 Viaduct
Gardens, London SW11 7BW

Quadrille Publishing Limited is part of the Penguin Random House group of companies whose addresses can be found at global.penguinrandomhouse.com

Copyright © 2025 by Alison Roman
Photography © 2025 by Chris Bernabeo
Artwork © 2025 by Rosie McGuinness

Alison Roman has asserted her right to be identified as the author of this Work in accordance with the Copyright, Designs and Patents Act 1988

No part of this book may be used or reproduced in any manner for the purpose of training artificial intelligence technologies or systems. In accordance with Article 4(3) of the DSM Directive 2019/790, Penguin Random House expressly reserves this work from the text and data mining exception.

Published by Quadrille in 2025
www.penguin.co.uk

A CIP catalogue record for this book is available from the British Library

ISBN 9781837834891

Colour reproduction by F1

printed in Estonia by Print Best OÜ

10 9 8 7 6 5 4 3 2

The authorised representative in the EU for product safety and compliance is Penguin Random House Ireland, Morrison Chambers, 32 Nassau Street, Dublin D02 YH68

Penguin Random House is committed to a sustainable future for our business, our readers and our planet. This book is made from Forest Stewardship Council® certified paper.

For Charlie, inside and out

RECIPES

SNACKS
& THINGS TO START WITH

- 19 Artichoke Hearts with Anchovies & Parmesan
- 21 Green Bagna Cauda
- 23 Lupin Beans with Garlic & Parsley
- 27 Lentil Dip with Toasted Garlic & Crispy Herbs
- 28 Labneh with Caramelised Harissa
- 30 Herbed Artichoke Dip
- 36 Snail Butter
- 37 Calabrian Chilli Butter
- 37 Anchovy Butter
- 38 Cracked Spiced Olives
- 40 Spanish Tortilla & Friends
- 45 Aioli for Everything

SOUPS & STEWS

- 51 Chicken Broth, the Long Way
- 52 Chicken Noodle Soup with Lots of Lemon
- 54 Ginger & Greens Noodle Soup
- 57 Chicken Soup for Summer Colds
- 60 Kimchi-Tomato Soup with Rice & a Soft Egg
- 62 Very Classic Split Pea Soup
- 65 Dilly Bean Stew with Cabbage & Frizzled Onions
- 67 Pork Noodle Soup with Toasted Garlic & Greens
- 68 Summer Vegetable Soup with Hominy & Lime
- 73 Potato Leek Soup with Dark Leafy Greens
- 75 Spiced Squash & Lentil Soup with Fried Shallots
- 77 Matzo Ball Soup
- 80 Spicy Pork Soup with Pasta & Parmesan
- 82 Buttered Tomato Soup with Lentils & Fennel
- 84 Creamy Clam Chowder with Celery
- 87 Cold Borscht
- 88 Golden Mushroom Soup with Orzo & a Pat of Butter

VEGETABLES
& HOW TO MAKE THEM TASTE EVEN BETTER

- 95 Deeply Roasted Fennel & Capers
- 96 Wine-Braised Romano Beans with Anchovy
- 98 Long-Cooked Potatoes, Garlic & Lemon
- 101 Spiced, Butter-Roasted Carrots with Walnuts
- 104 Forever-Roasted Squash with Browned Butter Dates
- 106 Vinegar-Braised Greens
- 109 Vinegar'd Wax Beans with Dill & Cheddar
- 113 Perfect Oil-Roasted Tomatoes
- 120 Salty Sungolds with Sesame & Soy
- 120 Spicy Tomatoes with Pickled Peppers & Onions
- 121 Savoury Tomatoes with Toasted Garlic & Fried Capers
- 125 Crunchy Green Beans Dressed in Chilli Oil
- 127 Quick Chilli Oil
- 129 Barely Cooked Cime Di Rapa with Calabrian Chilli & Garlic
- 131 Beetroot with Celery, Apple & Tahini
- 132 Picnic Salad with Cucumbers & Fennel
- 134 Salty Celery Salad with Anchovy
- 137 Fruit Salad with Chives & Sticky Walnuts
- 138 Tuna Salad Salad
- 140 Browned Butter Potato Salad
- 142 Jammy Egg Salad
- 148 Leafy, Herby Salad with Sherry Vinegar
- 149 An Excellent Mustard Dressing
- 150 A Caesar for All Occasions

BEANS & GRAINS

- 158 Long-Cooked Brothy Chickpeas with Shallot & Chilli
- 160 Caramelised Beans with Tomato & Cabbage
- 162 Chilli Beans
- 165 Spiced Chickpeas & Greens
- 166 Almost Cassoulet
- 173 Tiny White Beans in Green Bagna Cauda
- 175 Crispy Baked Beans with Mushrooms & Parmesan
- 177 French Onion Beans & Greens
- 178 A Chilli, Because You Asked
- 180 Olive Oil–Fried Lentils with Harissa & Herbs
- 184 Spelt with Mushrooms, Frizzled Leeks & Sour Cream
- 187 Spelt & Pea Salad with Preserved Lemon
- 189 Buttered Polenta with Fresh Corn
- 191 Toasted Rice Pilaf with Crushed Walnuts & Dates

PASTAS & NOODLES

- 196 Walnut Pesto Pasta
- 199 Lemon Pepper Pasta with Browned Butter
- 202 Saucy Roasted Aubergine Pasta
- 204 Creamy Cauliflower Pasta with Pecorino Breadcrumbs
- 208 Winter Squash Pasta with Chilli & Toasted Garlic
- 210 Carbonara for Two
- 213 Caramelised Shallot Pasta
- 216 Secret Ingredient Pasta Salad
- 218 Pasta Salad with Courgette, Lemon & Walnuts
- 221 Brothy Vinegar Noodles with Mushrooms & Sesame
- 225 Chicken Noodle Salad with Spicy Lime Dressing
- 226 Shrimp Scampi
- 228 Linguine & Clams with Spicy Breadcrumbs
- 232 Snail Butter Pasta (Snails Optional)
- 237 A Very Good Tomato Sauce
- 239 Baked (But Not Stuffed) Shells
- 240 A Little Aubergine Parm
- 244 Weeknight Lamb Ragù with Anchovy
- 246 Bolognese with Fennel

MEATS & FISHES

- 256 Olive Oil-Roasted Chicken & Chickpeas
- 259 Spicy Vinegar Chicken Over Tomatoes
- 261 Braised Chicken Piccata
- 262 Crisp, Hot Roast Chicken with Leeks
- 266 Crushed-Olive Chicken with Turmeric
- 269 Saucy, Wine-Roasted Chicken with Mushrooms
- 270 Chicken Pot Pie (A Real Classic)
- 276 Overnight Lamb & Potatoes in White Wine
- 278 Spicy Braised Short Ribs with Garlic & Lemon
- 283 Braised Pork Stew with Cabbage, Olives & Lemon
- 284 Tangy Braised Brisket with Shallots & Horseradish
- 288 Goodbye Meatballs
- 293 Steak Like Tartare
- 296 Crispy Schnitzel with Browned Butter Radishes
- 299 Crunchy Chicken Parmesan with Burst Tomatoes
- 301 Crispy Fish with Dill & Fried Capers
- 303 Slow-Roasted Salmon with Preserved Lemon & Sesame
- 304 A Skillet of Prawns in Anchovy Butter (with a Baguette)
- 307 Slow-Cooked Tuna with White Beans & Aioli
- 308 Tomato-Poached Fish with Crispy Chilli Oil

HELLO, AGAIN

Someone very close to me texted me out of the blue one day: 'I just made your olive chicken. Every time I make your recipes, I'm amazed how I could make something so good from basically nothing.' Chicken and a jar of Castelvetrano olives is not *nothing*, but I know what she was trying to say. Even after all these years, I still struggle to succinctly describe my cooking style, but 'something from nothing' is as close as I've come.

I'm not a lazy cook, really, but I am obsessed with being productive and efficient, which makes me pretty frugal with both my ingredients and my time. I don't soak my beans, and I enjoy doing in two steps what's usually done in five. I save the scraps of my vegetables to make soup to avoid going shopping, and one of my favourite snacks on planet Earth is the softened, chicken fat–soaked celery leftover in the pot from making broth, because why waste perfectly good celery? Both as a cook and an eater, I'm turned off by needless complications, and as particular and fussy as I can be, my food remains quite the opposite.

Since my last book, I met, fell in love with, got married to and had a baby with a wonderful man. In his vows, he told me that his favourite nights at home were when we didn't have time to go grocery shopping and I made something out of what we had in the pantry, because it was in those thrown-together moments that he got to see how my imagination worked. I cried very hard, of course – never had I considered that someone might interpret my affinity for practicality as creativity. Gorgeous meals come together easily with perfect produce and well-marbled meats, but nothing gives me more pleasure than rooting around the cans and tins of a dimly-lit kitchen and emerging with the best tomato soup of my life.

Coincidentally, I wrote and shot this book in tandem with opening a tiny pantry store in upstate New York called First Bloom. It's a longtime dream fully realised: a grocery store of my very own, a physical manifestation of all my favourite things about cooking, shelves stocked with tins of anchovies, both expensive and cheap pasta, the nice-looking beans from California and, in the centre of the room, a large wooden table of rotating seasonal produce (plus lemons). Everything you need to make a perfect meal; a room full of the practical things that make me happiest in the world. (This is less a plug for the store and more just to illustrate how dedicated I am to the pantry-staple lifestyle.)

I would be remiss if I didn't mention that I was also pregnant through much of the writing and making of this book. (It was a big year.) I didn't plan it that way, but I like the idea that my son, Charlie, will one day be able to cook from this book, knowing it's what fuelled me while he grew in my belly – the foods I had the energy to make (lots of brothy soups) and the ingredients I craved (capers).

I feel both proud of and nervous to admit that this book could potentially be described as . . . adult. Mature, even. There's a quiet confidence in recipes that have so few ingredients, take so little time and yet promise so much. What the recipes here lack in bells and whistles, they make up for in soul and unimpeachable deliciousness. Some are old classics I've reinterpreted (I add garlic to my carbonara and there's no cheese in my Caesar dressing), some are recipes that are classic to me (Caramelised Shallot Pasta, page 213, is undeniably more famous than I am), some aren't classic at all (yet!) and all are easy to make with the help of a well-stocked pantry. Throughout, the complexity of the recipes stays low and the ingredient lists are minimal, all the while encouraging you to go off script, to adapt and make them your own. An extended love letter to simplicity, this book is about finding joy and satisfaction in the tiny miracles of cooking – all of the deliciousness that comes from making something from nothing.

SNACKS *and* THINGS *to start with*

Before you dive into this chapter, know that I have skipped over some of the more obvious snacks one might make from the contents of their pantry. I know you know how to pop open a tin of fish, slice some cured meats, put out the nice cheese to pair with your crackers and fancy almonds and a pickled thing or two, and have a great time. As far as I'm concerned, that's a perfect, unimpeachable snack platter.

But sometimes we need (or simply want) more for those predinner, in-between-meal times: maybe a dip made from tinned vegetables, another use for all those anchovies, or a wedge of Spanish tortilla – tender potatoes and soft onions held together with eggs and olive oil to eat with spoonfuls of aioli. You'll find all those in the pages that follow, as well as some non-recipes, simple reminders of what great snacks can be made using little more than the contents of your pantry and perhaps one splurge item: high-low pantry, let's call it. Grocery-store radishes and the nice, salted butter. Expensive anchovies and a jar of pickled peppers. Potato chips and caviar. Humble little pantry ingredients waiting to be brought to life with a little special something, reminding you why you keep them around in the first place.

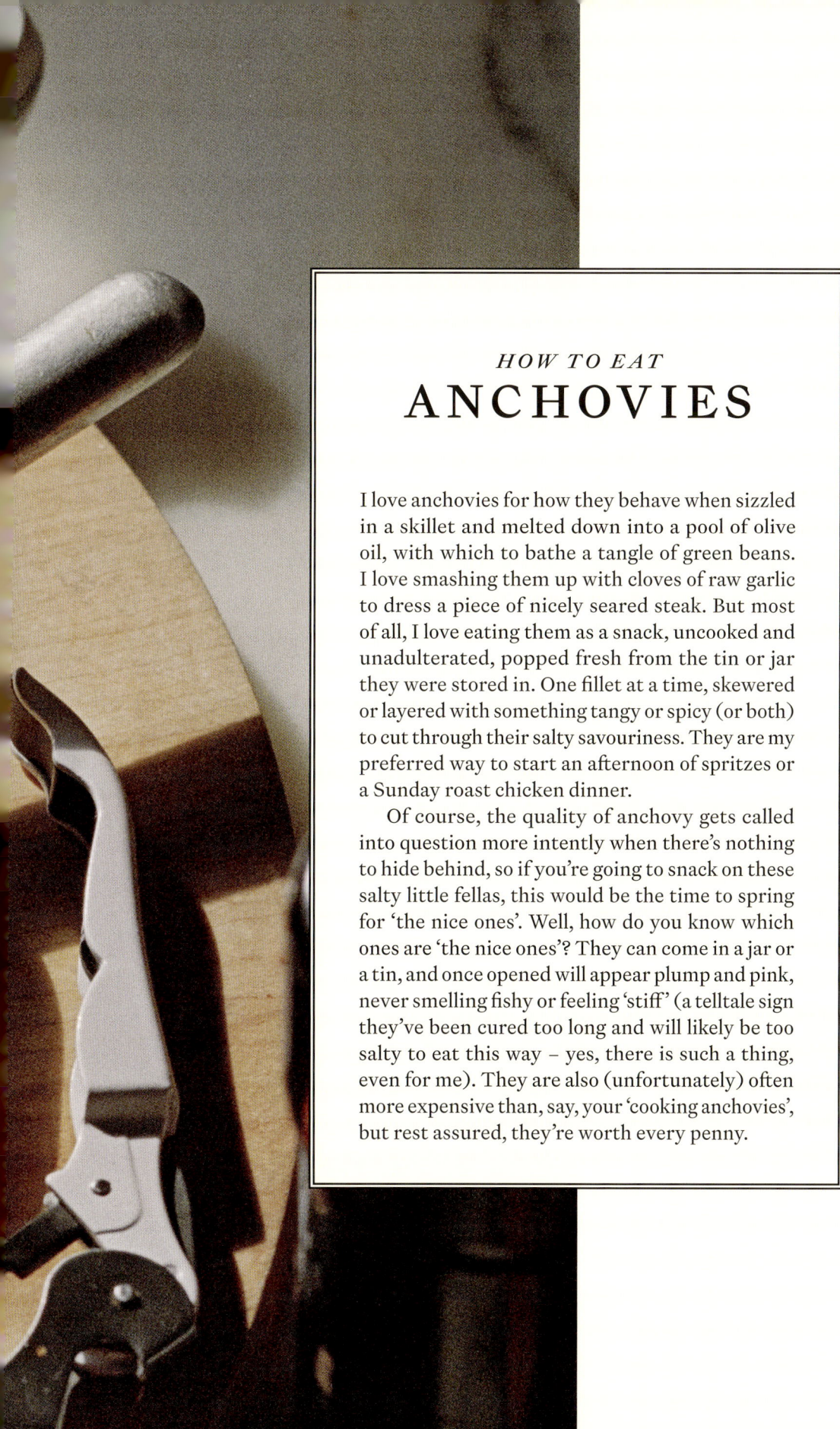

HOW TO EAT
ANCHOVIES

I love anchovies for how they behave when sizzled in a skillet and melted down into a pool of olive oil, with which to bathe a tangle of green beans. I love smashing them up with cloves of raw garlic to dress a piece of nicely seared steak. But most of all, I love eating them as a snack, uncooked and unadulterated, popped fresh from the tin or jar they were stored in. One fillet at a time, skewered or layered with something tangy or spicy (or both) to cut through their salty savouriness. They are my preferred way to start an afternoon of spritzes or a Sunday roast chicken dinner.

Of course, the quality of anchovy gets called into question more intently when there's nothing to hide behind, so if you're going to snack on these salty little fellas, this would be the time to spring for 'the nice ones'. Well, how do you know which ones are 'the nice ones'? They can come in a jar or a tin, and once opened will appear plump and pink, never smelling fishy or feeling 'stiff' (a telltale sign they've been cured too long and will likely be too salty to eat this way – yes, there is such a thing, even for me). They are also (unfortunately) often more expensive than, say, your 'cooking anchovies', but rest assured, they're worth every penny.

PEPPERS & ANCHOVIES

TOGETHER FOREVER

I'll admit fresh peppers have long been at the bottom of my list of favourite vegetables. That said, peppers, when crunchy and pickled in brine, or roasted and preserved in oil, serve as the backbone of one of my favorite snacks: peppers and anchovies. I enjoy both the crunchy pickled variety (fancy guindillas, which are worth the trouble to seek out, or basic grocery-store-friendly pepperoncini), skewered on a toothpick with an olive for a classic Gilda, and the roasted ones, cut into strips, layered in a small bowl, dressed with a touch of vinegar and eaten with a dainty fork (as seen on page 12). Peppers and anchovies come alive when popped open and eaten as one: A salty, plump fillet is the perfect foil to the acidity of pickled peppers or the sweetness of roasted ones. I consider this pairing as iconic as peas and carrots, one you can count on to both stave off hunger at apéro hour and serve as a makeshift light lunch when coupled with a good hunk of bread and a wedge of firm, salty cheese. All said, a snack match made in heaven.

One of the most iconic examples of this pairing are Gildas, the classic Basque snack ('pintxo') served as an accompaniment to drinks and other tiny little bites. Traditionally, it's a trio of your basic green olives, anchovies and pickled peppers (specifically, a small, long, thin pepper, like the aforementioned guindilla or pepperoncini). But I like to throw in other pickled things or crunchy vegetables (not traditional, but delicious): Pickled pearl onions, chunks of fresh cucumber or tiny, boiled potatoes are my favourite options. The anchovies are typically the salted-and-oil-packed kind, not the white, vinegared 'boquerones', but both work. I've seen these prepared as almost an appetiser-size portion (double anchovies, peppers, and olives on a thick skewer) and as a more delicate version with only a single pepper and anchovy on a thin little toothpick. If neither skewer nor toothpick is an option, combine all the things on a sweet little plate and call it a snack platter. Whatever works!

ARTICHOKE HEARTS
with ANCHOVIES & PARMESAN

SERVES 4–6

1 × 400 g (14 oz) tin of unmarinated artichoke hearts, drained (quartered, if whole)

2 tablespoons white distilled vinegar

flaky sea salt and freshly ground black pepper

60 g (2 oz) hunk of Parmesan cheese, coarsely chopped into bite-size pieces

8–12 anchovy fillets

1 handful parsley, tender leaves and stems

Artichokes are one of my favourite vegetables, but even I can (reluctantly) admit they're kind of annoying to prepare, especially if it's just the tender heart you're after. For convenience alone, tinned artichokes are a blessing, one of the best shelf-stable vegetables you can buy. Together with anchovies (incidentally, one of the best shelf-stable fishes you can buy) and some good Parmesan, you get an elegant snack worthy of the finest wine bar, on the most exquisite European vacation.

Whether I'm cooking or snacking, I generally prefer to start with unmarinated artichoke hearts. They taste like a more pure expression of the vegetable, plus I can better control the acidity and saltiness without any additional flavours. But if the marinated ones are all you can find, you have my blessing – just skip the vinegar bath and the extra salt and pepper.

1. Scatter the artichoke hearts on a plate (or divide between two small snack plates) and douse with the vinegar. Season with flaky salt and pepper.

2. Pile the Parmesan next to the artichoke hearts, and the anchovies next to the Parmesan. Scatter with the parsley and serve with small forks or toothpicks for eating.

    Alternatively (I like to do this for parties): After seasoning the artichoke hearts with vinegar, salt and pepper, pierce one piece of artichoke, one anchovy and one hunk of Parmesan on a small wooden skewer. Chop the parsley and scatter over before serving.

GREEN BAGNA CAUDA

SERVES 6–8

125 ml (4 fl oz/½ cup) olive oil
120 g (4 oz) unsalted butter
10 garlic cloves (8 thinly sliced, 2 finely grated)
4 spring onions (scallions), finely chopped, white and green parts separated
10–12 anchovy fillets (from approximately 1 × 55 g/ 2 oz tin or 95 g/3 oz jar), finely chopped
1 large bunch parsley, tender leaves and stems, very finely chopped (about ¾ cup)
kosher salt and freshly ground black pepper
vegetables, for dipping (steamed artichokes, boiled potatoes, thinly sliced fennel, radishes, blanched asparagus, etc.)

DO AHEAD
—
Bagna cauda can be made 5 days ahead, stored wrapped and refrigerated. Rewarm over a low heat before serving.

EAT WITH
—
A whole, steamed artichoke is my dream pairing here. Otherwise, set out a mélange of bite-size raw or briefly cooked vegetables of your choosing: thinly sliced fennel, halved radishes, blanched asparagus, artichoke hearts, boiled potatoes, carrot spears or quartered turnips. Also good with crusty bread, over roasted potatoes or as a dressing for roast chicken.

Many versions of bagna cauda (translation: 'hot bath') exist, from the creamy to the buttery, but all contain a generous portion of anchovies, which get melted down into whatever fat is being used, providing not only a meaty saltiness but also the body needed to qualify it as a dip. This particular one is decidedly buttery (no heavy cream here), very green, extremely garlicky and contains an entire tin of anchovies. The low and slow process of cooking everything down together in a small pot allows all the flavours to meld, each ingredient softening into the others and creating a luscious dip for whatever raw or cooked vegetables you fancy.

1 Combine the olive oil, butter, sliced garlic and white parts of the spring onions in a small pot over a low heat. Cook until the garlic and spring onions are completely tender and almost melted into the combined fats, 10–15 minutes. (If necessary, lower the heat even further to maintain a subtle simmer – you don't want the garlic or onions browning.)

2 Add the anchovies and continue to cook on the lowest heat possible, stirring occasionally, until they're completely broken down into a nice golden paste and smelling a little nutty (not unlike browned butter), 15–20 minutes.

3 Add the green spring onion tops and raw grated garlic. Continue to cook until the onion tops are wilted and bright green and the garlic is fragrant, another minute or so. Remove from the heat, add the parsley and season with salt and pepper as needed. Serve with vegetables of your choosing.

LUPIN BEANS
with GARLIC & PARSLEY

SERVES 4–6

2 tablespoons olive oil
½ teaspoon chilli flakes
1 × 450 g (1 lb) jar lupin (lupini) beans, drained and rinsed
kosher salt and freshly ground black pepper
2 garlic cloves, finely chopped
small handful of parsley, tender leaves and stems, finely chopped
flaky sea salt, to finish

EAT WITH
―

A few spritzes, some potato chips and a deck of cards.

I don't remember the first time I had lupin (lupini) beans, but I'm going to assume it was in Italy, and I'm going to assume I was drinking something fizzy over ice, and I'm going to assume I was having a fabulous time. Eaten as a sort of drinking snack or prelude to a meal, lupin beans are similar to edamame in that they are a good little blank canvas from which to start your evening. Salty and garlicky, quick to make, tiny and easy to love, lupin beans make an appearance at 96 per cent of my dinner parties, aperitivo hours, spritz gatherings, barbecues, birthday celebrations and so on.

I don't know why they aren't more popular, though I have started seeing little bags of them – promising a low-glycaemic, keto-friendly source of protein – sold at airport kiosks, so I guess they are catching on? Anyway, those are *not* what I suggest buying here. The lupin beans you want are sold in jars. They're fully cooked, usually stored in some sort of liquid and seasoned with nothing but salt. They can be found at most Italian groceries or, if you need, online – I have no brand loyalty and have found most to be the same in texture and flavour. When it comes to eating them, while I've only ever been served lupin beans basically straight from the jar, I like to do more. If you could do more, wouldn't you? I would, so I do.

Sautéing them in a quick little chilli oil and finishing them with some raw garlic and lots of parsley makes for a supremely addictive snack. Adding the garlic at the end, so it stays punchy and raw, is important here – if that makes you worried in the company of others, I think you need new company. I'm not entirely sure if you're 'supposed' to eat the tender outer shell or not, but I find the texture pleasing, so I do. (It's more of a 'skin' than a 'shell', but you can easily pop it off, if it's not for you.)

1. Heat the olive oil in a large skillet over a medium-high heat. Add the chilli flakes and swirl to toast for a minute or two. Add the lupin beans and season with salt and pepper. Give them a toss, letting them settle into the skillet to sizzle in the oil. Cook, tossing occasionally, until lightly golden at the edges, 3–5 minutes.

2. Remove from the heat, add the garlic and parsley, and toss to coat. Finish with flaky salt and serve warm (also good at room temperature).

POTATO CHIPS

FOR A GOOD TIME

There are people in this world who will make their own crackers from the sourdough starter they care for, or fry their own potato chips from farmers' market spuds in seed-free oil. I am not really either type of person. I believe that, in the same way the best ketchup comes from a bottle, the best potato chips come from a bag. I also believe that potato chips are one of the finest pantry staples you can have when it comes to snacking. They're salty, sturdy and satisfying in a way most crackers could never be. If you are completely unprepared for guests, having a bag of potato chips on hand will make you appear a little bit put together. It says: 'I know what people like, I have a good time and I don't take myself too seriously.'

As for what type of potato chip, there are pros and cons to consider. On the positive side, kettle chips are sturdier (great for dipping), while conventional chips have a nicer, larger size (better for eating anchovies on). On the other hand, kettle chips tend to need salt, and conventional chips are so fragile that most end up broken in the bag before you can even open it. Six of one, half a dozen of the other, really. Either way, salted is best. (Outrageous flavours are a gamble, though I suppose it depends on usage: Salted says simple and elegant dinner party, spicy BBQ says outdoor potluck, so whatever you are trying to say, say it.)

While a bowl of perfectly salted, unbroken potato chips fits into most people's snack fantasy, it's also nice to offer things to go alongside. Tins of fish (especially anchovies, spiced mussels and smoked sprats) or sheets of thinly sliced cured meats (especially jamón or prosciutto) are both great. But for me, potato chips are best paired with the extremely high- or extremely low-brow, and there is no greater example of this than caviar and sour-cream-and-onion dip made from a packet of Lipton Recipe Secrets (a perfect recipe). There are some things in between, but why bother?

I want to mention two things. One: Of course it's absurd to mention caviar in the context of a pantry-focussed book. But because so much else in this book is modestly priced and requires so little labour, I feel empowered to sneak in a little caviar (for a special occasion). Two: Yes, in the pursuit of excellence, I've made sour-cream-and-onion dip from scratch. I've caramelised onions for hours, built complex layers of flavour in a skillet and crossed my fingers that by the end of that painstakingly long process, I would have something more delicious and perfect than something store-bought. And guess what, I never did. I can say with full confidence that no onion dip made from scratch is better than the one from the packet! This is okay and something I accept because I have nothing to prove.

LENTIL DIP
with TOASTED GARLIC & CRISPY HERBS

SERVES 4–6 / MAKES ABOUT 480 ML (16 FL OZ/2 CUPS)

---

250 g (9 oz/1 cup) yellow lentils
kosher salt
2 tablespoons fresh lemon juice, plus more to taste
4 tablespoons olive oil
4 garlic cloves (2 finely grated, 2 thinly sliced)
8–10 sage leaves, or 1 tablespoon thyme or oregano leaves
freshly ground black pepper or chilli flakes

DO AHEAD
—
Lentil dip can be made 5 days ahead, stored wrapped and refrigerated.

EAT WITH
—
As a snack, I like this as a dip with any sort of bread and/or with raw or blanched vegetables. I also find it a delightful side, sitting somewhere between a starch and a sauce. It would be perfect with Overnight Lamb (page 276) and a pile of Vinegar-Braised Greens (page 106).

This is my best interpretation of 'fava', the classic Greek dip you're able to get at any taverna across the country. Each version I've had, made with yellow lentils (not favas), lots of lemon, garlic and olive oil, is wonderful, and I love them all. I suspect they're using a different technique, as the ones I've had in Greece were sublimely smooth, and this version is charmingly lumpy (intentional). The best part about this dip is that you don't need a food processor or blender: The lentils cook in just enough water to fully break them down into mush. Season aggressively, and – if making this ahead – know it'll firm up as it sits. (You can always thin it out with more lemon juice, olive oil, or a touch of water as needed.)

1. Bring 650 ml (22 fl oz/2¾ cups) water to the boil in a small pot. Add the lentils and season with salt. Reduce the heat to medium-low and simmer until the lentils are completely tender and cooked through and then pass into total mush. As they cook and break down and the water evaporates, stir them pretty constantly to encourage them to further break down into what looks to be a coarse paste (not watery or soupy). This whole process should take 20–25 minutes.

2. Once the lentils are the perfect mush/dip texture, remove them from the heat. Add the lemon juice, 2 tablespoons of the olive oil and the grated garlic. Season with salt, plus more lemon juice if you want. Let cool while you make the topping.

3. Heat the remaining 2 tablespoons olive oil in a small skillet or pot over a medium-high heat. Add the sliced garlic and herbs. Cook, swirling occasionally, until the garlic has toasted, crisped and browned, and the herbs are crispy, 2–3 minutes. Remove from the heat and season with salt and the pepper of your choosing.

4. To serve, transfer the dip to a bowl, spooning the toasted garlic-herb mixture over.

LABNEH WITH CARAMELISED HARISSA

MAKES 480 ML (16 FL OZ/2 CUPS)

2 tablespoons olive oil
2–4 tablespoons harissa
500 g (1 lb 2 oz/2 cups) labneh or full-fat Greek yoghurt
1 tablespoon fresh lemon juice, plus more to taste
kosher salt and freshly ground black pepper

NOTE

How much harissa you use will depend on the brand. Start with 2 tablespoons for the very spicy type that comes in a tube, closer to 4 tablespoons for the milder type that comes in a jar.

DO AHEAD

This dip comes together so quickly I wouldn't worry about making it ahead, but you can do it a few hours in advance; store it wrapped and refrigerated until ready to serve.

EAT WITH

Anything you'd eat with dip: flatbreads, raw vegetables, crackers, toast. Also great as a sauce with lamb or chicken, or dolloped on top of Brothy Chickpeas (garbanzos) (page 158) or next to Rice Pilaf (page 191).

Labneh, all thick, tangy and lightly salted, could be served to me out of the container as is and I would say, 'Wow, that's a perfect dip.' But of course, there's always a chance for more. Without doing too much, harissa paste – spicy and spiced, complex and nuanced – is the perfect out-of-the-jar ingredient to give you something, well . . . more. It would be a shame to upstage it by adding needless ingredients, so I won't, and you shouldn't. While more ambitious recipes exist, sometimes the best things in life require a lot less from you.

Different brands of harissa will have different ingredient lists and therefore different levels of spiciness, so think of the amount called for here as a suggestion, using your best judgement to add more or less. Some brands make a more mild harissa, the bulk of which is made from something like tomato purée (paste) or bell peppers, and you can use a lot more of those types in this recipe. Other brands stick to a more minimal ingredient list, containing only chilli peppers, garlic and various spices; these tend to come in a tube and are a lot spicier and more potent, so you may want to use less. Either way, both types benefit from the frying in oil that happens here. Not unlike how you'd typically cook tomato purée, this process takes the raw edge off, caramelises the sugars and deepens its flavour – a good tip anytime you're using harissa (see Olive Oil-Fried Lentils, page 180).

1. Heat the olive oil in a small pot or skillet over a medium-high heat. Add the harissa and cook, stirring occasionally, until it is properly frying in the oil, caramelising at the edges and turning a darker shade of red, 2–4 minutes, depending on the paste. Remove from the heat and set aside.

2. Place the labneh in the serving bowl of your choosing and add the lemon juice. Season with salt, pepper and more lemon juice if you like. Swirl in the fried harissa, making sure to drizzle some of the oil on top.

HERBED ARTICHOKE DIP

MAKES 480–750 ML (16–25 FL OZ/2–3 CUPS)

1 × 400 g (14 oz) tin of artichoke hearts (unmarinated preferred), drained and chopped
2 garlic cloves, finely grated
1 tablespoon finely grated lemon zest, plus 2 tablespoons fresh lemon juice (from about 1 lemon)
kosher salt and freshly ground black pepper
250 g (9 oz/1 cup) sour cream, full-fat Greek yoghurt or labneh
120 g (4 oz/½ cup) cream cheese, at room temperature (or more sour cream, full-fat Greek yoghurt or labne)
25 g (1 oz/½ cup) finely chopped chives
10 g (½ oz/¼ cup) finely chopped dill
1 × 225 g (8 oz) tin of water chestnuts, drained and finely chopped (very much optional)

DO AHEAD

This can be made 5 days ahead, wrapped tightly and refrigerated.

EAT WITH

As a dip, it's perfect with steamed artichokes, soft, fluffy bread and any variety of cold, crunchy, raw vegetables (carrot sticks). I also like to thin it out with a touch more lemon juice or splash of water and eat it as a sauce alongside things like a Roast Chicken (page 262) or Slow-Roasted Salmon (page 303).

This is not hot spinach-artichoke dip, so if that's what you came for, keep it moving. Just kidding, please stay – you'll love this. This is almost a tzatziki, almost a cold spinach-artichoke dip in a loaf of Hawaiian bread, but without cucumbers, without spinach, and without a loaf of Hawaiian bread, unless you desire. It's a refreshing little number, garlicky and lemony, punchy in the right ways. Really, this is simply another way for me to convince you that tinned artichoke hearts are an incredible and completely necessary addition to your pantry.

Not for nothing, it's also maybe the one and only time I'll suggest you seek out water chestnuts, which always appeared in my spinach-artichoke dip as a small California child. They're a very 'if you know, you know' ingredient, which is to say, if you grew up with a certain type of chilled spinach-artichoke dip, you might find them non-negotiable. They aren't always easily found, so feel free to leave them out, although they do provide a delightful crunchy texture and pleasantly neutral yet nutty flavour. To me, this is first and foremost a dip, ripe for celery sticks, crackers and hunks of soft bread, but perhaps most of all, nothing beats this with a freshly steamed artichoke. Too much artichoke? Truly no such thing.

1. Combine the artichoke hearts, garlic, lemon zest and lemon juice in a medium bowl; season with salt and pepper and let sit for a few minutes to marinate.

2. Add the sour cream, cream cheese, chives, dill and water chestnuts, if you're lucky enough to have them. Mix well, so that the dip takes on a gorgeous green tint. Season with salt, pepper and more lemon juice if you want. Refrigerate until ready to eat.

SEVERAL VARIATIONS ON
RADISHES WITH BUTTER & SALT

This is not a recipe for radishes with butter and salt. This is something else: a flagrant abuse of power, wherein I am writing a book and have the ability to use one whole page of that book to talk about how much I love radishes and butter together. What better combination of ingredients to remind you that something can truly come from nothing? Every time I slather a crisp, spicy radish with salty, creamy butter, I am floored at the exquisite simplicity and amount of pleasure two things can bring. Crunchy and soft, spicy and sweet.

It is also, I'll admit, a cheap trick. At pretty much any dinner party I have, radishes and butter start us off – not because I'm unimaginative, but because I have good taste, and radishes and butter are a perfect, elegant snack. Like me, the seemingly straightforward radishes-and-butter combination in fact contains multitudes. Watermelon radishes, cut into thick coins with a schmear of butter on the side of the plate, indicate I like to go above and beyond while shopping at the farmers' market. Breakfast radishes, halved with the leafy stem left on and dipped into a blob of too-soft butter, let my guests know I'm casual and easygoing. Regular grocery-store radishes cut into wedges, served with a slab of the very yellow, very expensive butter say that I am the very embodiment of the high-low lifestyle.

In the niche radishes-and-butter discourse that I happen to participate in, there's a good amount of back-and-forth on whether you should season your radishes before serving them with the butter, perhaps tossing them with lemon juice or sprinkling them with flaky salt. I am a practical realist and know that while tossing a radish with lemon juice or sprinkling it with salt might seem like a good and sophisticated idea, seasoning raw vegetables will cause them to sweat and become watery. Anyone who's done it will tell you that it's a nightmare to try to slather a wet radish with butter, and you probably shouldn't try. Of course, you do want to sprinkle your butter with plenty of flaky salt (even if the butter is salted, it likely needs to be saltier) – and maybe even some chives.

Through it all, you may be tempted to gussy up the humble radish or apologise for its simplicity. But remember: This is your home. Who are you there to impress? Snacks, especially when eaten at your own table, do not need to be cool; they need to be delicious. But if you're looking for more (and who isn't sometimes?), you can make the Anchovy Butter, Snail Butter (no actual snails involved), or Calabrian Chilli Butter (pages 36–37). The integrity of the radish-and-butter concept is preserved, though it seems less like 'radishes and butter' and more like an elevated snack you might pay $14 for at a cute new wine bar. Everyone wins.

GOOD BUTTER
AS A SNACK

SNAIL BUTTER

MAKES ABOUT 225 G (8 OZ/1 CUP)

---

120 g (4 oz) unsalted butter, at room temperature
1 large shallot, finely chopped
2 garlic cloves, finely grated
½ bunch parsley, very finely chopped (do this either by hand or in a food processor; you should end up with a heaping ½ cup)
1 bunch chives, finely chopped (about ½ cup)
kosher salt and freshly ground black pepper

There are no snails in this butter, but rather it's the flavour of the butter that you eat with snails. As a snack: This is a good, garlicky, herby butter smeared on a simple slice of well-toasted sourdough, best served next to some saucisson and a plate of briny olives. It's also nice with sardines on a cracker. To cook with it: See Snail Butter Pasta (page 232).

Using a fork, smash the butter, shallot, garlic, parsley and chives together in a small bowl and season with salt and pepper. Store wrapped and in a small container in the refrigerator until ready to use. Bring to room temperature before serving (unless you're using it to cook with or melt, then it can be used straight from the fridge).

CALABRIAN CHILLI BUTTER

MAKES 170 G (6 OZ/¾ CUP)

---

120 g (4 oz) unsalted butter, at room temperature
6–8 Calabrian chillies, finely chopped (or 3–4 tablespoons chopped Calabrian chillies)
zest of 1 lemon
kosher salt and freshly ground black pepper

This is 'The Spicy One'. The fermented, funky heat from the chillies is offset with fresh lemon zest – an Italian fever dream. As a snack: This is very good with crackers and thinly sliced cured ham or flakes of smoked trout. To cook with it: Melt it over grilled chicken or toss it with sautéed leafy greens, roasted cauliflower or caramelised carrots.

Using a fork, smash the butter, as many Calabrian chillies as feels right to you (they vary in size, and so does one's tolerance for heat) and lemon zest together in a small bowl and season with salt and pepper. Store wrapped and in a small container in the refrigerator until ready to use. Bring to room temperature before serving (unless you're using it to cook with or melt, then it can be used straight from the fridge).

ANCHOVY BUTTER

MAKES 170 G (6 OZ/¾ CUP)

---

120 g (4 oz) unsalted butter, at room temperature
10–12 anchovy fillets (from approximately 1 × 55 g/ 2 oz tin or 95 g/3 oz jar), finely chopped
2 garlic cloves, finely grated
kosher salt and freshly ground black pepper

My favourite butter (surprise). I will eat this by the spoonful with little to no regret. As a snack: It's perfect on a radish (the thinking man's potato chip) with a cold glass of wine and a hunk of the finest baguette you can find. To cook with it: Smear this butter onto a whole chicken before roasting (classic), or simply toss into pasta, à la buttered noodles. It's also good with steak (medium-rare) and blanched broccoli.

Using a fork, smash the butter, anchovies and garlic together in a small bowl and season with salt and pepper. Store wrapped and in a small container in the refrigerator until ready to use. Bring to room temperature before serving (unless you're using it to cook with or melt, then it can be used straight from the fridge).

CRACKED SPICED OLIVES

SERVES 6–8

350 g (12 oz/2 cups) olives, such as Castelvetrano, Cerignola, or Gordal (with pits)
60 ml (2 fl oz/¼ cup) olive oil
2 garlic cloves, very well crushed
1 tablespoon fennel seeds
1 tablespoon mild, finely ground chilli flakes, such as Aleppo pepper or gochugaru
1 teaspoon smoked or sweet paprika

DO AHEAD
—
Olives can be made a week or so ahead of time. Keep them refrigerated until ready to eat, then reheat them slightly before serving to awaken the chilli.

EAT WITH
—
Thinly sliced cured meats. A glass of cold red wine. Friends on a blanket. Oysters (if you're eating oysters at home). Spanish Tortilla (page 40).

I want to be flexible in my recipes, but I also want to give you the best possible experience. As arbitrary as it seems, I truly think olives with the pits taste better than pre-pitted olives. I can't quite explain it (at least not scientifically), but pitted olives always make me think of a boneless, skinless chicken breast: You can tell it's been through something. . . . Something . . . is missing. And just as with boneless, skinless chicken breast, sure, there is a time and a place for pitted olives (Crushed-Olive Chicken, page 266). But olives to be served during snack hour is not one of them.

Snacking olives are not meant to be popped casually like chips. They deserve to be intentionally nibbled, a little pit fished out to be discarded into a small, thoughtfully provided dish. Any olive will do – large olives, briny olives, tiny olives, salted olives – preferably tossed in an oily concoction of spices to be enjoyed as the whole olive, pit and all. It's part of the ritual, the process of olive eating. To make things slightly more approachable to the pit-averse, I do like to crack the olives with the side of a knife, exposing the insides ever so slightly before tossing them in that spiced, oily concoction. This makes it easier to get the pits out without sacrificing the flavour and integrity of the olive, a good thing for all involved.

1   Using the side of a large knife, smash the olives against a cutting board to expose their insides. (If the pit falls out, you can remove it, but otherwise leave it in for the eaters to remove themselves.) You don't want the olive totally intact – it's good to have craggly, irregular edges here.

2   Heat the olive oil in a small pot or medium skillet over a medium heat. Add the olives, garlic, fennel seeds, chilli flakes and paprika. Reduce the heat to low and cook, swirling occasionally, until the olives get a little browned and wrinkled at the edges, 10–15 minutes. Remove from the heat and set aside until ready to eat.

SPANISH TORTILLA & FRIENDS

SERVES 6–8

FOR THE TORTILLA

675 g (1½ lb) King Edward potatoes, peeled and sliced 5 mm (¼ inch) thick
1 medium yellow onion (about 225 g/8 oz), thinly sliced
kosher salt
480–750 ml (16–25 fl oz/2–3 cups) olive oil, maybe more (don't worry, you can reuse it)
6 large eggs
Aioli for Everything (page 45)
¼ teaspoon hot, sweet, or smoked paprika (optional)

NOTE

If you're going to use the leftover oil to make Aioli (page 45), please make sure the oil is at least room temperature (pop it in the fridge to expedite the process if needed). Warm oil will cause the aioli to break and you'll never get a proper emulsion – not a good time!

DO AHEAD

Tortilla can be made 2 days ahead, stored wrapped and refrigerated. Eat straight from the fridge or brought to room temperature, no need to reheat.

FRIENDS (EAT WITH)

Sliced jamón or other cured meats, pickled or roasted peppers, anchovies, trout or salmon roe, Gildas (page 16).

Much like when you bake a pie crust or biscuits, you learn a lot each time you make a Spanish tortilla – a perfect dish of potatoes cooked in olive oil and mixed with eggs – which is likely why I love making it. Tricks and little techniques reveal themselves to you with each attempt. No two are ever really alike: Each one is unique to your physical space, your personal touch, your specific preferences. In a world where we love to have the same exact thing as everyone else, isn't it so special to have something so perfectly your own?

There are lots of ways a Spanish tortilla can be made and eaten. It could be thick, sturdy, towering slices, grabbed like a piece of cake. Or it could be custardy omelettes, thin as pancakes and broken up with a small fork. It could be with onions, or without, eaten alongside aioli or simply one perfect anchovy. This recipe is just one way – a way I love and think you'll have success with in your own kitchen. From there, make another one. Then another. Do one thing differently next time, if you want. Increase the heat for more browning. Add another egg for a different ratio. Make it in a larger skillet for a thinner tortilla. Or change nothing. Feel it out as you cook through your tortillas, knowing that it might turn out a bit different from last time. The potatoes are a little waxier, the eggs a little larger, the skillet a little smaller, the heat a little lower: Whatever the differences may be, embrace them. Tortillas aren't meant to be perfect; they're only meant to be yours.

1 Layer the potatoes and onions in a small saucepan or pot, seasoning with salt as you go. Add 480 ml (16 fl oz/2 cups) of olive oil, plus more as needed to totally submerge the potatoes and onions. Bring to a gentle simmer over a medium heat (you should see only a few tiny bubbles – it should never look like it's sizzling or frying) and reduce the heat to low. Continue to cook until the potatoes are completely cooked through (but not falling apart), 15–20 minutes (fish out a thicker slice with a fork or knife to test for doneness).

2 Meanwhile, whisk the eggs and a nice pinch of salt in a medium bowl until well blended; set aside until the potatoes are cooked through. Once they are, use a strainer or slotted spoon to transfer the potatoes and onions to the eggs, trying to leave behind as much oil as possible. Using a spatula (and maybe your hands), mix everything until well combined, taking care not to break the potatoes apart. Season again with salt. (I keep pepper out of this, but you can add some if you like.)

3   To cook the tortilla, heat 1½–2 tablespoons of the leftover oil in a medium (preferably 20-cm/8-inch) non-stick skillet over a medium-high heat. Carefully add the egg mixture, smooth the top with a spatula, and give the skillet a few shakes so everything settles evenly.

4   Reduce the heat to medium and use your spatula to scrape up the bottom a few times to bring the uncooked egg to the bottom of the pan. Give it another shake to let everything settle once more, then let it continue to cook, shaking occasionally, until the edges are set, the sides and underside are nicely browned (you can peek on the underside to see that the bottom is browning to your liking), and the whole thing easily pulls away from the sides of the skillet, 5 minutes or so. (This process is not unlike making an omelette or frittata, and if you have a non-stick skillet, it will be rather effortless. If you don't and it sticks, it won't be the end of the world.)

5   To flip the tortilla: Grab a plate or platter larger than the skillet and carefully place it over the skillet. Then, using a dish towel to hold the sides of the skillet firmly, flip the tortilla (with confidence!) onto the plate (it should be stunning!). (If you don't want to flip, transfer the skillet to a 230°C/220°C fan/450°F oven for 5–7 minutes, until the top is browned and everything is set. Carefully slide the tortilla from the skillet onto a cutting board or plate.)

6   Add 1 tablespoon of oil to the skillet and return it back to a medium-high heat. Gently slide the tortilla off the plate and back into the skillet, browned-side up (for extra credit, use a spatula to gently tuck the sides underneath the tortilla to make everything nice and round). Cook until the bottom is set and golden brown, another 2–3 minutes or so. Slide the tortilla back onto the (clean) plate and let it rest while you make the aioli (the tortilla will be best sliced and served after it's rested for at least 30 minutes).

7   Serve the tortilla in thick wedges, topped with a dollop of aioli and some or all of the friends. Dust with the paprika if the spirit moves you.

42　　　　　　　　　　　　　　　　SOMETHING FROM NOTHING

SNACKS & THINGS TO START WITH

AIOLI FOR EVERYTHING

MAKES ABOUT 300 ML (10 FL OZ/1¼ CUPS)

175 ml (6 fl oz/¾ cup) neutral oil, such as grapeseed or rapeseed (canola)
60 ml (2 fl oz/¼ cup) olive oil
1 large egg yolk
1 teaspoon Dijon mustard
1–2 garlic cloves, finely grated, plus more to taste
1 tablespoon white distilled vinegar or fresh lemon juice, plus more to taste
kosher salt

DO AHEAD
—
The aioli will keep in the fridge for about a week.

EAT WITH
—
I use aioli on lots of things, including toast with tomatoes, smeared onto hard-boiled eggs, and as something to dip cold roast chicken into as a snack while I think about what to make for dinner.

This aioli is for you. It should be as thick (or thin) as you want, as heavy on the garlic as you want, as tangy as you want. That said, it's a pretty classic aioli: thick and creamy and made with lots of olive oil and raw garlic. It's my preference to make it by hand, and I think once you do, you'll enjoy the fact that you don't need anything other than a whisk and a bowl to pull it together.

It goes with nearly everything, which is especially handy for those who don't do dairy but want a little creamy something with their Perfect Oil-Roasted Tomatoes (page 113), Wine-Braised Romano Beans (page 96), or Crisp, Hot Roast Chicken (page 262). You can always add things at the end, like finely chopped herbs, capers or anchovies, or make a spicy aioli by stirring in a little Quick Chilli Oil (page 127).

1. Combine the oils together in a bowl or measuring cup with a spout.

2. Place the egg yolk, mustard, and garlic in a medium bowl. Slowly whisk in a few teaspoons of oil. Become more confident and whisk in a little bit more oil, stopping to make sure it's fully emulsified each time. Thin it out with a little vinegar or lemon juice if it becomes too thick. Whisk in more oil until it's all been added. Add the rest of the vinegar or lemon juice, then season with salt and more garlic, if you think it needs it.

3. While I love the thickness of aioli, it can also be thinned with more vinegar or lemon juice (or water), if you prefer this as more of a saucy dressing.

SOUPS *and* STEWS

It might sound dramatic to say that this book exists because of soup, but it's true. Soup is far and away my most-cooked category of food, and usually comes about from rooting around in my pantry. If you're thinking pots bubbling away for hours on end or multi-step broths and soups, well, these are not that. These are casual bowls made with items you likely already have on hand, which come alive with the addition of one or two fresh ingredients: a caramelised fennel bulb here, a squeeze of fresh lemon there.

My soups and stews are as impatient as I am, most ready in an hour or less, many relying on stock from a jar (one of the great gifts), a dash of fish sauce or a nice pat of butter for depth of flavour and the illusion of a long simmer. These are brothy celebrations of all the tins, jars and bottles of things I keep on hand, those seemingly mundane yet magical ingredients that allow you to make layered and complex-tasting soups and stews out of (almost) thin air.

CHICKEN BROTH, THE LONG WAY

MAKES 2.35–2.85 LITRES (80–96 FL OZ/10–12 CUPS)

1.8–2.25 kg (4–5 lb) bone-in, skin-on chicken (parts or a whole chicken)
2 large yellow onions, unpeeled, quartered
2 garlic heads, unpeeled, halved widthways
6 celery stalks, chopped
1–2 carrots, unpeeled, or 1 large fennel bulb, chopped
2 teaspoons black peppercorns
1 fresh or dried bay leaf (optional)
kosher salt

NOTE

You can purchase a whole chicken and cut it up, have the butcher do it for you, or simply purchase parts (wings, backs, legs, etc.). Or use a whole, uncut chicken and plop it right in there. You can also save up the carcasses from your whole roasted or rotisserie chickens and make broth that way, using two or three carcasses instead of one fresh chicken.

DO AHEAD

Broth can be made 5 days ahead and refrigerated, or several months ahead and frozen.

This is my basic and very general recipe for chicken broth. It is also extraordinary, in the way that only chicken broth, made with love, care, salt and plenty of bone-in, skin-on chicken can be. While the golden-brown, schmaltzy, salty, savoury broth is perfect as-is for soups like classic Chicken Noodle (page 52) or Matzo Ball (page 77), it's also ripe for innovations and modifications based on its final destination. Add a knob of sliced ginger here, some whole chillies there – whatever you like to suit your needs and desires.

I like to use a cut-up chicken, rather than a whole, uncut one. It's something I learned in Oaxaca, watching cooks prep soup in a market stall – a romantic, if fuzzy, memory. Cutting up the chicken does two things. First, it allows you to remove the chicken parts at different times, so that the breast can come out once it's poached, while the legs/thighs can continue to simmer and become more tender. Second, hacking up the chicken exposes the inside of the bones, which releases all that collagen and marrow into your broth, making it richer and more flavourful. If your preference is to purchase parts instead (and you're just after broth, no meat), I would go for all wings – or backs, if available, which are cheaper, less wasteful and have the highest ratio of skin and bone to meat.

1. Place the chicken, onions, garlic, celery, carrots, peppercorns and bay leaf (if using) in a large pot and cover with 2.85–3.35 litres (96–112 fl oz/12–14 cups) water. (Basically, you want to fill your pot to the top with water.)

2. Season with a good amount of salt (not quite salty like the sea, but you can really season it well, keeping in mind it will reduce down a bit) and bring to the boil. Reduce the heat to medium-low (the broth should be gently simmering) and continue to simmer until the chicken is cooked through and falling apart, the vegetables are nearly mush (but still taste good) and the broth is as seasoned and delicious as you'd want it to be when serving, about 1½ hours or so. If you want to pluck the leg/thigh pieces out and pick the meat from them for later use, you should (I do!).

3. Strain the broth. (I use a basic fine-mesh sieve/strainer – no need for muslin/cheesecloth.) Keep it hot if using right away or let it cool before refrigerating.

SOUPS & STEWS

CHICKEN NOODLE SOUP with LOTS OF LEMON

SERVES 4–6

2.85 litres (96 fl oz/12 cups) Chicken Broth, the Long Way (page 51)
kosher salt and freshly ground black pepper
450 g (1 lb) boneless, skinless chicken breasts or thighs
120 g (4 oz) egg noodles or other small pasta noodle shape
2–3 medium carrots, thinly sliced
1 small yellow onion, very thinly sliced
1 teaspoon fish sauce, plus more to taste (optional)
handful of parsley, tender leaves and stems, very finely chopped
20 g (¾ oz/½ cup) dill, tender leaves and stems, very finely chopped
2 lemons, halved for squeezing
saltine crackers, for serving (optional)

DO AHEAD
—
Chicken soup can be made 3 days ahead, stored in the refrigerator. *Sans* noodles, it can be made and frozen up to 3 months ahead (simply reheat and add the noodles when you're ready to eat).

Among all the ways that soup can be exciting, sometimes all you want is for soup to be whatever the opposite of that is. Comforting. Calming. Soothing. Basic. Expected. Frankly, I don't want any surprises from my chicken noodle soup. I want tender, puffy, nearly overcooked noodles swimming in a savoury, golden broth, lightly sweetened from little coins of carrots. I want dill and parsley floating on top of a thin layer of chicken fat, I want perfectly cooked shredded bits of chicken throughout, I want it pleasantly sour from tons of lemon, I want it to taste like the best version I've ever had at my favourite diner, and I want it to make me feel better, even if I'm not all that sick.

It goes without saying (but I'll say it anyway) that this soup will only be as good as your broth, and this recipe alone is worth the hours of simmering that it takes to make your own. If you were waiting for a sign to make a batch of chicken broth, consider this that sign.

1. Bring the chicken broth to a simmer in a large pot. Season with salt and (lots of) pepper and add the chicken. Cook the chicken at a gentle simmer until cooked through, 12–15 minutes.

2. Meanwhile, cook the noodles in a separate large pot of salted boiling water until just before al dente (if using egg noodles, this will happen faster than pasta, around 4 or 5 minutes). Drain and set aside.

3. Once the chicken is cooked through, pluck it from the broth and let it cool slightly on a cutting board or plate. As soon as it's cool enough, shred it with your hands or two forks and set it aside.

4. Add the carrots, onion and fish sauce (if using) to the broth and simmer for a few minutes, until the carrots and onion are tender. Add the noodles, chicken, parsley and dill to the broth. Bring to a simmer and season again with salt, pepper and a dash more fish sauce if you like. Add the lemon juice and remove from heat.

5. To serve, divide among bowls, maybe serving with saltines on the side.

GINGER & GREENS NOODLE SOUP

SERVES 4–6

1 large bunch coriander (cilantro) or parsley, leaves and tender stems, very finely chopped (about 1½–2 cups)

4 spring onions (scallions), very finely chopped

3–4 tablespoons finely grated fresh ginger (from about a 7.5-cm/3-inch piece)

4 garlic cloves, finely chopped or grated

1 teaspoon fish sauce, plus more to taste

90 ml (3 fl oz/⅓ cup) olive oil

kosher salt and freshly ground black pepper

1.9–2.35 litres (64–80 fl oz/ 8–10 cups) chicken or vegetable stock (or water plus Better Than Bouillon, see page 58)

2 bunches leafy greens, such as kale, mustard greens or Swiss chard, thick stems removed, leaves well chopped (about 6 cups)

175 g (6 oz) dried pasta, such as bow ties or ditalini, or 370 g (13 oz/2 cups) cooked rice

280 g (10 oz/2 cups) cooked chicken, shredded or cut into bite-size pieces (optional)

2 limes or lemons, halved for squeezing over

DO AHEAD

Noodle soup can be made 3 days ahead and refrigerated. It can be made, *sans* noodles, and frozen several months ahead.

When I'm not feeling well, I want to combine the things that make me feel best: chicken noodle soup and lots of ginger and greens. This soup does that, heavy on both the ginger and the greens, and yes ... it heals me. I like the noodles here to either be very large, behaving almost like a dumpling (an excellent use for those oft-maligned bow ties), or something very small that can crowd onto your spoon (ditalini, fregola or cooked rice). As for the greens (kale, Swiss chard, spinach), you really want them to cook down in the soup, going from bright green to almost olive green in colour and taking on the softened texture of braised or stewed greens. This way, they almost melt into the broth, becoming the most tender, sweet versions of themselves. Finally, the ginger – spicy and very much alive – gets added both to simmer in the broth and to finish on top, keeping the soup perky and restorative. If this doesn't heal you, I don't know what will.

1 Combine the herbs, spring onions, ginger, garlic, fish sauce and olive oil in a small bowl. Season with salt, pepper and more fish sauce if you want; set aside.

2 Heat the stock in a large pot and add the leafy greens and half of the herb-ginger mixture. Bring to a simmer and season with salt and pepper. Simmer gently until the broth is very gingery and the greens have gone from perky and bright green to completely tender and dark green (looking more like braised than blanched greens), 15–20 minutes.

3 Meanwhile, cook the pasta in a pot of salted water until al dente; drain and add the pasta and chicken (if using) to the broth when it's ready, simmering for a few minutes to finish cooking. (Add the cooked rice here, if going that route.)

4 Ladle the soup into bowls and top each with the remaining herb-ginger mixture. Squeeze over lots of lime or lemon.

CHICKEN SOUP FOR SUMMER COLDS

SERVES 4–6

3 tablespoons olive oil, plus more to serve
1 medium leek (the whole thing!), thinly sliced
4 garlic cloves, thinly sliced
kosher salt and freshly ground black pepper
healthy pinch of chilli flakes, plus more to taste
675–900 g (1½–2 lb) tomatillos (or tomatoes), husks removed, quartered or chopped
1 large bunch kale or Swiss chard, stems removed and leaves torn into bite-size pieces (about 6 cups)
1.9–2.35 litres (64–80 fl oz/ 8–10 cups) chicken or vegetable stock (or water plus Better Than Bouillon, see page 58)
white distilled vinegar, sherry vinegar, fresh lemon or lime juice (optional)
280 g (10 oz/2 cups) cooked chicken meat or tofu, cut into bite-size pieces (optional)
60 g (2 oz/2 cups) basil, coriander (cilantro), and/or parsley, torn
hot sauce or chilli oil, for serving

Soup is an all-seasons, any-time-of-day food for me. Although it's forever associated with cold winter evenings, I would happily have it for breakfast or in the dead of summer – both, if that were an option. Sometimes it's not just an option but a necessity, like when you think, 'I couldn't possibly feel a cold coming on – it's summertime,' but alas. This is the soup for such occasions: It has all the restorative properties of chicken soup but is tangier, spicier, herbier – dare I say, summery-er – and, incidentally, easily made without chicken.

While you could cook this any time of year (or day), the fresh tomatillos really make it, so embrace the soup-year-round lifestyle, won't you? Their acidity is unrivalled, and the pectin content (the stuff that makes jam jammy) really thickens the soup in an excellent, extremely satisfying way. In case you can't find them, fresh tomatoes are an option, too, but they're sweeter and less acidic, so be sure to adjust the final soup with a splash of vinegar, lemon or lime juice as needed.

1 Heat the olive oil in a large pot over a medium-high heat. Set a little bit of the white part of the leek aside to top your soup later and add the remaining leek and all the garlic to the pot. Season with salt and pepper. Cook, stirring occasionally, until the leek and garlic are completely softened and starting to get a little colour, 8–10 minutes.

2 Add the chilli flakes, let them sizzle in the oil for a few seconds, then add the tomatillos and season again with salt and pepper. Cook, stirring occasionally, until the tomatillos are falling apart, almost jam-like in texture, 5–8 minutes. Add the leafy greens and season again with salt and pepper. Cook them until they're just wilted, 3–4 minutes.

3 Add the stock and bring to a simmer. Taste every now and then and simmer until the broth is tangy, a little salty and very delicious, seasoning with salt, pepper and maybe a little bit more acidity from vinegar or citrus juice. If you can't taste anything because you have a cold, expect this to take 10–15 minutes.

4 Add the chicken or tofu (if using) and let warm through in the broth. Season one more time to taste, then divide among bowls and top with a few rings of the raw leek, all the herbs, a drizzle of olive oil and some hot sauce, chilli flakes or chilli oil.

BETTER *Than* BOUILLON IS BEST

Better Than Bouillon, a product I am not paid to extol the virtues of, is one of my favourite things in my pantry. More often than not, if I'm spending the effort and time to make my own broth from actual parts and bones, I feel like it's a true crime to use that precious liquid in something like a lentil soup, bolognese or, god forbid, to braise a pot of short ribs – the delicate nuance is almost always lost. I like to save my slow-simmered broth for when I'm effectively drinking it straight: things like chicken noodle soup, matzo ball soup, or … literally sipping it out of a mug with freshly grated ginger and maybe a sliced spring onion or two inside.

For the times my quick soups and stews need something more than water, I use Better Than Bouillon, a concentrated paste (there are many 'flavours', including several very good vegetarian/vegan ones) that comes in a little jar that you store in the fridge once open. It dissolves effortlessly into pots of water, soups, braises and stews, no 'blooming' or preparation required. While it's right there in the name that it's 'better than bouillon', trust me when I say it's not just better than regular bouillon, but SO much better than any sort of boxed chicken broth, which I almost never recommend using. It tastes so good straight from the jar (not a recommended use) that I've thought about tossing some of the chicken-flavoured one with buttered pasta as a sort of Top Ramen proxy. (I have not done this yet, but it's only a matter of time.)

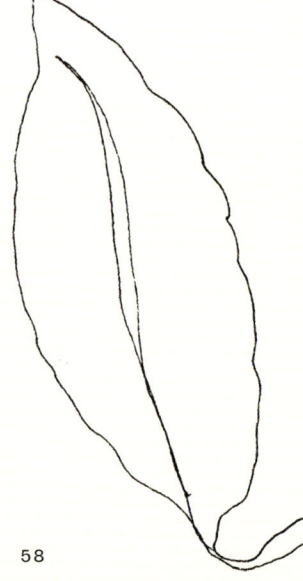

I BELIEVE IN
BAY LEAF

On my worktop, next to my stove, is a little clear glass plate with all my most loved ingredients: salt, my Unicorn pepper mill, olive oil, sherry vinegar, chilli flakes, fennel seeds and... bay leaves. When I travel to a place that offers fresh bay leaves (California, Greece, etc.), I bring them back in my luggage. If I'm making soup or stock or a pot of braised meat or beans, or some nice steamed rice, I add a bay leaf, two if I'm feeling flush.

For reasons I can't understand, people love to disrespect bay leaves, asking, 'But what does a bay leaf even do?' Well, do they look great in a little jar next to my flaky salt? Of course, but they're more than that. Not as strong as other herbs like thyme or rosemary (a compliment), bay leaves have a sort of green eucalyptus-y flavour, herbaceous and almost medicinal, like the botanical flavours in a fancy amaro, if that makes sense. While their presence is subtle, their absence is felt, leaving my broths and soups and beans and rice feeling a little lacking in *je ne sais quoi*. While I almost exclusively use fresh herbs, I don't mind dried bay leaves (although fresh is my preference – even if I do then dry them myself, which I do).

SOUPS & STEWS

KIMCHI-TOMATO SOUP WITH RICE & A SOFT EGG

SERVES 4

2 tablespoons olive oil
½ large yellow onion, finely chopped
4 garlic cloves, thinly sliced
kosher salt and freshly ground black pepper
450 g (1 lb) fresh tomatoes (any type), chopped (or 2 × 400 g/14 oz tins whole plum tomatoes, drained, tomatoes crushed by hand)
5 cm (2 inch) piece of fresh ginger, peeled or not, finely chopped
1 × 350 g (12 oz) jar kimchi, chopped (about 1½ cups), plus any liquid
60 ml (2 fl oz/¼ cup) soy sauce or tamari, plus more to taste
1 tablespoon fish sauce, plus more to taste
100 g (3½ oz/½ cup) jasmine or basmati rice, well rinsed
sesame oil or a few pats of unsalted butter, for serving
4 six-minute eggs (page 144), for serving (optional)
thinly sliced spring onions (scallions), for serving (optional)

NOTE

Place the rice in a mesh strainer and rinse with cold water until the water runs clear. This rids the rice of excess starch, which could otherwise make the soup murky or gluey, versus having nice individual grains.

DO AHEAD

The soup can be made 3 days ahead and refrigerated.

I am such a fan of tomato soups that I decided to put two in this book. The smooth, creamy, from-a-can variety feels, to me, more like puréed sauce than something I'd want to eat a whole bowl of, so know that this is decidedly different, proving (mostly to myself) that tomato soup can be so much more. Like the other one in this book (Buttered Tomato Soup with Lentils & Fennel, page 82), it doesn't require a blender and is full of texture and *joie de vivre*.

This one is just as much about the kimchi as it is the tomato, heavy on the tanginess and full of delightful bits and pieces to scoop up with your spoon. It's brothy but nicely thickened by plump little grains of rice that cook right in the soup. As with many soups in this chapter, the liquid you add here is water (not broth), so the soy and fish sauces pull their weight big-time. It almost feels like cheating, using this many umami-heavy ingredients in one soup, but that's the beauty of having a well-stocked pantry, no?

For the tomatoes, this is a good time to use those ugly, bruised, end-of-year sorts you might find, or maybe ones that overstayed their welcome on your kitchen counter. If fresh aren't an option, you can of course go full pantry and use tinned.

1 Heat the olive oil in a large pot over a medium-high heat. Add the onion and garlic and season with salt and pepper. Cook, stirring occasionally, until the onion and garlic are lightly browned and the edges are starting to frizzle, 8–10 minutes.

2 Add the tomatoes and ginger and season with salt and pepper. Cook, stirring occasionally, until the tomatoes break down and start to become jammy, 8–10 minutes (same if using tinned tomatoes).

3 Add the kimchi and its liquid, soy sauce, fish sauce and 1.4 litres (48 fl oz/ 6 cups) water. Bring to a boil and add the rice. Cook, stirring occasionally, until the rice is completely cooked through and tender and the broth has thickened nicely, 15–20 minutes. Season with salt, pepper and more soy or fish sauce as needed. Ladle into bowls and top with a drizzle of sesame oil or a pat of butter, an egg and some sliced spring onions, if you like.

VERY CLASSIC SPLIT PEA SOUP

SERVES 4

225–280 g (8–10 oz) bacon, pancetta or guanciale, chopped
1 yellow onion, 2 large shallots or 1 large leek (225–280 g/ 8–10 oz), finely chopped
5 garlic cloves (4 thinly sliced, 1 finely grated)
kosher salt and freshly ground black pepper
1 swede (rutabaga) or 2 large waxy potatoes, sweet potatoes or carrots (225 g/8 oz), peeled and chopped
450 g (1 lb/2 cups) split dried peas, yellow or green
1.9 litres (64 fl oz/8 cups) vegetable or chicken stock (or water plus Better Than Bouillon, see page 58)
bay leaf or thyme (optional)
handful of parsley, finely chopped
olive oil, for drizzling
1 lemon, halved for squeezing over

NOTE
—
To make this without any pork products, simply use 2 tablespoons of olive oil in place of the bacon.

DO AHEAD
—
This soup will keep in your fridge for at least 5 days, speaking from personal experience. It also freezes well (minus the toppings, of course).

EAT WITH
—
This soup is one of my favourite diner orders. I like to treat it as such even when I'm at home. It wants a grilled cheese or extra-toasted rye bread slathered with butter and a Tuna Salad Salad (page 138).

Split pea soup might not be known as a beautiful soup, but it is beautiful to me. As with many iconic recipes, I don't feel the need to overexplain why it's worth making, so I'll provide only the facts here: You don't need a pressure cooker or a soak or hours of your day to make this. This will not be puréed or blended. You can make it with or without pork, and nearly any sort of cured or salted pork will do. A bay leaf really does add 'a special something' here, but is optional. If your own broth is not available, this is an excellent use of Better Than Bouillon (see page 58), but even made with water, this soup will be delicious. Most importantly, perhaps: swede (rutabaga). Swede is a root vegetable, long ago made by crossing a cabbage and turnip. It's less sweet than a parsnip or carrot and less starchy than a potato, but carries characteristics of both. A swede is the correct vegetable to use in this recipe, but a potato, sweet potato or carrot can stand in.

1 Place whatever pork product you're using in a large pot and cook over a medium heat. Cook, stirring occasionally, until the meat is crisped and there is a generous pool of fat inside your pot, 6–10 minutes.

2 Leaving all the fat behind, remove the meaty bits with a spoon and set them aside on a plate or in a small bowl. (If you're not using pork, do none of the above and instead drop 2 tablespoons or so of olive oil into your pot.)

3 Add the onion and sliced garlic to the fat and season with salt and pepper. Increase the heat to medium-high and cook, stirring occasionally, until the onions are tender and lightly browned at the edges, 5–7 minutes.

4 Add the swede and season with salt and pepper. Cook, stirring occasionally, until the onions are deeply browned, 10–12 minutes.

5 Add the split peas, stock and either a bay leaf or a few sprigs of thyme, if you've got it. Bring to a strong simmer, then reduce the heat to medium-low. Continue to simmer gently until the swede and split peas are so tender, they're practically falling apart, 45–55 minutes. At this stage, I like to use a wooden spoon to gently smash some of the swede and peas against the side of the pot to create a slightly thicker and creamier soup. If you are finding it still too soupy, keep simmering.

6 Add the grated garlic, stir, and season the soup with salt and pepper. Ladle into bowls and top with crispy pork, parsley, olive oil and lemon.

DILLY BEAN STEW with CABBAGE & FRIZZLED ONIONS

SERVES 4

2 tablespoons unsalted butter, plus more (or more olive oil) to serve
2 tablespoons olive oil, plus more to serve
1 large yellow onion, thinly sliced
kosher salt and freshly ground black pepper
2 × 400 g (14 oz) tins white beans, such as haricot (navy), butter (lima) or cannellini, drained and rinsed
1 litre (34 fl oz/4 cups) vegetable or chicken stock (or water plus Better Than Bouillon, see page 58)
¼ head cabbage, core removed, coarsely chopped (about 225 g/8 oz)
2 tablespoons white distilled vinegar or fresh lemon juice, plus more to taste
40 g (1½ oz/1 cup) dill, coarsely chopped
sour cream, for serving (optional)

DO AHEAD
—
Dilly Bean Stew can be made 5 days ahead, sealed and refrigerated. It also freezes beautifully, sealed and frozen up to 2 months ahead (probably more).

Some recipes are born from cooking something I think is delicious, and some are born from a name that I think sounds good. The latter is the case with Dilly Bean Stew, which contains beans and dill (lots of it) and is tangy like a jar of pickled dilly beans. I thought this was very clever: 'A star is born,' I said out loud, to nobody in particular.

As with any pantry-staple situation, the low number of deceptively modest ingredients in this recipe might lead you to believe that it doesn't have what it takes to be your new favourite stew – but I assure you, it does. Two secrets: The onions must be frizzled (somewhere between caramelised and fried) for the correct depth of flavour, and the beans must be cooked and lightly crushed before any liquid is added (or your stew will forever be a soup). While it might seem like overkill, I do highly recommend the pat of butter at the end, which truly takes this stew from humble to luxurious.

1   Heat the butter and olive oil in a medium pot over a medium-high heat. Add the onion and season with salt and pepper. Cook, without stirring too much or too frequently, so the onions get nicely browned and frizzled, 5–8 minutes. You do not want jammy, caramelised onions, but you also do not want burnt onions, so just adjust the heat and stir as needed. Using a slotted spoon, transfer one-quarter of the onions to a small bowl; set aside.

2   Add the beans and season with salt and pepper. Using a spoon, smash some of the beans, breaking them up to release the creamy, starchy interior (this is what will thicken your stew). I say 'some of' because we are not making refried beans, nor are we making bean purée. Think whole, tender beans swimming in a pot of creamy, broken-down, lightly brothy beans.

3   Add the stock and bring to a simmer. Simmer until the texture is to your liking (soupier, stewier – you choose) and everything is tasting nice and savoury, 15–20 minutes. Add the cabbage and vinegar, stirring to wilt. Simmer until the cabbage is tender and all the flavours have melded, 10–15 minutes. Season with salt, pepper and more vinegar if you like.

4   Remove from the heat and stir in half of the dill. Divide among bowls and top with more dill and some frizzled onions. Add a teeny knob of softened butter – live a little – or a drizzle of olive oil and, if the mood strikes, some sour cream.

PORK NOODLE SOUP
with TOASTED GARLIC & GREENS

SERVES 4

2 tablespoons neutral oil, such as grapeseed or rapeseed (canola)

8 garlic cloves, thinly sliced

450 g (1 lb) minced (ground) pork (or turkey or chicken, if you don't do pork)

kosher salt and freshly ground black pepper

1½ teaspoons chilli flakes, plus more to taste

60 ml (2 fl oz/¼ cup) soy sauce or tamari, plus more to taste

100 g (3½ oz/2 cups) coriander (cilantro), tender leaves and stems, coarsely chopped

1 large bunch pea shoots, spinach, Swiss chard or kale, thick stems removed, leaves torn or chopped

2 tablespoons finely grated fresh ginger (from about a 5 cm/2 inch piece)

1–2 teaspoons fish sauce

175 g (6 oz) rice noodles (thick or thin cut)

½ medium red, yellow or white onion or 4 spring onions (scallions), very thinly sliced

DO AHEAD
—
This soup is best eaten the day it's made, since rice noodles tend to bloat too much when they sit awhile. It can be made, *sans* noodles, onion and herbs, 3 days ahead and refrigerated.

This is one of the soups I make most often, as it hits all my personal pleasure receptors: spicy, salty, brothy, herby and just a little bit meaty. I've published a few versions of this in my time (all of them fan favourites), but I truly can't help myself since it's always exactly what I want to eat, consisting almost entirely of things I already have on hand. It's also extremely flexible, good for the days when you're excited to make something but might be out of, say, 30 per cent of the ingredients.

While this is called pork noodle soup, you can certainly use turkey or chicken, but add a few more tablespoons of fat when browning the meat. The 'greens' here can be any you like. Pea shoots are tender, sweet and perfect, but can be elusive depending on where you're shopping, so feel free to use other leafy greens that wilt down effortlessly: I love the more delicate spinach and Swiss chard, but kale works, too.

1. Heat the oil in a large, heavy-bottomed pot over a medium heat.

2. Add the garlic and cook, stirring occasionally, until the slices become nicely toasted and golden brown, 2–3 minutes. Using a spoon (preferably slotted, to make life easier), transfer the garlic to a small bowl and set aside.

3. Add the pork to the pot and season with salt and pepper. Cook, using a wooden spoon or spatula to break up large pieces (you aren't making meatballs here), until the pork is very well browned and in small, bite-size pieces, 10–12 minutes. Add the chilli flakes and cook for a minute or so, just to bloom the chilli in the hot fat.

4. Add the soy sauce, about half of the coriander and 1.4 litres (48 fl oz/ 6 cups) water. Bring to a simmer and cook until the pork is very tender and the broth tastes impossibly good, 5–8 minutes. (Give it a taste and season with more salt, pepper, chilli flakes and soy sauce if needed.) Add the pea shoots and ginger, stirring to wilt and soften the leaves. Taste the soup and season with fish sauce; remove from the heat.

5. Cook the rice noodles according to the package instructions. (I usually just boil them like pasta, cooking for 2–4 minutes.) Drain and divide among bowls (or keep in the pot to serve it that way).

6. To serve, ladle the soup over the noodles if the noodles are in the bowl, or simply divide the noodle soup among bowls. Either way, top each bowl with onion, the remaining coriander and the toasted garlic chips.

SUMMER VEGETABLE SOUP with HOMINY & LIME

SERVES 4

2 tablespoons olive oil
2 large yellow or white onions, finely chopped
4 garlic cloves, chopped
¾ teaspoon ground cumin
kosher salt and freshly ground black pepper
675–900 g (1½–2 lb) courgettes (zucchini) or other summer squash, cut into large chunks
1 jalapeño, very thinly sliced (seeds in or out, your preference)
1.9 litres (64 fl oz/8 cups) vegetable or chicken stock (or water plus Better Than Bouillon, see page 58)
2 × 400 g (14 oz) tins hominy, drained and rinsed
3 corn cobs, shucked and kernels removed (about 375 g/13 oz/ 2½ cups corn kernels, if using frozen)
1 bunch coriander (cilantro), finely chopped
2–4 limes, halved for squeezing over

DO AHEAD

This soup makes fantastic leftovers, kept in the fridge for up to 3 days (without coriander or lime) or frozen several months ahead.

With so few ingredients, this soup could easily become very boring very quickly, but . . . it doesn't. While summer vegetables are meant to be added in as you see fit (lots of options below), the majority of the flavour and texture in this soup comes from a tin in your pantry. Hominy (also known as 'pozole', famously used in the classic Mexican soup that's called . . . pozole) gives this soup an irreplaceable, pleasantly bouncy, chewy texture and a toasty corn-chip flavour. While it traditionally anchors meat-forward dishes and stews (like . . . pozole), hominy is such a good tin to have around for quick, brothy soups, especially of the vegetarian sort. I love cooking it from dried (which I WILL soak, as it takes much longer to cook than beans), but for anyone looking to explore hominy as an ingredient, the already-cooked kernels in a tin are a great (and easy) introduction.

As for the vegetables, you can throw in a variety of whatever bounty you find yourself with. That said, if you pick two, go with barely cooked corn (which can be fresh or, honestly, frozen) for tenderness and a delicate sweetness and lots of courgette (zucchini), cut into large chunks to sort of braise and soften in the broth (making this my all-time favorite way to use up and eat 'how can there be so much' courgette).

1 Heat the olive oil in a large pot over a medium-high heat. Add about three-quarters of the onion (reserve the rest to add at the end), the garlic and cumin, and season with salt and pepper. Cook, stirring occasionally, until the onion is softened and starting to brown at the edges, 5–8 minutes.

2 Add the courgettes and half of the jalapeño and season again with salt and pepper. Cook, stirring occasionally, until the courgettes have started to soften and brown around the edges, 8–10 minutes.

3 Add the stock, hominy and corn and bring to a simmer. Cook, stirring occasionally, until the courgettes have completely softened and started to break down a bit (without totally turning to mush), 20–25 minutes. Add the remaining jalapeño and half of the coriander. Season again with salt and pepper. Ladle into bowls and top with the remaining onion and coriander and serve with limes for squeezing over the top.

VEGETABLES
ARE PART OF YOUR
PANTRY, TOO

There are a few vegetables I consider to be 'pantry vegetables'. These are the vegetables that can stay on your counter, in your fridge or in your literal pantry for much longer than you thought possible without degradation.

There's a wide range: Cured alliums meant to be stored indefinitely, like onions and garlic, are a given. 'Cellar-temperature' root vegetables, like potatoes and squash, qualify, followed by slightly less sturdy root vegetables like carrots, beets and turnips. I also count heartier refrigerator vegetables, the ones stored in the drawers and toward the back behind some jar of pickles you probably forgot about until one day you rediscovered them and asked yourself, 'How does this still look so good? It's been weeks. Can I still cook with it?' (Yes – it's fine.) Things like cabbage, fennel, some radishes and celery (which, despite being made almost entirely of water, is shockingly hardy) all fall into this latter category.

I try to keep any or all these vegetables on hand so that I don't feel like all I eat are lentils and pasta – because even the starchiest potato or most wrinkled head of cabbage, when perked up via the magic of roasting, braising, caramelising or stewing, will comfort me, knowing I've had my vegetables. When in doubt, turn these vegetables into soup or stock (especially if compost is not an option), simmering whatever life they have left out of them and into a fabulous broth.

POTATO LEEK SOUP with DARK LEAFY GREENS

SERVES 4

2 tablespoons olive oil
900 g (2 lb) waxy potatoes, such as King Edward or La Ratte, sliced about 1 cm (½ inch) thick
2 leeks (the whole thing!), chopped
kosher salt and freshly ground black pepper
1.4 litres (48 fl oz/6 cups) vegetable or chicken stock (or water plus Better Than Bouillon, see page 58)
1 large bunch (or 2 small bunches) leafy greens, such as kale, spinach or Swiss chard, stems removed, leaves torn into bite-size pieces
60 ml (2 fl oz/¼ cup) sour cream, plus more to serve
2 teaspoons white wine vinegar, plus more to taste
4 spring onions (scallions), thinly sliced
40 g (1½ oz/1 cup) dill, tender leaves and stems, coarsely chopped

DO AHEAD
—
This soup can be made *sans* sour cream and herbs 3 days ahead and refrigerated, or several months ahead and frozen. This is a very popular feel-better-soon or postpartum meal to have on hand in the freezer.

I am irrationally thrilled by this soup. It has so few ingredients, it has no right to be as delicious as it is. I attribute this miracle mostly to the dill, but also to the small amount of white wine vinegar (a hero) at the end, which gives the whole thing a sort of perky flair that no pot of cooked-down potatoes and leeks has ever been accused of having. It's definitely heavy on the leeks, which is great for flavour, but also texture – the white and light green parts almost melt into the potatoes, while the usually tougher dark green parts behave like an oniony extension of the wilted dark leafy greens, becoming perfectly tender.

This soup is a beauty as written, but know there is some flexibility here. Don't have waxy potatoes? You can use russets. No greens? Cabbage would be good, too. Before the sour cream is added, this soup is technically vegan, but it doesn't have to be. Use butter instead of olive oil, chicken stock instead of vegetable, yoghurt instead of sour cream. Want to add a crispy cured pork situation? Sure! This would also be excellent topped with smoked trout, sardines or salmon. But whatever you do, don't skip the dill. Nothing can replace the dill.

1   Heat the olive oil in a large heavy-bottomed pot over a medium-high heat. Add the potatoes and leeks and season with salt and pepper.

2   Cook, stirring occasionally, until the leeks are bright green and have begun to sweat, 5–8 minutes. Add the stock and bring to a simmer. Simmer until the liquid has reduced a bit and the potatoes are basically falling apart, 30–40 minutes. With a little encouragement from your wooden (or whatever) spoon, I want you to smush the tender potatoes so that they fall apart even more. (This will thicken the soup, turn it creamy and make the potatoes a nice uneven, chunky texture.)

3   Add the greens, stirring to wilt them into the soup.

4   Add the sour cream and vinegar and simmer for another minute or so. (Adding the sour cream later in the cooking process keeps a 'fresher' sour cream flavour and prevents any curdling.) Season with salt, pepper and maybe a little more vinegar.

5   Ladle the soup into bowls and top with more sour cream if you're going that route. Scatter the bowls with spring onions and lots of dill, then grind some more pepper over everything.

SPICED SQUASH & LENTIL SOUP with FRIED SHALLOTS

SERVES 4–6

2 tablespoons unsalted butter (or more olive oil)

2 tablespoons olive oil, plus more to serve

3 large shallots or 1 large red onion, thinly sliced

kosher salt and freshly ground black pepper

1 teaspoon cumin seeds, or ¾ teaspoon ground cumin

½ teaspoon chilli flakes, plus more to serve

1 small acorn, kabocha or butternut squash (800–900 g/1¾–2 lb), peeled, seeded, cut into 2.5 cm (1 inch) pieces

4 garlic cloves, thinly sliced

375 g (13 oz/1½ cups) red or yellow lentils

1.9 litres (64 fl oz/8 cups) water or stock (or water plus Better Than Bouillon, see page 58)

2 teaspoons sherry vinegar or white wine vinegar, plus more to taste

100 g (3½ oz/2 cups) coarsely chopped mixed herbs, such as coriander (cilantro), dill, chives and/or spring onions (scallions)

yoghurt or sour cream, for serving

DO AHEAD
—
This soup keeps remarkably well (without herbs), either in the fridge for up to 5 days or in the freezer for up to 2 months (possibly longer).

EAT WITH
—
This is the sort of soup that doesn't really need anything to go with it. That said, it would be nice with some flatbread or toast, and maybe a Leafy, Herby Salad (page 148).

More squash than lentil, this soup has a similar texture to split pea: smooth with visible bits of vegetables and legumes here and there. While absolutely savoury, it does have a lovely little sweetness (curbed by a good splash of vinegar) and just enough cumin to remind me of eating soup from a co-op – a very specific, niche, yet evocative reference for a select few. Like most of my soups, this one is also very flexible, but I do think acorn squash is the right squash for the job: It's mild in flavour (an asset here) with a mushy texture once cooked. The way it truly melts and falls apart makes the creaminess of this soup possible without the need for a blender or machine of any sort.

1. Heat the butter and olive oil in a large pot over a medium heat. Add the shallots and season with salt and pepper. Cook, stirring occasionally, until the shallots are starting to turn a nice golden-brown, 10–12 minutes.

2. Add the cumin and chilli flakes. Stir, cooking for a minute or two to bloom the spices a bit in the fat. Using a fork or slotted spoon, remove about half of the shallots and set aside.

3. Add the squash and garlic to the pot and season with salt and pepper. Cook, stirring every now and then, until the garlic is tender and the squash starts to fall apart (it should look like a very coarse mash), 15–20 minutes.

4. Add the lentils and water or stock and season with salt and pepper. Bring to a gentle simmer, letting the squash melt into the stock as the lentils become tender and follow suit, 30–35 minutes. Things should be getting to split-pea-soup texture – not entirely smooth (this isn't a purée) but creamy with bits of squash here and there. If it feels watery or too thin for your soup preference, continue simmering until you've reached the texture that's pleasing to you.

5. To serve, season the soup with the vinegar and more salt and pepper, if needed (it should be nicely acidic to balance the sweetness of the squash). Ladle soup into each bowl, and top with the herbs, stirring to let them wilt into the soup a little (which will really perk up the aroma, especially if using a mix of dill and coriander, as I would). Spoon yoghurt or sour cream into the soup (if using) then top with the reserved shallots, a drizzle of olive oil, and maybe another grind or two of pepper or a pinch of chilli flakes.

SOUP THAT *HEALS*

The story of matzo ball soup is, for me, a story about love. It was the first food I fell in love with – the first food I associated with care and tenderness. Every time I was sick, my parents or grandparents would order it from Solly's, the now-defunct Los Angeles diner, right off the 101 in Sherman Oaks, where my grandpa would take me every morning when I was a baby. He'd let the waitresses carry me around the dining room and ask them to change me in the bathroom because he didn't want to. I guess you could say it was the first restaurant where I was a regular.

You'd think that since I only had this soup when I was sick, I might have developed a cognitive distaste for it, but quite the opposite. Arriving in a plastic quart container leaking all over the place, one giant, fluffy ball floating in some salty, schmaltzy chicken broth flecked with not nearly enough dill, full-sour dill pickles in a plastic bag on the side, it healed me time and time again. Even though there is no empirical evidence that this soup (or any soup) can cure what ails you, I at least associated it with the attempt, always making me feel loved and cared for, cradled and looked after.

As an adult living in New York, I admit I struggled to find any version of matzo ball soup in the city that I thought was all that good. The balls too big, the broth underseasoned. Noodles floating around and a singular carrot coin as garnish, always feeling like an insult. Don't get me wrong, I'll order it (a subpar matzo ball soup still gives me a serotonin boost), but still, for me, nothing compares to the one I make (possibly arrogant, definitely true).

I guess it's funny to have 'your favourite food' be something you only make when you're sick or for holidays twice a year, but it is. I have to assume my now husband understood this on a deep, cellular level, because he made it for me the night he proposed. Not a cook himself, he told me he was terrified to mess it up, but the soup truly was undeniably wonderful, as if I had made it myself (my highest compliment?). The matzo balls perfectly sized, seasoned and cooked; the broth that gorgeous golden colour we all dream of. No carrots, ample dill. I would have said yes even if it had turned out inedible, because with or without my favourite soup, he, too, makes me feel loved and cared for, cradled and looked after.

MATZO BALL SOUP

SERVES 6-8

150 g (5½ oz/1 cup) matzo meal (not matzo ball mix) or finely ground matzo boards (from 3–4 matzo boards)
15 g (½ oz/¼ cup) finely chopped chives, plus more for garnish
10 g (½ oz/¼ cup) finely chopped dill, plus more for garnish
1¾ teaspoons kosher salt, plus more to taste
5 large eggs
90 ml (3 fl oz/⅓ cup) chicken fat or 75 g (2½ oz) unsalted butter (if not keeping kosher), melted
60 ml (2 fl oz/¼ cup) club soda or seltzer
1.9 litres (64 fl oz/8 cups) Chicken Broth, the Long Way (page 51)
2 celery stalks, thinly sliced, plus any leaves for garnish
freshly ground black pepper

DO AHEAD
—
This soup can be made 3 days ahead and refrigerated.

Of all the recipes in this book, this might be my finest work. If you are looking for heavy, dense, softball-size matzo balls, please find another recipe – you will be disappointed here. These are light, they are ethereal, they taste deeply of chicken fat, and of course, they've got so much dill. The soup itself is heavy on the celery, a tragically underappreciated vegetable that does so much for both the chicken broth and the matzo balls. (Someone once told me, 'You've gotta really like celery to enjoy this soup,' which I take as high praise.)

1 Combine the matzo meal, chives, dill and salt in a medium bowl. Using a fork, incorporate the eggs until well blended. Add the chicken fat, followed by the club soda, mixing until everything is evenly soaked. This mixture will look upsettingly loose. It will firm up as it sits. Trust the matzo ball.

2 Cover with cling film (plastic wrap) and refrigerate until the mixture is firm and fully hydrated, at least 2 hours (and up to 24 hours). It should have the texture of wet clay: malleable and shapeable.

3 Bring the chicken broth to a simmer in a large pot; set aside but keep hot.

4 Separately, bring another large pot of well-salted water to a boil. Using your hands, roll the matzo mixture into balls, somewhere between the size of a ping-pong and a golf ball. (Please resist the urge to make the matzo balls larger. They double in size and will be perfect once cooked – this I promise you.) Place them on a plate or parchment-lined sheet pan as you go. (You should have 12–24 matzo balls, depending on size.) If the mixture starts to feel too soft, you can put it back in the fridge to firm up. I have also been known to just roll directly into the pot of boiling water – they always somehow end up perfectly spherical.

5 Gently plop all the matzo balls into the boiling water and cook until floating, puffed and cooked through, 12–15 minutes. (Pluck one from the water at 12 minutes and cut it in half to see how it's doing – it should be uniform in colour and texture and lighter in colour than it was in its raw state. It should look fluffy, not dense.) Using a slotted spoon, transfer the matzo balls to the chicken broth to give them a final brief simmer.

6 Add the celery and season again with salt before ladling the soup into bowls. Top each bowl with plenty of dill, chives, celery leaves if you've got them, and a crack of freshly ground pepper.

SPICY PORK SOUP with PASTA & PARMESAN

SERVES 4

1 tablespoon olive oil, plus more for drizzling
450 g (1 lb) minced (ground) pork or turkey
kosher salt and freshly ground black pepper
4 garlic cloves, thinly sliced
1 tablespoon fennel seeds
½ teaspoon chilli flakes, plus more to taste
1.4 litres (48 fl oz/6 cups) chicken or vegetable stock (or water plus Better Than Bouillon, see page 58)
175–225 g (6–8 oz) dried pasta (a short, tube-y noodle or something fun like radiatori)
1 bunch cime di rapa or kale, thick stems removed, chopped
Parmesan or pecorino cheese, for grating or shaving (lots of it)
1 lemon, halved for squeezing (optional)

NOTES

In place of the pork, you can use fresh sausage (hot Italian, turkey, chicken), casing removed, leaving out the fennel seed and chilli flakes.

DO AHEAD

Soup can be made 3 days ahead. Keep the noodles separate to prevent soggy pasta.

This soup is salty and porky, cheesy and garlicky. There are little whimsical bits of pasta floating about, soaking up all that salty, porky, cheesy, garlicky broth. It's what I'd call an undeniable 'crowd-pleaser'. There is also cime di rapa, a vegetable I've come to learn is shockingly divisive (shocking to me, as it's a personal top five). So here's what I'll say: The cime di rapa is important here. It has a unique ability to be everything at once: delicate and sturdy, bitter and sweet. Simmering it in the fatty, seasoned broth mimics the effect of blanching, which mellows out the bitterness some people find so off-putting, so I'd love for you to take a leap of faith even if you don't think you like it. If you REALLY hate it, okay, use kale.

1 Heat the olive oil in a large pot over a medium-high heat. Add the pork and season with salt and pepper. Cook, resisting the urge to break it up too much at first. As it browns, break it up into small pieces; some of the pork will get very small (these bits will get very brown and crispy), and some will stay larger, in sausage-like clumps (these will be tender and juicier). Once the pork is about 80 per cent browned to your liking, 8–10 minutes, add the garlic. Continue cooking until the pork is well browned throughout and the garlic is softened and starting to brown around the edges, another 4–5 minutes.

2 Add the fennel seeds and chilli flakes. Give them a stir to toast in the pork fat, cooking for a minute or two. Add the stock, season with salt and pepper and bring to a simmer.

3 Meanwhile, cook the pasta in a medium pot of salted water until just before al dente. (It'll continue to cook in the soup, but it's good to give it a head start. I don't love cooking raw pasta in a brothy soup – it makes the broth too starchy and cloudy.)

4 Once the soup has simmered for a few minutes, add the cime di rapa and the pasta, stirring to wilt the cime di rapa. Simmer until the rabe is tender and the flavours have mingled appropriately, another 5–8 minutes or so. Season with salt, pepper and more chilli flakes if you like.

5 To serve, ladle into bowls and top with a drizzle of olive oil and tons of cheese. Sometimes I squeeze lemon over, but not always (doesn't need it, but it can be nice).

BUTTERED TOMATO SOUP with LENTILS & FENNEL

SERVES 4

2 tablespoons unsalted butter (or more olive oil)
2 tablespoons olive oil, plus more to serve
4 garlic cloves, thinly sliced
1 large fennel bulb, thinly sliced
1 medium yellow or red onion or 2 large shallots, thinly sliced
kosher salt and freshly ground black pepper
2 teaspoons fennel seeds
½ teaspoon chilli flakes, plus more to taste
185 g (6½ oz/¾ cup) red lentils
2 × 400 g (14 oz) tins whole peeled tomatoes, crushed by hand
1.4 litres (48 fl oz/6 cups) water, vegetable or chicken stock
sour cream, full-fat yoghurt, or Parmesan cheese if you like

NOTE
—
I enjoy the extra texture of thinly sliced fennel and onion here, but if you prefer a more uniformly textured soup, you can finely chop them.

DO AHEAD
—
The soup can be made 5 days ahead and refrigerated, or 3 months ahead and frozen.

EAT WITH
—
Good slices of cheddar cheese on oiled toast or a classic grilled cheese. A few links of nice, spicy sausage. A big, broad-leaf, endive (escarole) salad.

Imagine, for a moment, a tomato soup that needs no blender to produce an impossibly creamy result, all without a drop of dairy; a lentil soup vibrant and gorgeous enough to grace the cover of a cookbook yet humble enough to eat alone at your kitchen counter for a Tuesday lunch. Seasonally agnostic (tinned tomatoes here!), this soup thrives in winter with the best of your pantry staples, as cosy as Potato Leek Soup (page 73) and made in half the time.

Once this soup comes together, you may forget there are lentils in here at all. They magically melt into the pot, nearly disappearing (that's the idea), giving you creamy texture and luscious body: tomato (and lentil) soup utopia.

1 Heat the butter and olive oil in a large pot over a medium-high heat. Add the garlic, fennel and onion. Season with salt and pepper and cook, stirring occasionally, until the fennel and onions are completely softened and start to caramelise a bit, 12–15 minutes. (This builds a lot of flavour for your soup – don't rush it.)

2 Add the fennel seeds and chilli flakes, stirring to encourage contact with the pot so the spices have a chance to toast for a minute or two. Add the lentils, crushed tomatoes and liquid of your choosing. (I make mine with water, and it's perfect, but if you have some broth to use or want to add some Better Than Bouillon to your water, go for it.)

3 Season everything with salt and pepper and bring to a strong simmer. Reduce the heat to medium-low and continue to cook until the lentils have nearly disappeared into the pot, 45–50 minutes. Stir every now and then (especially toward the end of cooking) to encourage the lentils and tomatoes to break down and into one another. If the soup doesn't feel quite thick enough or the lentils are somehow still not near-mush, increase the heat slightly and continue to cook until it happens. It will happen!

4 To serve, give the soup one more season with salt and pepper. Ladle the soup into bowls and finish with more olive oil, pepper and chilli flakes. I am continually shocked at how good this soup is with nothing else (no squeeze of lemon, no fresh herb in sight!), but I do like to spoon a little dollop of sour cream or yoghurt into the bottom of my bowl and top it with the soup. What a treat that is, a little buried puddle of melting sour cream at the bottom of your bowl. A true gift!

CREAMY CLAM CHOWDER WITH CELERY

SERVES 6–8

2 × 185 g (6½ oz) tins whole or chopped clams (or 1.8–2.25 kg/ 4–5 lb fresh clams, such as littlenecks or cockles), or a mix of both tinned and fresh

175 g (6 oz) slab or sliced bacon, cut into 1 cm (½ inch) pieces (or 4 tablespoons olive oil)

6 garlic cloves, thinly sliced

2 large leeks (the whole thing!) or 1 large yellow or white onion, chopped

kosher salt and freshly ground black pepper

4 celery stalks or 1 fennel bulb, thinly sliced (celery leaves or fennel fronds reserved)

675–900 g (1½–2 lb) potatoes (King Edward preferred), unpeeled, cut into 2.5 cm (1 inch) pieces

950 ml (32 fl oz/4 cups) double (heavy) cream

1 fresh or dried bay leaf, or a few sprigs of thyme (optional)

parsley, salted crackers, hot sauce and/or lemon wedges, for serving

DO AHEAD
—
Clam chowder can be made 2 days ahead, wrapped and refrigerated. It can also be frozen (*sans* clam shells) 2 months ahead (probably longer).

EAT WITH
—
A cold beer and a gentle breeze running through your hair.

If you're expecting a thick, gloopy chowder experience, you've come to the wrong place. There is no roux here, no flour, no blending. This chowder is more of the soupy, light and ethereal variety. The potatoes fall apart into the broth to thicken it just so, and bits of clam and smoky bacon bob among abundant slices of bright green celery and leeks – a real chilly New England summer evening sort of chowder. But I'm burying the lede: The beauty here is that you don't need fresh clams for this. Much like the clam pasta on page 228, it can be made entirely with tinned clams (chopped or whole, brine and all), an excellent (if often overlooked) pantry staple.

1. If you're using fresh clams, scrub them well and let them soak in cold water while you make the chowder.

2. Heat a large pot over medium heat. Add the bacon (if not using, heat butter or olive oil in the pot and skip ahead to step 3) and cook, stirring occasionally, until the fat has rendered considerably, 10–12 minutes.

3. Increase the heat to medium-high and add the garlic and leeks to the pot. Season with salt and pepper and cook, stirring occasionally, until the leeks are bright green and softened, 6–8 minutes. Add the celery and potatoes and season with salt and pepper. Cook, stirring occasionally, until the vegetables are on their way to tender (but not yet falling apart), 8–10 minutes. Add the cream, bay leaf (if using—and you should!), and 1.2 litres (40 fl oz/5 cups) water. Season with salt and lots of pepper and bring to a simmer.

4. Reduce the heat to medium and cook until the potatoes are very tender, nearly falling apart, 20–25 minutes. Taste the broth: It should already taste wonderful and feel a bit thicker.

5. Add the clams (fresh or tinned) and cover the pot. Bring back to a simmer and cook, without peeking, for 5 minutes or so. If using fresh, the clams should start to steam open, give up their juices and further flavour the broth. Season the soup again with salt and lots of pepper.

6. To serve, finely chop parsley and/or celery leaves and sprinkle over the top. Serve alongside salted crackers, hot sauce and/or lemon.

COLD BORSCHT

SERVES 4–6

450 g (1 lb) red beetroot (beets), tops removed, scrubbed well (unpeeled)
60 ml (2 fl oz/¼ cup) white distilled vinegar, plus more to taste
kosher salt
small pinch of sugar (optional)
2 baby (Persian) cucumbers, thinly sliced or chopped
2 spring onions (scallions), thinly sliced
40 g (1½ oz/1 cup) dill, tender leaves and stems, finely chopped
2 lemons, halved for squeezing over
sour cream or full-fat yoghurt, for dolloping

DO AHEAD
—
Cold borscht, *sans* toppings, can be made 3 days ahead and refrigerated.

EAT WITH
—
I'd eat this either as a little lunch with some rye toast and a jammy egg, or as the start of a fancy meal, featuring brisket and ice-cold martinis.

This is an elegant, brothy soup made from very few ingredients – beetroot (beets) and the water they are cooked in being two of them. It relies heavily on toppings (dill) and will likely be enjoyed most by those who think of pickles as a desert island food. (I do.) I am historically not on the side of cold soups, but since this one tastes like pickles (desert island food) and isn't puréed, I have lots of affection for it. To call it a brothy salad would really turn me off, so I won't, but know that I'm thinking it. In a chapter full of 'cosy' soups, this one is chilled and a little austere but somehow still familiar and comforting. Try not to overthink it, and simply be amazed that such a wonderfully flavourful bowl can come from nearly nothing.

1   Place the beetroot in a large pot and cover by at least 10 cm (4 inches) of water. Add the vinegar, season with salt and bring to a boil. Reduce the heat so the beetroot are gently (not violently) boiling and cook until the tender and completely cooked through, 60–70 minutes. (The best way to tell that the beetroot are done is to make sure you can easily pierce them with a knife – it should feel like inserting a knife into a ripe peach, not a radish. This is the only time the beetroot get cooked, so they need to be as tender as you'd want them to be.) Saving the water in the pot, remove the beetroot, and let them cool slightly. Using a paper towel, peel them. (The skin should slip right off – if it's feeling stubborn, the beetroot might not be as cooked through as you think.)

2   Chop or grate the beetroot (fine chop, coarse chop, box grater, anything goes) and place in a large bowl. Measure out whatever liquid is left in the pot – you need at least 950 ml (32 fl oz/4 cups) (supplement with water if you're short) – and add to the bowl with the beetroot. Season with salt, a pinch of sugar if necessary and more vinegar. Right now, it should taste good – not overly acidic like actual pickle brine, but pleasantly tangy, well seasoned with salt and with just enough sugar to enhance the natural sweetness of the beetroot. It should be delicious enough to drink because, well, you will be drinking it. Chill this mixture until absolutely frigid (overnight is best).

3   Each person will tell you that cold borscht should be garnished a different way, and nobody is wrong here. I like a minimal approach, with plenty of thinly sliced cucumbers and spring onions, LOTS of dill, a healthy squeeze of lemon (different acidity than vinegar) and a modest amount of sour cream.

GOLDEN MUSHROOM SOUP
with ORZO & A PAT OF BUTTER
SERVES 4

3 tablespoons olive oil, plus more as needed

350 g (12 oz) mushrooms, a good mix of the more exotic cultivated or wild foraged varieties, if you can, torn or cut into bite-size pieces

kosher salt and freshly ground black pepper

6 garlic cloves, thinly sliced

½ teaspoon ground turmeric

¼ teaspoon chilli flakes, or to taste

1.4 litres (48 fl oz/6 cups) water or stock (or water plus Better Than Bouillon, see page 58)

225 g (8 oz/¾ cup) dried orzo

2 teaspoons fish sauce or soy sauce, plus more to taste

2 tablespoons unsalted butter, plus more to serve

flaky sea salt, for finishing

NOTE

Oyster, maitake, chanterelle or king trumpet mushrooms would all be wonderful here.

DO AHEAD

This soup can be made a few days ahead and refrigerated, if you want. The orzo will continue to absorb the flavours of the broth and the mushrooms, so one might argue this gets better with age. Thin with water as needed.

EAT WITH

In keeping with the monastic theme, I like to eat this soup alone (often for lunch), but for dinner (maybe even with others), I think a giant piece of toasted bread or baguette to dunk into the broth would be nice.

This is the type of soup that, at first glance, might seem a little ... unexciting. But what you're likely underestimating is the power of mushrooms (naturally high in umami, a fever dream of mixed textures, visually dazzling in all their shapes and sizes), which are doing most if not all of the heavy lifting here. Technically this recipe can be done with all button or chestnut (cremini) mushrooms, but I can't say it will look or taste as good as it does with a mix of the more exotic types, such as oyster, maitake or chanterelle.

The simplicity of this soup means you do have to be vigilant about seasoning (especially if you're so bravely using water instead of stock), salting, peppering and adjusting with fish sauce as you go. That said, I really enjoy the monk-like restraint of the mushroom-garlic-water magic that occurs (with a fish sauce assist, of course), creating a broth that is delicate and earthy, evoking a very good, robust mushroom tea.

1. Heat the olive oil in a large pot over medium-high heat. Add half of the mushrooms and season with salt and pepper. Cook, stirring occasionally, until they're starting to brown around the edges, 6–8 minutes. Add more olive oil if the pot is looking a little dry (mushrooms really soak it up), followed by the remaining mushrooms and all the garlic. Season again with salt and pepper. Cook, stirring occasionally, until all the mushrooms are nicely browned and have started to leave a little fond (the brown, sticky parts where a lot of the flavour is) on the bottom of the pot, another 6–8 minutes.

2. Add the turmeric and chilli flakes and stir to bloom the spices in the fat for a minute or two. Add the water or stock and bring to a simmer. Add the orzo and fish sauce and season again with salt and pepper.

3. Simmer until the broth is deeply flavourful and the orzo has cooked through, 15–20 minutes. The end soup should be brothy enough that you can see bits of orzo and mushrooms floating close to the surface – my simmer might not be your simmer, so keep simmering if it's feeling a little thin.

4. Once the broth is where you want it and the orzo is good and plumped, add the butter to the pot and season again with salt, pepper and more fish sauce. Divide among bowls and top with more chilli flakes, some flaky salt and ... more butter. Because it looks nice and tastes so good.

VEGETABLES
and how to make them taste even better

I subscribe to the idea that a plain, mostly unadulterated piece of perfectly cooked, pristine produce is one of life's greatest pleasures. A small, waxy boiled potato with a smear of good butter; a just-blanched spear of nice broccoli squeezed with an absurd amount of lemon; a nicely ripened tomato topped with a bit of flaky salt.

That said, often we are not working with pristine produce, and our vegetables need a little help to truly sing. That, or those romantic waxy potatoes are all that's been in season for months, and we need something more than a smear of butter to get us through. That's where your pantry comes in.

These recipes don't depend on perfection from the earth. Rather, they make the most of what you have, working a little magic from your (well-stocked) pantry. Still simple but with a nice *je ne sais quoi*, the vegetables and salads in this chapter will exceed your expectations: They might be enhanced by fermented Calabrian chillies, they might be braised with a whole tin of anchovies, they might make you fall in love with sherry vinegar (if you're not already). Examples of small additions (olive oil, especially) to the equation going a long way, these vegetable-based dishes are loving expressions of how to make something from nothing.

DEEPLY ROASTED FENNEL & CAPERS

SERVES 4–6

2 large or 3 medium fennel bulbs (about 550 g/1¼ lb), including stems and fronds, if available
30 g (1 oz/1 cup) parsley, tender leaves and stems, finely chopped (optional)
1 lemon, zested
flaky sea salt
3–4 tablespoons olive oil
40 g (1½ oz/¼ cup) capers, drained, coarsely chopped
1 tablespoon fennel seeds
a good pinch of chilli flakes or whole *chile de árbol* (optional)
kosher salt and freshly ground black pepper

DO AHEAD

You can roast this fennel a few hours ahead and reheat in the oven when you're ready to eat, but it's also a great room-temperature side.

EAT WITH

Because I really love fennel, I love this dish (fennel with fennel) with something like a big bowl of pasta that's also got a kiss of fennel in it (like the Bolognese on page 246). For those for whom that sounds like overkill, this really is perfect as a side for the Overnight Lamb (page 276) or Slow-Roasted Salmon (page 303). It's also nice over a bed of greens or cooked grains for a little salad with some crumbled feta over the top.

The most convincing thing I could say about this dish is that it is, hands down, the best and most delicious way to eat fennel. If you've never had transcendent fennel, then I am thrilled to present you with the opportunity to make it yourself by following this recipe. Capers and fennel seeds roast alongside the wedges, sizzling in the oil, both getting extremely crunchy and crispy, adding an additional layer of wonderful that you might never have thought possible. It's a vegetable side you don't have to worry about pairing with something because it truly goes with everything: roast chicken, braised beef, pork chops, lamb, salmon – all of god's creatures.

1 Preheat the oven to 220°C/200°C fan/425°F.

2 If the fennel bulbs have the stems and fronds, great: Thinly slice some of the stems, finely chop a bit of the fronds, and combine both in a small bowl with the lemon zest and a pinch of flaky salt; set aside. (This will go on fresh and raw at the end, before serving.) If you don't have fennel stems or fronds, use the parsley (nice to have something green and fresh at the end) – or skip altogether and just use lemon zest and flaky salt.

3 As for the bulbs, cut them into wedges about 1 cm (½ inch) thick – not too thick, not too thin. I prefer wedges to slices since wedges have a thicker end and thinner end, which results in different textures once roasted.

4 Toss the fennel in a large baking dish or on a rimmed baking tray with the olive oil, capers, fennel seeds and chilli flakes and season well with salt and pepper. Roast, tossing once or twice, until the fennel is deeply, impossibly caramelised, 45–55 minutes. As with all deeply roasted vegetables, it will first steam and become tender but look pale and not all that interesting – you must stay the course! Eventually, it'll properly caramelise and start to crisp up in spots, becoming pleasantly chewy in others. It's the deep brown colour and frizzled edges you're looking for. When in doubt, keep going.

5 Once the fennel is properly roasted and deeply caramelised and the capers are looking dark, frizzled and crisped, remove from the oven. Serve in the baking dish or transfer to a large plate, bowl or platter; scatter with the reserved stem-frond-and-zest mixture before serving.

WINE-BRAISED ROMANO BEANS with ANCHOVY

SERVES 4–6

60 ml (2 fl oz/¼ cup) olive oil, plus more to serve
8 garlic cloves, thinly sliced
8–10 oil-packed anchovy fillets
a good pinch of chilli flakes
550–675 g (1¼–1½ lb) helda beans, green beans or yellow wax beans, stems trimmed
kosher salt and freshly ground black pepper
250 ml (8 fl oz/1 cup) dry, acidic white wine

NOTE
—
While you can do these in a skillet, my preferred vessel for cooking these is a casserole (Dutch oven) or high-sided pot. It will always look like too many beans, but they do eventually shrink as they soften and wilt. Giving them enough space in a larger pot prevents them from prematurely breaking, ensuring they stay as intended: a wild mess of long, entangled beans.

DO AHEAD
—
These beans will keep for several days in the fridge. You can reheat them gently when ready to serve, but they're also great cold, room temperature for a picnic or sun-warmed at the beach.

EAT WITH
—
A gorgeous vegetarian spread with Long-Cooked Brothy Chickpeas (page 158) or Olive Oil–Fried Lentils (page 180) next to a Leafy, Herby Salad (page 148) and Labneh with Caramelised Harissa (page 28).

Hopefully each time I say, 'This is one of the best-tasting things in the book,' it doesn't come off as disingenuous because I'd like to say it again, here and now. I know you know I rely on anchovies a great deal for lots of things, but it's remarkable how differently they show up each time I reach for a little tin or jar. Here, they take a back seat to the acidity of the wine but provide an undeniable savouriness that can't easily be replaced (and that you'd miss if it weren't there). White wine, garlic and anchovy are an obviously delightful combination, especially when used as the cooking liquid to braise something like a Romano bean (or green bean or yellow wax bean), simultaneously being absorbed by the vegetables, seasoning them from the inside out, and giving them a little saucy something to sit in.

1 Heat the olive oil in a large, high-sided pot, casserole (Dutch oven) or a large, wide skillet over a medium-high heat. Add the garlic and cook until toasted and nicely browned, 3–5 minutes. Add the anchovies and stir to melt for a minute or two. (Using a wooden spoon or tongs to smash them into the oil can be helpful if they need it.) Add the chilli flakes and let them bloom in the hot oil for a few seconds.

2 Add the beans, tossing them in the anchovy oil (I like tongs for this), and season with salt and pepper. They'll be really stiff and inflexible to start with, but give them time and they'll start to soften and bend, making them easy to periodically stir and toss.

3 Add the wine and stir to coat. Once the wine comes to a simmer, reduce the heat to medium. The fun part of cooking beans this way is that you get to decide the texture. If you like them on the al dente side with a bit of a brothy situation (I do), you'll cook them for 10–15 minutes. If you prefer a bean that is saucier, softer and falling apart (I do, too), cook for 25–30 minutes. If you've never cooked beans this way before, just taste one periodically. They can be eaten raw, so there's no danger in sampling early on.

4 Season again with salt and pepper and transfer to a large plate or bowl, making sure to get all the sauce spooned over. Drizzle with a bit of olive oil and give a grind or two of pepper before serving.

LONG-COOKED POTATOES, GARLIC & LEMON

SERVES 4-6

675 g (1½ lb) small, waxy potatoes, halved or quartered depending on the size
4 *chiles de árbol*, crumbled, or 1 teaspoon chilli flakes (optional)
8 garlic cloves, smashed
2 lemons, cut into wedges, seeds removed
20 g (¾ oz/½ cup) finely chopped dill
kosher salt and freshly ground black pepper
360 ml (12 fl oz/1½ cups) olive oil, chicken fat or duck fat
flaky sea salt

NOTE

Don't panic about the leftover garlicky dill-flecked oil you're left with (there will be a lot). Pour into a jar and keep refrigerated to use next time you're making these potatoes, roasting a chicken, slow-cooking tuna (page 307), or even, dare I say, making an aioli.... The possibilities are endless.

DO AHEAD

These potatoes can be made 5 days ahead, stored in their oil, wrapped, and refrigerated. Reheat in a 180°C/160°C fan/350°F oven until warmed through, or in a skillet on the stove.

EAT WITH

A tin of sardines and some pickles, a gorgeous Leafy, Herby Salad (page 148), and some Slow-Cooked Tuna (page 307) or Crispy Schnitzel (page 296).

Potatoes are a well-behaved pantry vegetable, save for the occasional brown spot or rogue sprouts that tend to arise when they are particularly young (dug from the ground early in the season) or especially old (left to languish in your pantry for two-plus months). While basic roasted potatoes are a wonderful thing, I've since discovered something better (on accident, almost): potatoes submerged in fat, long-cooked with whole cloves of smashed garlic and wedges of fresh lemon. This gives you potatoes with golden brown edges and a custardy, creamy interior nearly reminiscent of a french fry (it's true), plus cloves of garlic, tender and sweet, and wedges of lemon, bright and jammy, both soft and mellow enough to eat whole. Perhaps best of all, these potatoes love to be ignored, roasted low and slow enough to never burn, requiring only a toss or two if it suits you (if not, that's okay, the potatoes will still thrive). It all sounds too easy and too good to be true, but I assure you, it works. What bliss!

1 Preheat the oven to 190°C/180°C fan/375°F.

2 Combine the potatoes, *chiles de árbol* (if using), garlic, lemons and half of the dill in an oven-safe baking dish or large cast-iron skillet. Season with salt and pepper and toss. Pour the olive oil over and place in the oven. (It's okay, good even, if the potatoes aren't fully submerged in the oil.) Roast, stirring halfway or so, until the potatoes are completely tender and starting to brown where exposed at the top, 80–90 minutes.

3 Remove from the oven and finish with the remaining dill while the oil is still hot. Using a spoon, remove the potatoes and garlic and lemon bits from the oil and transfer to a serving platter, plate, or bowl. Drizzle with more of the dilly oil and sprinkle with flaky salt before serving.

SPICED, BUTTER-ROASTED CARROTS with WALNUTS

SERVES 4

2 bunches small carrots (about 450 g/1 lb), unpeeled, tops trimmed

75 g (2½ oz/¾ cup) walnuts, coarsely chopped

2 tablespoons olive oil

kosher salt and freshly ground black pepper

¼ teaspoon ground cinnamon

¼ teaspoon ground coriander

½ teaspoon chilli flakes

1 tablespoon fennel seeds

2 tablespoons unsalted butter, cut into tiny pieces (or more olive oil)

1 garlic clove, finely chopped or grated

DO AHEAD

The carrots can be roasted a few hours ahead of serving, gently rewarmed in the oven if your kitchen is cold and the butter has solidified.

EAT WITH

Crisp, Hot Roast Chicken (page 262) and a bowl of spelt (farro) tossed with herbs, or alongside brothy beans or chickpeas (garbanzos) (page 158) and a perky salad.

I am not a very heavy-handed spice user in my savoury cooking, but there is something about sweet, earthy carrots that calls for it. Instead of getting toasted beforehand, the spices (and walnuts!) are roasted with the carrots (and an extremely generous knob of butter), blooming in the fat as they cook, the butter lightly browning as the spices come alive, the walnuts toasting, the carrots tenderising, then caramelising – all at once.

I'm admittedly wary of sweet vegetables, so I always like to anchor them in something deeply savoury. Here, raw garlic adds that intensity, but don't worry, the heat from the just-roasted carrots gently tames its bite.

1 Preheat the oven to 220°C/200°C fan/425°F.

2 For fun and if you feel like it, thinly slice some of the carrots into coins. Halve the remaining ones lengthways, quartering them if they're especially large or thick (don't overthink this!) – it's just nice to have different shapes that lead to different textures once roasted.

3 Toss the carrots, walnuts and olive oil together on a baking tray and season with salt and pepper. Add the cinnamon, coriander, chilli flakes and fennel seeds and toss to coat. Scatter with the butter (or more olive oil). Roast, tossing every 15 minutes or so, until the carrots are deeply browned, well past the point of tender and starting to frizzle at the edges, 30–35 minutes.

4 Remove from the oven and toss with the raw garlic (the warmth of the carrots will soften the raw bite). Serve warm or at room temperature.

THE GORGEOUS SIMPLICITY OF
ROASTED SWEET POTATOES

Sweet potatoes occupy a very special and unique place in my heart. While I almost never cook with them (they're mushy and sweet, two things I'm not so attracted to), I have to admit that on occasion, I crave them so intensely that I barely recognise myself. But I don't want them disguised; I don't want to force them into being something they're not. (I'd never pretend they're a potato – sweet potato fries are a punishable offence.)

I want them as they are, in all their mushy, sweet glory, celebrated and prepared exactly one way and one way only. (My relationship with sweet potatoes represents the most contrarian part of my personality: not liking something for certain traits, then loving it for the exact same reasons… I am who I am!) They should be roasted at 200°C/190°C fan/400°F for about an hour, until they're cooked through and tender, their papery skin all wrinkled and shrivelled with little bits of caramelised pieces poking out, looking like hardened sap from a tree. I split them open (lengthways, from top to tail) while they're still warm, almost always burning my hands (but I don't mind), top them with a generous pat of salted butter (the good kind that's bright yellow with salt crystals evenly dispersed throughout) and finally, drizzle them with just enough maple syrup to help the butter move around to adequately dress the sweet potato. They should always be finished with several grinds of black pepper and maybe, if that salted butter isn't salted enough, a good pinch of flaky salt.

As far as I know, there is not a more simple and delicious snack available. This is my little special treat, one that I have never ever served to anyone else, one that I might make at 2:30 in the afternoon with a cup of black coffee, or that I might eat for breakfast while I stare at my phone, a blissful seventeen minutes alone to begin the day. This sweet potato is for me and me alone, and there's nothing about it that I would change. I do recognise that there is something silly about turning your oven on for one lonely potato, but special little treats are not meant to be practical. They exist only to delight. Isn't that nice?

FOREVER-ROASTED SQUASH with BROWNED BUTTER DATES

SERVES 4–6

- 900 g (2 lb) winter squash, such as acorn, butternut or honeynut (about one or two squash), quartered lengthways and seeded
- 6 Medjool dates, pitted and torn in half
- 2 tablespoons olive oil
- kosher salt and freshly ground black pepper
- 2 tablespoons light or dark brown sugar
- 8 garlic cloves, peeled or not, well smashed
- ½ bunch sage (thyme, marjoram or oregano also work)
- 6 tablespoons unsalted butter

DO AHEAD

The squash can be roasted a few hours ahead; gently rewarm in the oven in the baking dish it's roasted in before serving.

EAT WITH

These squash really are fantastic as a Thanksgiving side. That said, this dish also deserves to be eaten year-round. It's great with other large hunks of slow-cooked celebratory meats that aren't turkey, especially red meat like Brisket (page 284) or Short Ribs (page 278). Serve with a salad that's both bitter and salty, like chicories with toasted nuts or the Fruit Salad on page 137.

While I rarely specifically seek out sweeter vegetables, squash are certainly my favourite of the genre. I truly love how soft and sweet they can be, especially when roasted for a very long time (maybe even forever), going past merely tender, into sticky, almost chewy territory.

I know the squash, sage and browned butter combination can feel a little 'ravioli special at the local Italian restaurant', but damn, there's a reason it's always the ravioli special. These three ingredients are perfect together, a true gift of sweet, earthy and rich. To gild the lily of that perfect trifecta, there's a handful of dates – a stealthy pantry ingredient I love adding to select roasted vegetables. It might seem like overkill, but somehow doubling down on the sweetness and amplifying the chewy textures is just right. The best part about this particular recipe is that you don't have to brown the butter or crisp the sage – they brown and crisp, respectively, all on their own in the oven. (They are in there forever, after all.)

1. Preheat the oven to 140°C/120°C fan/275°F.

2. Place the squash and dates in a large baking dish (whatever size accommodates, but a standard 1.9- to 2.85-litre/2- to 3-quart dish should do the trick). Drizzle all over with the olive oil and season with salt and pepper. Scatter the cut side of the squash with the brown sugar and flip the squash so it's all cut-side down (this helps the squash almost steam while it roasts, cooking through without drying out).

3. Tuck the garlic and sage under and around the squash and top with the butter. Roast, without touching or flipping or turning, until all the squash is impossibly tender (when you poke it, it should feel like it's about to collapse), 2½–3 hours (approximately forever). The butter will be browned, the garlic will be jammy, the sage will be crisp, the squash and dates will be caramelised and soft, and you will be happy.

4. Serve the squash in or out of the skins (you can eat the skin!), scattered with the dates, garlic, sage and browned-butter-and-brown-sugar business that's pooled at the bottom of the dish.

VINEGAR-BRAISED GREENS

SERVES 4–6

2 tablespoons olive oil
6 garlic cloves, well smashed
½ teaspoon chilli flakes, plus more to taste
2 large bunches leafy greens, thickest part of the bottom stems removed, chopped (6–8 cups)
kosher salt and freshly ground black pepper
60 ml (2 fl oz/¼ cup) white distilled vinegar, plus more to serve

DO AHEAD
—
These can be made a few hours ahead of time and left at room temperature – no need to refrigerate.

EAT WITH
—
These go with everything but are especially good with large hunks of fatty meat or big roast chickens.

This is a very good solution for anyone who finds themselves with an obscene amount of dark, leafy greens. While the most popular ones (kale, Swiss chard, spinach, cime di rapa) available in nearly any big-box or grocery store will do, the best ones to use here are the special freaky greens you see at niche groceries or the farmers' market. My favorite is spigarello, which looks like long curly pasta and tastes like kale and broccoli together, but this is a good chance to experiment with nearly any you've seen and wondered, 'How should I cook these?'

The goal here isn't to 'just cook' the greens but to cook them until they've surpassed tender, giving you something that could almost be described as 'melted'. Doing this in a bath of vinegar with plenty of garlic keeps them punchy and interesting, leaving you with a long-cooked vegetable that's somehow the perkiest thing on the table (the magic of vinegar at work).

1 Heat the olive oil in a large pot or skillet over a medium-high heat. Add the garlic and cook, stirring occasionally, until golden brown, 2–3 minutes. Add the chilli flakes and half of the greens and season with salt and pepper. Cook, tossing occasionally, until the greens have wilted to make room for the remaining half, 3–4 minutes. Add the remaining greens, season again with salt and pepper, and continue to cook until all the greens are wilted and fitting nicely in the pot.

2 Add the vinegar and 250 ml (8 fl oz/1 cup) water (or stock if you want/ have it, but it's not necessary) to the pot and reduce the heat to medium-low. Cook, tossing occasionally, until the greens are impossibly tender and the liquid has all but evaporated from the bottom, 15–20 minutes. Remove from the heat and season again with salt, pepper, chilli flakes and a splash of vinegar if you feel the greens need it (they likely won't!).

VINEGAR'D WAX BEANS with DILL & CHEDDAR

SERVES 4–6

60 ml (2 fl oz/¼ cup) white distilled vinegar
2 garlic cloves, finely grated
kosher salt and freshly ground black pepper
450 g (1 lb) wax beans, green beans, string beans or haricots verts (a bean by any other name . . .), stems trimmed
40 g (1½ oz/1 cup) dill, finely chopped, plus more to taste
60 g (2 oz) firm, salty cheddar or feta cheese, crumbled
olive oil, for drizzling

DO AHEAD
—
These beans are great eaten immediately but will admittedly get better with time to sit. They can be made, *sans* cheddar, 3 days ahead (expect some oxidisation and colour change in the green varieties), stored wrapped and refrigerated.

EAT WITH
—
Tuna Salad Salad (page 138) or a bowl of Buttered Tomato Soup with Lentils (page 82).

I don't use a ton of cheese when cooking with vegetables, but something about a pile of crunchy, very vinegary, garlicky green beans showered with dill just begs for a hard, salty, aged cheddar crumbled over them. A candidate for 'best thing at the barbecue', they taste like fresh dilly beans (an affectionate name for pickled green beans with dill, not to be confused with the dilly bean-inspired Dilly Bean Stew on page 65, which contains no actual green beans).

While you can get there any number of ways, I think the green beans for this dish are best tenderised in a pot of salted boiling water (another argument for the humble blanch). But please, soften them by any means necessary (steam, quickly sauté, even roast or barbecue using a grill basket), just as long as they're dressed with plenty of vinegar while warm. Borrowing the technique from potato salad, dressing them fresh from the pot (or skillet, or . . .) will give you the tangiest, most flavourful beans possible, the vinegar marinating the beans to the core without overstepping. This technique for seasoning and dressing still-warm vegetables is, perhaps, the most compelling argument for keeping white distilled vinegar in your pantry.

1 Combine the vinegar and garlic in a large bowl. Season with salt and plenty of pepper; set aside.

2 Bring a large pot of salted water to a boil. Blanch the beans until just tender, 3–5 minutes. (Smaller, more delicate beans will take less time than the older, larger ones – you can always test one and see if it needs another minute before removing them all.)

3 Drain (do not rinse or transfer to an ice bath) and immediately add to the bowl with vinegar and garlic, tossing to coat. Let sit, tossing occasionally, until they're cooled to room temperature, 30 minutes or so.

4 Add the dill, tossing to coat and evenly distribute those little fronds over each bean. Taste one or two and season again with salt and pepper as needed. Using tongs or two forks, transfer the beans to a serving platter or bowl and top with the cheese, a nice drizzle of olive oil and another few grinds of pepper before serving.

COOKING WITH

WHITE DISTILLED VINEGAR

Quiet, unassuming white distilled vinegar can wear many hats, which is precisely why it's my most-used vinegar. It's rare to praise an ingredient for having no taste, but white distilled (the vodka of the vinegar world) has acidity without discernible flavour, meaning you can add it to anything that needs a light puckering tang without causing a distraction. Lacking the glamour of its counterparts (sherry, red or white wine, apple cider, etc.), it's more of a 'cooking vinegar', versus a fancier, more flavourful one that might be used for, say, seasoning or finishing a salad dressing. I love it for braising rich, fatty meats, dressing fresh wax beans or cucumbers, or lending brightness (without that more specific lemon flavour) to creamy things like aioli or tahini dressing. It's the highest in acidity of all the vinegars, so a little bit goes a long way, which means the bottle you bought on sale (it's already very cheap) might last you perhaps a full calendar year.

YOU NEED SO MUCH
OLIVE OIL

If I told you how much olive oil I went through in a month, you might be horrified or delighted, depending on how you feel about olive oil. To be fair, I cook a lot, and nearly every time I cook, I'm using olive oil. I use it to sear meat at a high temperature, to simmer my beans low and slow, to sweat out my onions and garlic for soups, stews and sauces. It's a miracle ingredient, and aside from salt, I can't think of a single more important thing in my pantry. Unlike salt, where I keep two types on hand (kosher salt, flaky salt), I really only need one olive oil. I need one that's nice enough to eat out of the bottle, to finish salads or a roast chicken, and I need that same olive oil to be not so expensive I can't use it to sweat my leeks for a soup. It's not that I don't enjoy a fancy, freshly pressed olive oil, radioactive green and tasting exactly like an olive plucked from the tree. (I do.) It's just that in my own kitchen, I'm more likely to need only one type: the sort that comes in a giant (reasonably priced) bottle or tin and could be described as 'pretty good', which I can use with wild abandon to save the tomatoes (page 113) or to slow-cook a skillet of potato and lemon wedges (page 98). I am a one-olive-oil kind of gal, needing only something that's practical and purposeful, just like the kind of cook I like to think I am.

SAVE THE TOMATOES

Through the magic of hothouse farming, it's easy to take tomatoes for granted as being available year-round (these days, you can get pretty decent tomatoes in the dead of winter, it's true). But still, nothing compares to the tomato picked at the height of summer. It's easy to get caught up in buying too many (we are trying to hold on to something by holding on to the tomatoes), but then what? Sauce is great and should be done; canning is great and should be done by those who know how to can. But what about something else, like slow-roasting them in a glut of olive oil with some tiny onions and dried chillies until shrivelled and concentrated, jammy and just juicy enough? Speaking from personal experience, this is a great way to save the tomatoes and a great way to not feel so sad three months later, when we're all back inside wishing it were too hot to be outside. (This is also a very good reason to keep one of those giant three-litre cans of olive oil on hand.)

I want my tomatoes, for this practice, to be imperfect and preferably on sale from a farm stand looking to offload some imperfect produce, a little bit ugly and possibly bruised. I want the ones that might taste a little fermented from being in the sun too long or the ones that got too much water and started splitting. I want to give these tomatoes a second life, to love them, to treat them right, and in return, to let them love me back. Remember, there is no such thing as 'past their prime' tomatoes – only tomatoes looking forward to being roasted.

As for what to eat them with or how to enjoy them, anything goes and you will find ways that even I have not yet discovered. They aren't quite sauce, but they are great to make a sauce with: I like to sauté them in a skillet with a splash of white wine and thinly sliced raw shallot. They're also great spooned onto toast rubbed with raw garlic like a sort of concentrated *pan con tomate* (with anchovies on the side, naturally). Try them plopped into a soft scramble with a little warmed tortilla, stir them into a bowl of brothy chickpeas (garbanzos) (page 158) or Olive Oil–Fried Lentils (page 180), or scatter them over some nicely browned chicken thighs. Chop them up and mix with herbs to spoon over roasted vegetables or sliced steak, or simply eat them straight, next to a tiny wheel of soft, creamy cheese. Or hell, stir them into that soft, creamy cheese and eat it like dip. Honestly, do whatever you want with them: They're agreeable and impossible not to love.

PERFECT OIL-ROASTED TOMATOES

MAKES ABOUT 600 G (1 LB 5 OZ/4 CUPS)

1.8 kg (4 lb) tomatoes of various sizes, colours and flavours (anything goes)

a few peeled and quartered shallots; spring onions; whole scallions; or thick wedges of peeled red, yellow, or white onions; or even longish slabs of leeks

4–6 garlic cloves, smashed

a few sprigs of thyme, marjoram or oregano

a few whole dried chillies (*chile de árbol*, New Mexican, guajillo, etc.)

kosher salt

250 ml (8 fl oz/1 cup) olive oil, possibly more

DO AHEAD

Keep them in their oil – they're good stored in the fridge for about a month, or up to 6 months in the freezer.

Aside from eating a tomato simply with salt or in any of the salads that follow, this is quite possibly the best use of tomatoes come late August or early September. Roasted in a not-insignificant amount of oil, the tomatoes become sweet and shrivelled, blistered and jammy. Don't feel precious about the amount of olive oil you're about to pour – use the tomato-y liquid to cook beans, start a roast chicken or season ricotta cheese for a little snack.

1 Preheat the oven to 150°C/140°C fan/300°F.

2 Prepare the tomatoes. Small tomatoes go in whole, medium ones get halved or quartered, and larger ones get cut into 5 cm (2 inch) pieces.

3 Pile the tomatoes in a large casserole (Dutch oven) or other oven-safe baking dish (like a 23 × 33-cm/9 × 13-inch Pyrex, for example; avoid cast iron because it'll react poorly with the acidity of the tomatoes). Add the shallots (or onions), garlic, herbs and dried chillies to the pot and season everything with salt.

4 Drizzle with a good amount of olive oil, and no, I don't mean several tablespoons – I am talking at least 250 ml (8 fl oz/1 cup). You will reuse this oil, so don't worry about wasting – we are not wasting! You're not poaching the tomatoes in the oil, but you do want to give them enough to swim in as they break down while roasting.

5 If you're doing this in a casserole, put the lid on; otherwise, cover the baking dish with foil. Pop them into the oven, letting them go for 2–2½ hours. Remove the lid (or foil) and let them go another hour or so until the tops have started to caramelise slightly and all the tomatoes look past jammy and into shrivelled territory – not quite sun-dried, but concentrated, wrinkled versions of themselves. (If you're doing a smaller batch – say, 900 g/2 lb – you can roast them uncovered, without a lid, for about the same amount of time.)

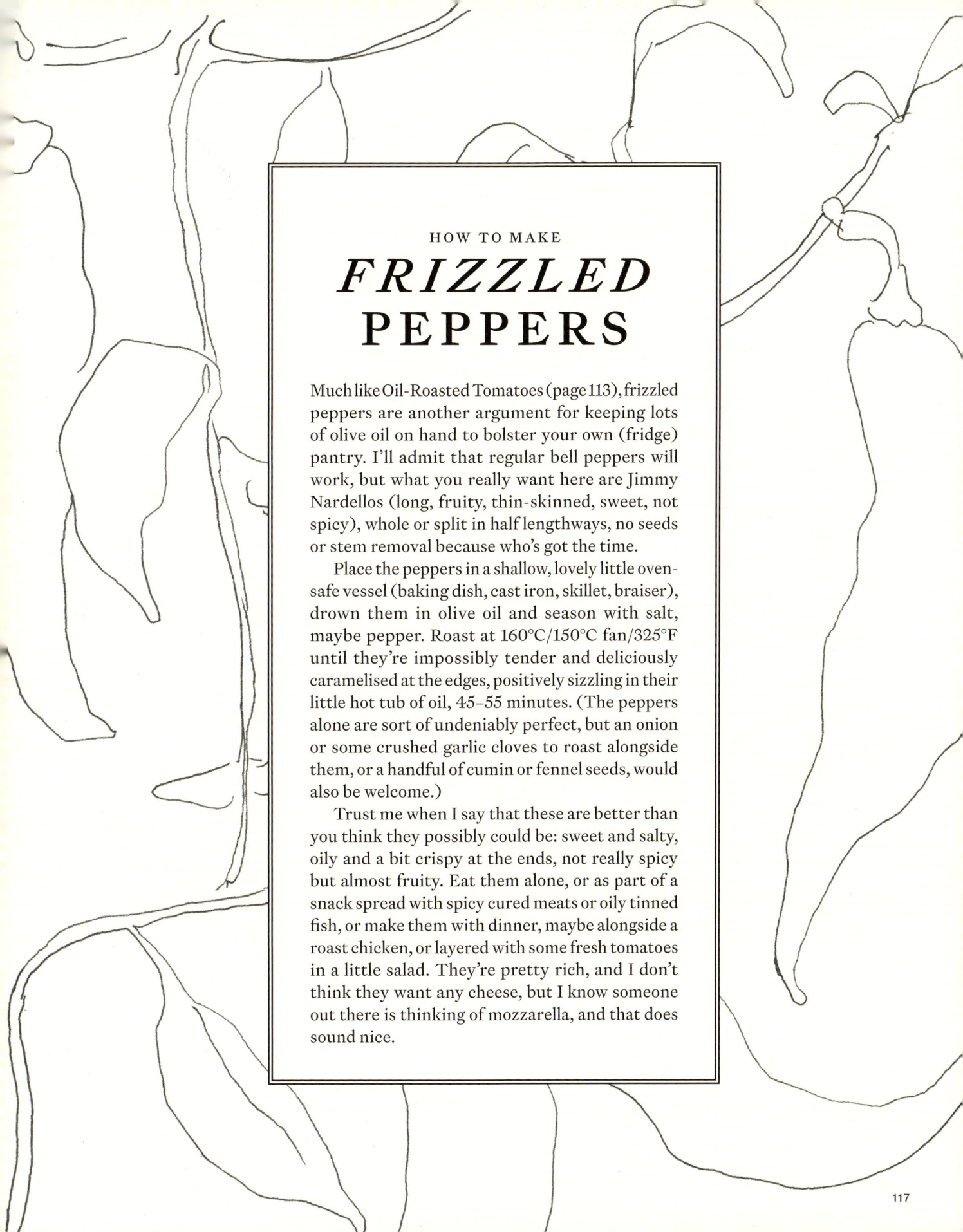

HOW TO MAKE

FRIZZLED PEPPERS

Much like Oil-Roasted Tomatoes (page 113), frizzled peppers are another argument for keeping lots of olive oil on hand to bolster your own (fridge) pantry. I'll admit that regular bell peppers will work, but what you really want here are Jimmy Nardellos (long, fruity, thin-skinned, sweet, not spicy), whole or split in half lengthways, no seeds or stem removal because who's got the time.

Place the peppers in a shallow, lovely little oven-safe vessel (baking dish, cast iron, skillet, braiser), drown them in olive oil and season with salt, maybe pepper. Roast at 160°C/150°C fan/325°F until they're impossibly tender and deliciously caramelised at the edges, positively sizzling in their little hot tub of oil, 45–55 minutes. (The peppers alone are sort of undeniably perfect, but an onion or some crushed garlic cloves to roast alongside them, or a handful of cumin or fennel seeds, would also be welcome.)

Trust me when I say that these are better than you think they possibly could be: sweet and salty, oily and a bit crispy at the ends, not really spicy but almost fruity. Eat them alone, or as part of a snack spread with spicy cured meats or oily tinned fish, or make them with dinner, maybe alongside a roast chicken, or layered with some fresh tomatoes in a little salad. They're pretty rich, and I don't think they want any cheese, but I know someone out there is thinking of mozzarella, and that does sound nice.

ONE MILLION TOMATO SALADS

(OR AT LEAST THREE)

Nobody needs a recipe for a tomato salad: It's a premise you're already familiar with and could execute without a single measurement. Cut, chop, slice a tomato. Season with some salt, maybe a dash of vinegar. Finish with some herbs or perhaps a little sliced onion and a good pour of olive oil. If your tomatoes are great, this tomato salad will be great. If your tomatoes are okay, this version will also be okay. And if the tomatoes are bad, well, I hate to say it: This basic version of a tomato salad will also be bad.

Unfortunately, very little will help truly bad, white, mealy tomatoes if you're determined to eat them raw – you're better off roasting them (page 113). But with the help of your pantry, okay tomatoes can be made great, and great tomatoes can be made transcendent. On the pages that follow are three of my favourite ways to dress tomatoes when they're nice enough to eat raw but still need a bit more than the purity of salt, vinegar and olive oil.

The measurements and instructions are flexible; tomato salads are meant to be casual. The second they become fussy, it ruins the alluring mystique of 'throwing together a tomato salad', which should be done with the kind of confidence that makes it look almost accidental.

SALTY SUNGOLDS with SESAME & SOY

SERVES 4-6

600–800 g (1 lb 5 oz–1 lb 12 oz/ 4–6 cups) Sungold (cherry) or other small tomatoes, halved

2 tablespoons soy sauce or tamari, plus more to taste

½ bunch chives or 2–3 spring onions (scallions), finely chopped

1 tablespoon toasted sesame oil, plus more to taste

olive oil, for drizzling (optional)

These tomatoes don't need salt or pepper: The soy sauce lends plenty of salinity to make these Sungolds 'salty'. Of all the tomato salads, this one is my favourite to make in advance – it really does get better with time.

Combine the tomatoes, soy, chives and sesame oil in a bowl and toss well. Taste a tomato and add more soy or sesame if you like. Finish with a bit of olive oil if the tomatoes are particularly acidic or salty and you want a touch more roundness without more sesame flavour.

SPICY TOMATOES with PICKLED PEPPERS & ONIONS

SERVES 4-6

675–900 g (1½–2 lb) tomatoes, chopped, sliced into rounds, or cut into wedges

½ small red or yellow onion, thinly sliced

35 g (1¼ oz/¼ cup) pickled peppers, such as guindilla or pepperoncini, chopped

2 tablespoons pickled pepper brine or white distilled vinegar, plus more to taste

kosher salt and freshly ground black pepper

hot sauce (optional)

olive oil, for drizzling

While the combination of tomatoes and onions is a beloved, tried-and-true classic, it's the pickled peppers here that really make magic (both the peppers themselves for crunchy texture and heat and the spicy vinegar brine they sit in as the dressing). This is a perfect salad for a Hot Dog Party.

1   Combine the tomatoes, onion, pickled peppers and brine in a large bowl and season with salt and pepper. Toss well, then taste a tomato or two, adding more brine or vinegar, salt, pepper and hot sauce if you like. (Sometimes the pickled peppers will lend enough heat and you won't need it, but you might, especially if you truly like it hot.)

2   Once the tomatoes are spicy and seasoned to your liking, finish with a bit of olive oil to round it all out.

SAVOURY TOMATOES WITH TOASTED GARLIC & FRIED CAPERS

SERVES 4

60 ml (2 fl oz/¼ cup) olive oil
6–8 garlic cloves, thinly sliced
2–3 tablespoons capers, drained
a good pinch of chilli flakes (optional)
675 g (1½ lb) tomatoes, chopped, sliced into rounds, or cut into wedges
1–2 tablespoons sherry vinegar or white wine vinegar, plus more to taste
kosher salt and freshly ground black pepper

The first time I had a fried caper was when I was nineteen, cooking at my first restaurant job. I can't remember whether they went on a beef tartare or tuna carpaccio, but either way, at the end of service, the cook who worked that station would slide the nine-pan of leftover fried capers (they would get soggy overnight) to my station, and I would eat the whole thing. It was one of the few signs that any of the line cooks gave that they didn't absolutely hate me.

Anyway, if you didn't know, capers are the pickled or salted unopened flower buds of the caper plant. When they're fried, each petal inside blossoms, crisping up in the hot oil: nature's salt-and-vinegar chip. I couldn't get enough then, and I can't get enough now.

Here, the capers fry alongside thinly sliced garlic, which also crisps up like chips. Between those two, this tomato salad has so much deeply salty, savoury texture, it's by far the 'heartiest' tomato salad here. This is the ideal companion for something grilled or roasted when it's warm out and you think, 'We should eat outside tonight,' even if that just means sitting in your kitchen with all the windows open.

1 Heat the olive oil in a small pot or skillet over a medium-high heat. Before the oil gets too hot, add the garlic and the capers and cook, swirling occasionally, until the garlic starts to brown and the capers begin to fry and sizzle – opening, blossoming, blooming and popping. This will happen quickly, within 2 or 3 minutes, so don't take your eyes off them. Remove from the heat, add the chilli flakes (if using) and let cool slightly in the oil. Once cooled, the garlic should be lightly browned and crisped and the capers should be shrivelled, dark green and crunchy.

2 Combine the tomatoes and vinegar in a medium bowl, season with salt and pepper, and toss well. Transfer to a large serving bowl or platter and top with the toasted garlic and crispy capers and the oil they fried in.

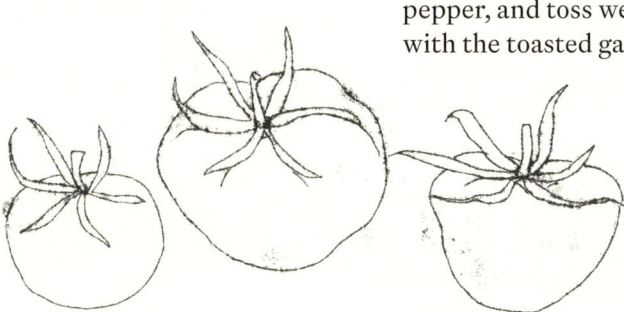

CRUNCHY GREEN BEANS DRESSED IN CHILLI OIL

SERVES 4–6

350–450 g (¾–1 lb) green beans or wax beans, stems trimmed
60 ml (2 fl oz/¼ cup) soy sauce or tamari
2 teaspoons fish sauce
3 tablespoons fresh lime or lemon juice, plus more to taste
6 spring onions (scallions), thinly sliced
kosher salt and freshly ground black pepper
chilli oil, your favourite brand or the one on page 127

DO AHEAD

I love these eaten immediately, but they really are great over the next few days – just expect some oxidisation in the colour. Store them wrapped and refrigerated.

EAT WITH

A tomato-poached or simply grilled piece of fish, some seared salt-and-pepper chicken thighs, or crispy bits of pan-seared tofu.

Do blanched beans sound boring to you? I get it, but think of the blanch as just a surprisingly delightful means to soften those harder-than-you'd-like green beans. These ones, sitting in a tangy, soy saucy bath, will get better as they sit, so feel free to make them as far as two days ahead of time. As for the chilli oil, everyone will have their favourite, any of which will fit in here perfectly. If you find yourself without your precious jar, you can make your own very quick version (page 127), but whichever you're using, don't be shy. These beans, after their nice little blanch and bath in soy, should be appropriately slicked with fiery oil before eating.

1 Bring a large pot of salted water to the boil. Blanch the beans until bright green and tender but with some snap, 90 seconds or so. (This will depend on how thick, old and large the beans are. Always test one to see if they need a little more time.)

2 Drain and transfer to a large bowl. Sometimes, I'll cut any egregiously large green beans in half lengthways, which exposes their cute little beans and gives some nooks and crannies for your dressing to pool into, which I like. (I do this after they are blanched so the little beans don't fall out in the water and they cook more evenly.)

3 While the beans are still warm, add the soy sauce, fish sauce, lime juice and a little more than half of the spring onions, and season with salt and pepper. Season with more lime juice, if needed. The beans should be as tart as they are salty.

4 Drizzle with chilli oil and top with the remaining spring onions to serve.

QUICK CHILLI OIL

MAKES 480 ML (16 FL OZ/2 CUPS)

360 ml (12 fl oz/1½ cups) neutral oil, such as grapeseed or rapeseed (canola)
1 large shallot, very finely chopped
4 garlic cloves, very finely chopped
1–2 tablespoons chilli flakes
1 tablespoon finely crushed chilli flakes, such as Aleppo or gochugaru
1 tablespoon fennel seeds
2 tablespoons raw white sesame seeds (optional)
2 teaspoons flaky salt (optional)

DO AHEAD
—
Chilli oil can be made and refrigerated 1 month ahead (or more). Since the chilli flakes and bits of shallot tend to sink to the bottom, I like to add more neutral oil to the jar as it gets low, letting it slowly infuse over days and weeks as it sits (meaning this chilli oil could potentially last a lifetime).

EAT WITH
—
Everything in this book.

There are a lot of chilli oils out there, and I love almost all of them. I'm including this recipe not to outdo the ones you can buy, but to remind you that if you don't have a jar on hand, you can make a pretty great version at home relatively quickly with ingredients you likely already have. This is my ideal ratio, equal parts spicy from the chilli flakes and fragrant from the fennel seeds and Aleppo pepper. Because I like the texture when spooned over things like cold, blanched green beans or a bowl of lentil soup, this version is heavy on the shallot and garlic. Cooked low and slow, they all but melt into the oily pool of dried chillies, giving almost jam-like bits floating throughout.

1. Combine the oil, shallot, garlic, chilli flakes, Aleppo pepper, fennel seeds and sesame seeds (if using) in a small pot. Heat over a medium-low heat until the shallot and garlic start to sizzle, 4–6 minutes, then reduce the heat all the way to low.

2. Continue to cook, swirling the pot occasionally, until the bubbles go from fast and furious to slow and quiet (almost nonexistent), the shallot and garlic turn a very nice golden brown, the oil is a bright, fiery orange, and the fennel seeds are toasted throughout, 20–25 minutes. Remove from the heat and let cool to room temperature. Add the flaky salt (if using; I like to season my chilli oil, but you may feel differently) and store in a glass jar or other airtight container.

BARELY COOKED CIME DI RAPA
with CALABRIAN CHILLI & GARLIC

SERVES 4–6

60 ml (2 fl oz/¼ cup) olive oil

8 garlic cloves, thinly sliced

2 bunches cime di rapa, torn into large pieces, or 3 bunches broccolini, tough ends trimmed, chopped in half

kosher salt and freshly ground black pepper

1–2 tablespoons Calabrian chilli paste (or 2–4 whole Calabrian chillies, finely chopped)

1 lemon, halved for squeezing over

finely grated pecorino, for serving (optional)

DO AHEAD
—

If you can avoid doing this cime di rapa ahead, you should – the barely cooked of it all sort of implies you want it barely (and just) cooked.

EAT WITH
—

Baked (But Not Stuffed) Shells (page 239), Bolognese with Fennel (page 246), or A Little Aubergine Parm (page 240).

'Barely cooked' is ambiguous here on purpose, as this recipe is great with cime di rapa that's barely cooked any which way: blanched, steamed, roasted, or, as here, quickly sautéed. (To that end, it's also great with baby broccolini and most hearty bunched greens like kale or Swiss chard.) Calabrian chilli is a friend to all barely cooked greens, giving a smack of fermentation along with salty spiciness, all dressed in an equally punchy oil. Regardless of how you're preparing the greens (or which ones you choose), the idea is to keep a bit of bite, which might be a stretch for those accustomed to cooking cime di rapa until army green and softened beyond recognition. In all its spicy, lemony, garlicky glory, this dish really walks the line between 'side' and 'salad', perfect for perking up a big dish of something classic and cheesy.

1 Heat the olive oil in a large skillet over a high heat. Add the garlic and cook, shaking the skillet occasionally, until the garlic is nicely toasted, 2–3 minutes. Add half of the cime di rapa and season with salt and pepper. Using tongs or a wooden spoon, toss until the leaves are bright green and the stems are just tender, 3–4 minutes. Add the remaining cime di rapa, season again with salt and pepper, and toss to coat. Cook for another 2–3 minutes so you have some cime di rapa slightly more wilted than others, giving you a nice variety of textures.

2 Once the cime di rapa is tender but still has some bite (and remains bright green), remove it from the heat and add the Calabrian chilli, tossing to evenly distribute. Transfer to a serving plate or bowl and squeeze lemon over with the optional pecorino sprinkled over top.

BEETROOT WITH CELERY, APPLE & TAHINI

SERVES 4–6

450 g (1 lb) red or yellow betroot (beets), scrubbed well, unpeeled, tops removed
3 tablespoons white distilled vinegar, plus more to taste
olive oil, for drizzling
kosher salt and freshly ground black pepper
4 celery stalks, thinly sliced, plus leaves if available
1 large apple (any sort), unpeeled, cored and sliced or chopped
½ small shallot, thinly sliced (optional)
120 ml (4 fl oz/½ cup) tahini
50 g (1¾ oz/½ cup) toasted walnuts, chopped (optional)

DO AHEAD

Beetroot can be roasted a few days ahead, stored wrapped and refrigerated. The tahini sauce can be made a week ahead, stored wrapped and refrigerated.

EAT WITH

This salad wants something a little rich and fatty to balance the tangy-sweet of it all – like Braised Pork Stew (page 283) or Tangy Braised Brisket (page 284). Also good with cold leftover chicken for a nice little lunch.

While I truly can't get enough of any salad that heavily features celery, this recipe really exists to show my love for a thick tahini sauce that serves as a bed for vegetables. One of the more magical ingredients in your pantry, tahini transforms from oily, shelf-stable paste to luscious, creamy dressing with little more than a few splashes of water and some acid of your choosing. Keeping it more neutral allows it to seamlessly blend in with just about any flavour profile (although feel free to add garlic or lemon, if you want), enhancing vegetables or salads with a creamy texture that you'd typically otherwise get from cheese or dairy. Here, the dressing serves as a sort of mayonnaise proxy, which, together with the fruit, celery and (optional) nuts, certainly qualifies this salad as Waldorf-adjacent – very elegant, no?

1 Preheat the oven to 200°C/190°C fan/400°F.

2 Place the beetroot in a large baking dish, give them a healthy splash of vinegar and a nice drizzle of olive oil, and season with salt and pepper. Cover with foil and roast until the beetroot are completely tender, 50–60 minutes. (To check, pierce one with a knife; it should slide in with little to no resistance.)

3 Let the beetroot cool slightly before using paper towels (or a kitchen towel that you don't care about) to gently rub the skins off. (Do this while the beets are slightly warm – the steam will help the skins slip off.)

4 Once the beetroot are cool enough to handle, slice, quarter or chop them – any shape is nice. Place in a large bowl along with the celery, apple, shallot (if using) and 2 tablespoons of the vinegar. Season with salt, pepper and more vinegar if you like (it should be rather acidic to counter the sweetness of the beets) and then give it a nice drizzle of olive oil; set aside.

5 Stir the tahini in a small bowl with the remaining 1 tablespoon vinegar and 1 tablespoon water. It should (counterintuitively) become thicker and more paste-like. Stir in another tablespoon of water (it should start to thin out a little), followed by another tablespoon of water. You should now have a thick, pale, creamy-looking dressing. Season with salt and pepper and spoon the tahini dressing onto a large serving platter or bowl. Top with the beet-celery-apple mixture, finishing with celery leaves.

6 Sprinkle with walnuts (if using) and drizzle with olive oil before serving.

PICNIC SALAD WITH CUCUMBERS & FENNEL

SERVES 4-6

675 g (1½ lb) cucumbers (I like either baby/Persian or English/long hot house cucumbers, but any type will do)
1 fennel bulb, thinly sliced
70 g (2½ oz/½ cup) pepperoncini or other pickled peppers, chopped
2 garlic cloves, finely grated
2 tablespoons white distilled vinegar, white wine vinegar or red wine vinegar, plus more to taste
1 teaspoon Aleppo pepper or gochugaru (optional)
kosher salt and freshly ground black pepper
20 g (¾ oz/½ cup) finely chopped dill
25 g (1 oz/½ cup) finely chopped coriander (cilantro) or parsley

DO AHEAD
—
The cucumbers, *sans* herbs, can be made 1 day ahead, wrapped and refrigerated (after that they get a little too soft and while they still taste very good, they lose a bit of their crunchy magic).

EAT WITH
—
A few tins of your favourite fish, a ripped baguette or box of crackers, a wedge of very aged Gouda – the kind with the crystals inside.

If you like pickles (and I do), you'll love this salad (I really do). It's got both actual pickled peppers and bracingly acidic, marinated cucumbers and fennel. The whole salad stays crunchy forever and only gets more delicious with time, thus making it the ideal 'eat me outside on a blanket' picnic salad. But even indoors, it's great for lunch with a tin of fish and torn baguette, or for dinner alongside grilled meat or a pot of herby orzo. It goes without saying that it might be the perfect Hot Dog Party accompaniment, taking the place of slaw or any other raw vegetable side.

Don't be put off by how juicy this salad gets: The blessing of a cucumber is how much liquid it gives off once cut, crushed and seasoned, creating its own dressing. The pickled peppers are there for textural contrast, tang and a delightful spiciness, packing a lot in without adding more liquid to the mix. They also have the ability to turn anything they touch into something that reminds me of my favourite turkey sandwich from Subway (turkey, mustard, iceberg lettuce, pickled peppers, onion, vinegar, salt and pepper on a roll).

1 Cut the cucumbers into about 2.5 cm (1 inch) pieces, and then crush each piece of cucumber until it bursts, exposing its juicy interior and creating craggly edges. (You can do this either by simply smashing each piece of cucumber between the side of your knife and a cutting board or by placing all the cucumber chunks in a large resealable plastic bag and crushing them with something heavy, like a rolling pin or small skillet.)

2 Transfer the cucumbers (and any juices they've released) to a large bowl. Add the fennel, peppers, garlic, vinegar and Aleppo pepper (if using). Season well with salt and pepper and toss to combine. Let everything sit for a few minutes if you can, tossing every now and then.

3 Taste the cucumbers again, then adjust with more salt and vinegar as needed. They shouldn't be as tangy and salty as, say, a pickle, but they should be pretty tangy.

4 Once you're closer to serving, add the herbs and toss to coat.

SALTY CELERY SALAD with ANCHOVY

SERVES 4

4 anchovy fillets, finely chopped

35 g (1¼ oz/¼ cup) pickled peppers (pepperoncini or guindilla), finely chopped

1 garlic clove, finely grated

2 tablespoons brine from the peppers (or white wine vinegar, sherry vinegar, or fresh lemon juice), plus more to taste

6 celery stalks, thinly sliced on a bias (leaves reserved)

kosher salt and freshly ground black pepper

2–4 handfuls of salad greens, such as Japanese greens (mizuna), rocket (arugula), even perky parsley leaves

a good handful of salty, crumbly cheese, such as Parmesan, pecorino, cheddar, or even a blue (optional)

EAT WITH
—
Crispy Schnitzel (page 296) and an ice-cold martini.

I am shocked by the number of people who feel comfortable letting me know they don't like celery. It's (proudly) one of my top five favourite vegetables (have you not had a celery stick with peanut butter?), unrivalled in refreshing crunchiness and mild yet present 'green' flavour. I keep it around for snacking, for adding to soup or stock, and most importantly, for very quick and extremely gratifying salads like this one.

While the bulk here is, of course, celery, this perfect little salad also has anchovies, garlic, pickled peppers and vinegar. It's a little (but not too) spicy and – as the name indicates – salty. It's the exact bracing, punchy salad you want scattered over schnitzel (page 296) or chicken Parmesan cutlets (page 299), but it's equally wonderful next to a casual pot of braised brisket (page 284) and classy enough for a special holiday (whichever one is your favourite). Eat it on its own with poached chicken breast for lunch, or with an open tin of tuna and a pile of saltine crackers. Point being: Celery salads are marvellous little chameleons, welcomed on every table for nearly any occasion, not to be underestimated.

1. Combine the anchovies, peppers, garlic and brine (or vinegar) in a large bowl. Add the celery, toss to coat, and season with salt, pepper and more brine if you want. It's nice to let this marinate a bit before adding the salad greens.

2. When ready to serve, toss with the greens, adding any celery leaves you've held on to. Top with or mix in the cheese, if you're doing that, and serve, topped with a bit more cracked pepper.

FRUIT SALAD
with CHIVES & STICKY WALNUTS

SERVES 4–6

2 tablespoons olive oil, plus more to serve

100 g (3½ oz/1 cup) walnuts or pecans, coarsely chopped

1 tablespoon fennel seeds (optional)

kosher salt and freshly ground black pepper

2 tablespoons honey

2 crisp, tart apples, such as Honeycrisp or GoldRush, thinly sliced

1 persimmon or pear, thinly sliced

2 tablespoons sherry vinegar, apple cider vinegar or fresh lemon juice, plus more to taste

2–3 handfuls of bitter greens, such as radicchio, chicory, endive or a peppery green like rocket (arugula)

25 g (1 oz/½ cup) finely chopped chives

DO AHEAD
—
The walnuts can be made a few days ahead and refrigerated. They're fine to use right from the fridge.

EAT WITH
—
This sort of salad loves to be the centre of attention, served in front of your finest company alongside a show-stoppy main course like Tangy Braised Brisket (page 284) or Saucy, Wine-Roasted Chicken (page 269).

The chopped walnuts on this salad, toasted in oil and caramelised in honey, just might be the best thing to ever happen to a slice of fruit or leaf of greenery. They're sticky and also crunchy, savoury but also sweet. They are, in short, a miracle – and maybe the best reason for making sure your pantry (or freezer) always has a bag of walnuts in it. I'm calling this a fruit salad because fruit is the lion's share here, but the savoury, bitter greens (radicchio, chicory, endive) are pulling a lot of weight in making this a salad and not just a pile of fruit and nuts (though I love a pile of fruit and nuts). You may be tempted to add a few shavings of cheese – and that would be good – but I promise you, with the nuts and honey, it really doesn't need it.

1 Heat the olive oil and walnuts in a small skillet over a medium heat. Cook, tossing occasionally, until the nuts begin to toast, about 2 minutes. Add the fennel seeds (if using) and season with salt and pepper. Continue cooking, stirring often and keeping a close eye so nothing burns, until the nuts are golden brown and well toasted, 4–5 minutes. Add the honey and give it a stir; it'll bubble up and start to caramelise a bit around the edges – this is good. Make sure all the nuts are evenly coated, then remove them from the heat and set aside.

2 In a large bowl, combine the apples and persimmon, toss with the vinegar, and season with salt and pepper. Let sit for a minute or two until the juices start to run.

3 Add the bitter greens and chives and toss to coat with the dressed fruit and their juices. Taste a leaf or two and season again with more vinegar, salt and pepper if needed. Add a little drizzle of olive oil and give everything a little tousle to coat. Transfer the salad to a serving platter or bowl and top with the sticky walnuts.

TUNA SALAD SALAD

SERVES 2

½ small red onion or 1 large shallot
1 lemon, zested and halved
kosher salt and freshly ground black pepper
1–2 celery stalks, finely chopped
10 g (½ oz/¼ cup) fresh dill leaves, coarsely chopped
2–3 tablespoons mayonnaise, plus more for the toast, if you like
1 × 135–200 g (5–7 oz) tin or jar tuna, drained
½ head iceberg or romaine lettuce, leaves torn into large pieces
2 tablespoons capers, drained (optional)
buttered toast (optional)

NOTE
—
The tuna can be whatever kind you want: packed in oil or spring water, purchased in Italy or at the grocery store, coming in a tin can or a glass jar. I like spring water-packed for tuna salad and oil-packed for eating solo.

DO AHEAD
—
Tuna salad (minus the iceberg) can be made 5 days ahead, stored wrapped and refrigerated.

EAT WITH
—
When it's not turned into a salad, I like to eat my tuna on top of a sturdy cracker, in the crevice of a celery stalk, or wrapped in a sheet of iceberg lettuce. When it's turned into a salad, I like it with a cup of soup, like I'm at my favourite diner.

In the same way that I do not want to explore the pizza with the 'creative toppings' (give me a margherita), I am not interested in a 'twist' on a tuna salad, which falls squarely in a style of food I like to ask to 'please just play the hits'. (See also: grilled cheese, ice cream, Caesar salad.) Classic cravings are specific, and the attempts to 'put a spin on' them are soul-crushing disappointments to me every time.

To me, the classic tuna salad means tuna, of course, but also lots of onion soaked in lemon juice, plenty of finely chopped crunchy celery, and just enough mayonnaise to hold it all together. There has to be (perhaps too much) dill, but the capers are optional (or, in this case, sprinkled on top, eaten as a sort of salad topping – the most innovation I can muster). The tuna is properly mashed just enough (not too chunky, never mushy), and be it sandwich or salad, iceberg lettuce is of course involved. The whole experience should be tangy and textured, borderline refreshing. It is, after all, a salad.

1   Finely chop half of the onion (or shallot). Thinly slice the remaining half and set aside. (You can also finely chop the whole thing if eating onions 'two ways' does not interest you the way it interests me.)

2   Combine the finely chopped onion in a medium bowl with the lemon zest and the juice from half of the lemon, and season with salt and pepper. Let sit for 5 minutes or so to kind of lightly pickle. (This is doing two things: mellowing out the raw onion and flavouring the lemon juice so that it can better dress the entire mixture.)

3   Add the celery, half of the dill and the mayo. Mix well, like you're making a dressing. (You're making a dressing!) Add the tuna to that and, using a fork, mix until it resembles the tuna salad you want to see in the world. (The end texture can be smooth and pâté-like, or chunky and dressed, and that is really personal preference.) Give it a taste and season again with salt and pepper.

4   Scatter the lettuce and remaining sliced onion onto a large plate, squeeze the other half of the lemon over, and season with salt and pepper. Spoon the tuna salad in and on the lettuce, like you're creating a little edible arrangement. Scatter with the capers (if using) and the remaining dill. Eat like lettuce cups, like a salad, or on a nice piece of buttered toast.

BROWNED BUTTER POTATO SALAD

SERVES 6–8

1.35 kg (3 lb) small waxy potatoes
8 tablespoons unsalted butter
60 ml (2 fl oz/¼ cup) olive oil, plus more to serve
1–2 × 100 g (3½ oz) jars capers, drained (I LOVE capers, so I like MORE capers)
1 large red onion, sliced into thickish wedges
kosher salt and freshly ground black pepper
60 ml (2 fl oz/¼ cup) apple cider vinegar, white wine vinegar or champagne vinegar, plus more to taste
60 ml (2 fl oz/¼ cup) whole-grain mustard
1½–2 handfuls dill, coarsely chopped

NOTE
—
If the potatoes are small enough – say, the size of a golf ball or smaller – I prefer to just boil them whole. If they're larger than that, halve or quarter them before boiling.

DO AHEAD
—
The potato salad can be made several days ahead – definitely two, but maybe more. Like many starchy salads, this gets better with time, although I do prefer it on the room-temperature side rather than chilled.

EAT WITH
—
Your best friends and many, many hot dogs.

My stepmom's mom's German potato salad was my introduction to the genre and, ever since, the gold standard. She made hers with small red potatoes, bacon, dill, finely chopped spring onions (scallions), lots of apple cider vinegar and maybe some mustard, but never mayonnaise. Instead of trying to re-create hers and inevitably missing the mark, I've reimagined it, as a tribute.

This version is vegetarian, with lots of browned butter (which is also used to lightly fry some onions before dousing them in vinegar) taking the place of the bacon fat. The result is a mess of just-cooked, kind-of still crunchy, lightly frizzled then almost pickled onions that really do bring something special to the could-be-ordinary potato salad. Not for nothing, there's at least an entire jar of capers, which also spend some time in the browned butter, losing their slipperiness and gaining some crispiness, a welcome texture among the creamy, crushed potatoes.

1   Bring a large pot of well-salted water to the boil. Boil the potatoes until very tender, 12–15 minutes; drain and let cool slightly.

2   Meanwhile, melt the butter in a medium skillet over a medium-high heat. Cook, stirring occasionally, until it starts to foam and then brown, 2–3 minutes. Add the olive oil and capers and cook until browned and starting to crisp, 5–8 minutes. (Capers have a lot of moisture in them, frying them until crisp is getting rid of that moisture, so it can take a while.) Add the onions, season with salt and pepper, and cook, tossing or stirring every so often, until the onions are tender and starting to brown at the edges and the capers are very crispy, 8–10 minutes.

3   Remove the pan from the heat, add the vinegar, and toss to coat. Transfer the butter-onion mixture to a large bowl and add the mustard and dill.

4   Once the potatoes are cool enough to handle, crush them to expose their insides. (I like to do this in my palm, but you can also smash them on a cutting board.) Add them to the bowl and toss very well to coat, crushing the potatoes further as you go, seasoning again with salt and lots and lots of pepper – more pepper than you think. More! Okay, that's good. Adjust with more vinegar or a drizzle of olive oil if you think it needs it.

JAMMY EGG SALAD

SERVES 4

8 large eggs
15 g (½ oz/¼ cup) finely chopped chives
10 g (½ oz/¼ cup) dill, tender leaves and stems, coarsely chopped
2 tablespoons mayonnaise
2 teaspoons whole-grain mustard
1 teaspoon apple cider vinegar, plus more to taste
kosher salt and freshly ground black pepper
2 cornichons or pepperoncini peppers, finely chopped (optional)
hot sauce (optional)

NOTE
—
I recognise egg salad does not include enough vegetables to be counted as a salad, but it is in fact a salad, thus, belonging with the other salads in this chapter.

DO AHEAD
—
The egg salad can be made a few days ahead and refrigerated.

EAT WITH
—
Serve on soft, untoasted white bread, on a large piece of crunchy matzo or out of little cups of iceberg lettuce or endive like it's 1992 – whatever you like.

Egg salad can be unremarkable, viewed as a food eaten only for sustenance, or it can be shockingly good – something to look forward to, and perhaps even serve for . . . company (gasp). I like to think that this one falls into the latter category. That's not because it's complicated but because it's made with barely set, still-jammy eggs, yielding a silky, almost luxurious texture that whispers *elegance*. It's meant to be served with pleasure at cocktail parties with little boats of endive, so very classique, but it's also good eaten out of a refrigerated container in times of need, or sandwiched between two slices of perfectly untoasted white bread on a sunny day.

1   Bring a medium pot of water to the boil. Gently lower the eggs into the boiling water (I use a large slotted spoon) and immediately set a timer for 6 minutes. (The boil may slow when the eggs are added; that's okay – still start your timer from this moment.) At 6 minutes, remove the eggs and transfer to a large bowl. Run the eggs under cold water for a minute or two. Don't fuss with an ice bath: Part of the 6-minute magic is allowing for a touch of carry-over cooking, rendering the need for an ice bath obsolete.

2   Once the eggs are cool enough to handle, peel and place them in a large bowl. Using a fork, crush them into smaller, bite-size pieces. (There's no need to pre-chop on a board – they're too jammy for that, anyway.) Add the chives, dill, mayonnaise, mustard and vinegar. Mix well and season with salt, pepper and more vinegar if you like. Decide if you want to add the cornichons or hot sauce and go for it (or not).

6 MINUTES IS THE PERFECT AMOUNT OF TIME FOR AN EGG

There was a time where everyone was 'putting an egg on it'. Every magazine cover (remember those) had an egg on it, every restaurant and 'all-day cafe' had eggs all over everything, including things that maybe didn't really need an egg. And I understand: They're beautiful (the golden, perfectly circular yolk!), provide a good dose of sauciness and texture thanks to both a runny yolk and a set white, and can make a lot of incomplete bowls of food feel like they could pass as dinner. Writing this book, I'll admit I stopped myself more than once from adding an egg to something, lest I look like I have one trick (putting an egg on it). But don't let that stop you. In fact, I encourage it.

When I say 'an egg', I'm mostly talking about a six-minute egg – to me, the perfect egg. The white is set, the yolk is runny, you can still slice it without it going all over the cutting board, and it holds its shape when placed atop a pile of beans or in a bowl of brothy rice. This is my morning egg on a thin piece of very seedy, buttered rye bread, the egg I eat as a midday snack with a sprinkle of salt and a few radishes. This is the egg I will turn into Egg Salad (page 142), the egg I will eat on top of a nicoise-y salad made from Slow-Cooked Tuna (page 307). This is the egg you see on the Kimchi and Rice Soup (page 60), and the egg that would be so good on a bowl of Crispy Baked Beans with Mushrooms (page 175).

To make these perfect six-minute eggs, bring a small pot of water to the boil. Using a small strainer or a regular spoon, gently lower in however many eggs you want. (I tend to do five at a time, since that's how many fit in my chosen small pot.) Once the eggs are in and your water is boiling, set your timer for six (6) minutes. Once the timer goes off, use that same strainer or spoon and remove the eggs, transferring them to a medium bowl. Run the eggs under cold water for a minute or two (an ice bath is not part of my plan) and let them cool. There will be some carryover since there is no ice bath – this is okay (this *is* part of my plan). When they're cool enough to handle, they are ready to peel and eat however you like: snack, salad, somewhere in between. They will keep in the fridge for a few days. (I like to label the outside of the shell with some sort of doodle, word or letter to indicate they are cooked and not raw.)

SOMETHING FROM NOTHING

VEGETABLES & HOW TO MAKE THEM TASTE EVEN BETTER 147

LEAFY, HERBY SALAD with SHERRY VINEGAR

SERVES 4–6

- 4 handfuls of spicy greens, such as rocket (arugula), Japanese greens (mizuna) or torn mustard greens
- tender leaves and stems from 1 bunch parsley
- tender leaves and stems from 1 bunch coriander (cilantro)
- 1 bunch chives, coarsely chopped
- dill or mint leaves (optional)
- 2–3 tablespoons sherry vinegar or fresh lemon juice
- flaky sea salt
- freshly ground black pepper
- olive oil, for drizzling

If there is any recipe in this book that will encourage you to buy a bottle of sherry vinegar and box of flaky sea salt, let it be this one. There are a lot of salads out there, and most of them will ask you to make a vinaigrette in a bowl and then use that to dress your lettuces. That's fine, but I prefer instead to dress and season lettuces or greens like any other thing I'm eating or cooking: bit by bit, adding a little of this, a little of that, adjusting until it tastes just how I want it. I'll start with my acid and a good bit of salt, then adjust from there – maybe more acid, definitely more pepper . . . finally finishing with a good pour of olive oil to round everything out, a generous but not overwhelming layer of fat to help carry all the other flavours.

While this method is how I dress nearly all my salads, this recipe is sort of my quintessential salad, the one I often serve with pastas and meats, fish and chicken, all on its own, or alongside a bowl of roasted potatoes and aioli. It's simple (a lot of this book is), meant to solidify your love and appreciation of a good bowl of leaves and nice vinegar. If you have a 'cool vinegar' you've been wanting to try, maybe something expensive or bespoke, this bowl of gorgeous greens and herbs is the place to let it shine. This is more of an idea than a recipe, so feel free to riff on what's involved, but things to know: It should have about a 1:1 ratio of salad greens to herbs, it should be very acidic, and it should not lack for crunchy salt.

1. Combine the greens in a large bowl along with the parsley, coriander and chives. Add the dill or mint leaves, if you have them on hand. (It's fine if you don't, but the more the merrier.)

2. Drizzle the vinegar all over everything (I'd start with 2 tablespoons), then season with flaky salt and plenty of pepper. Toss to coat, taste a leaf or two and season with more vinegar, salt and/or pepper. Once it tastes as good as you can imagine (on the tart, refreshing side with a nice bit of saltiness), finish with a nice drizzle of olive oil – the salad should only be lightly oiled.

AN EXCELLENT MUSTARD DRESSING

MAKES ABOUT 175 ML (6 FL OZ / ¾ CUP)

---

1 small shallot, finely chopped
1 garlic clove, finely grated
2 tablespoons white wine vinegar, red wine vinegar or sherry vinegar, plus more to taste
kosher salt and freshly ground black pepper
2 tablespoons whole-grain mustard or Dijon mustard (or a mix of both), plus more to taste
90 ml (3 fl oz/⅓ cup) olive oil, plus more to taste

NOTE
—
Whole-grain mustard will give you nice texture and look more like a 'dressing', while Dijon will look creamier, more like an emulsified vinaigrette. Both are great.

DO AHEAD
—
The mustard dressing can be made 1 week ahead, stored sealed and refrigerated.

I don't want to assume you're reading this whole book cover to cover, but let's say you are, and you're now wondering why, after I've said I don't really make vinaigrettes, I'm writing a recipe for one. Well, listen, it's more of a dressing than a vinaigrette, and sure, even I am not entirely clear on the differences between the two words, but I'm calling this a dressing, which – to me – indicates versatility.

Adding water to a dressing was something I gleaned from one of the more famous salads of our time, the insalata verde at the New York institution Via Carota. Once I noticed it in that recipe, I saw it appear elsewhere, usually in older cookbooks without photos (my favourite), and it makes sense: The dilution allows for more dressing to be applied, rather than having something so acidic that you are forced to limit your consumption of it. Not unlike its role in a well-shaken martini, water as an ingredient provides balance. Don't skip it.

I intend for you to use this all-purpose, excellent mustard dressing for things beyond a bowl of gorgeous greens. Perhaps you'll use it to coat black lentils served alongside a coil of browned sausage to pretend you're in France. Or spoon it over a little sliced chicken and lettuce, cosied next to a jammy egg and some crispy bacon for a Cobb-like experience. It can be tossed with sprigs of parsley served next to a baking dish of bubbling beans, or it can be treated as a sauce for just-cooked pieces of seared trout and a pile of steamed green beans. An Excellent Mustard Dressing is something everyone should have in their fridge, to dress any number of grains, proteins or vegetables at a moment's notice. The perfect vessel for storing it is, of course, an old mustard jar, but any sort of reusable container also works.

1 Combine the shallot, garlic and vinegar in a small bowl (or an old mustard jar). Season with salt and pepper and let sit for a few minutes to marinate the shallot and take some of the edge off the raw garlic.

2 Add the mustard and 1 tablespoon water and stir, whisk or shake to combine. Add the olive oil and stir, whisk or shake again to combine. Taste and season with salt, pepper or more vinegar, mustard or olive oil, depending on what you're needing or wanting from this dressing.

A CAESAR FOR ALL OCCASIONS

SERVES 4

FOR THE DRESSING

2 large egg yolks
6 anchovy fillets or 2 tablespoons capers, drained, finely chopped
2 garlic cloves, finely grated
1 teaspoon Dijon mustard, or to taste
2 tablespoons fresh lemon juice, or to taste
1 teaspoon Worcestershire sauce, or to taste
60 ml (2 fl oz/¼ cup) olive oil
60 ml (2 fl oz/¼ cup) rapeseed (canola) oil
kosher salt and freshly ground black pepper

FOR THE SALAD

60 ml (2 fl oz/¼ cup) olive oil
4 anchovy fillets, or to taste
60 g (2 oz/1 cup) panko breadcrumbs
1 garlic clove, finely grated
kosher salt and freshly ground black pepper
1 head romaine lettuce or 2–3 heads Little Gem lettuce, ends trimmed, leaves torn or cut into large pieces
a hunk of Parmesan cheese, for shaving or grating

NOTE

Torn kale leaves also make a great Caesar, and so does chopped radicchio, sliced endive or even a bowl of sliced fennel, if you were feeling especially nontraditional.

DO AHEAD

The dressing will keep for 3 days, covered and refrigerated.

This book is full of many classic recipes, things that have long existed, dishes that predate most cookbooks you or I likely own. But just know that before contributing my own version of a classic, I do ask myself, 'Does the world need another recipe for this?' and I have to come up with a good reason before deciding that it does.

This Caesar was born from always wishing that the dressing were less mayonnaise-y and more of a vinaigrette, creamy without being heavy, punchy without preventing you from wanting to lick the whole bowl. I wanted a true dressing, meant to evenly coat each leaf in a bowl, versus a dip or a thick, spoonable sauce. So while the list of ingredients will seem familiar, the ratios likely differ, and you might notice there isn't grated cheese *in* the dressing – I prefer to shower it on top. It's garlicky and tart, full of anchovies (but capers really are an honest-to-god good stand-in), and you would really miss the Worcestershire sauce if you had to skip it – the flavour is a little salty, a little sweet, and unmistakably 'Caesar'.

1 Make the dressing: Whisk together the egg yolks, anchovies or capers, garlic, mustard, lemon juice and Worcestershire sauce in a medium bowl. Gently whisk in the olive oil and rapeseed oil, without worrying if anything is going to break – it won't.

2 Season with salt and so much pepper it really ought to be in the recipe name. Taste and season with more mustard, lemon or Worcestershire as you like. (The dressing should be very acidic.) If you find it too punchy or too thin, whisk in a few more tablespoons of olive oil.

3 Make the salad: Heat the olive oil in a medium skillet over a medium heat. Add the anchovies, stirring just to melt. Add the breadcrumbs and stir to coat in the oil. Keep tossing or stirring until the panko is evenly coated and turning a nice golden brown, the colour of perfect toast, 4–5 minutes. Remove from the heat, add the garlic and toss it in the warm crumbs, just to take the edge off. Season with salt and pepper; let cool.

4 Place whatever greens you're dressing in a large bowl and add half of the dressing. Toss well, season with more salt, pepper or dressing as you (and the greens) see fit. Shower with cheese and breadcrumbs, tossing to encourage both to settle into the nooks and crannies. If you're me, top with more anchovies.

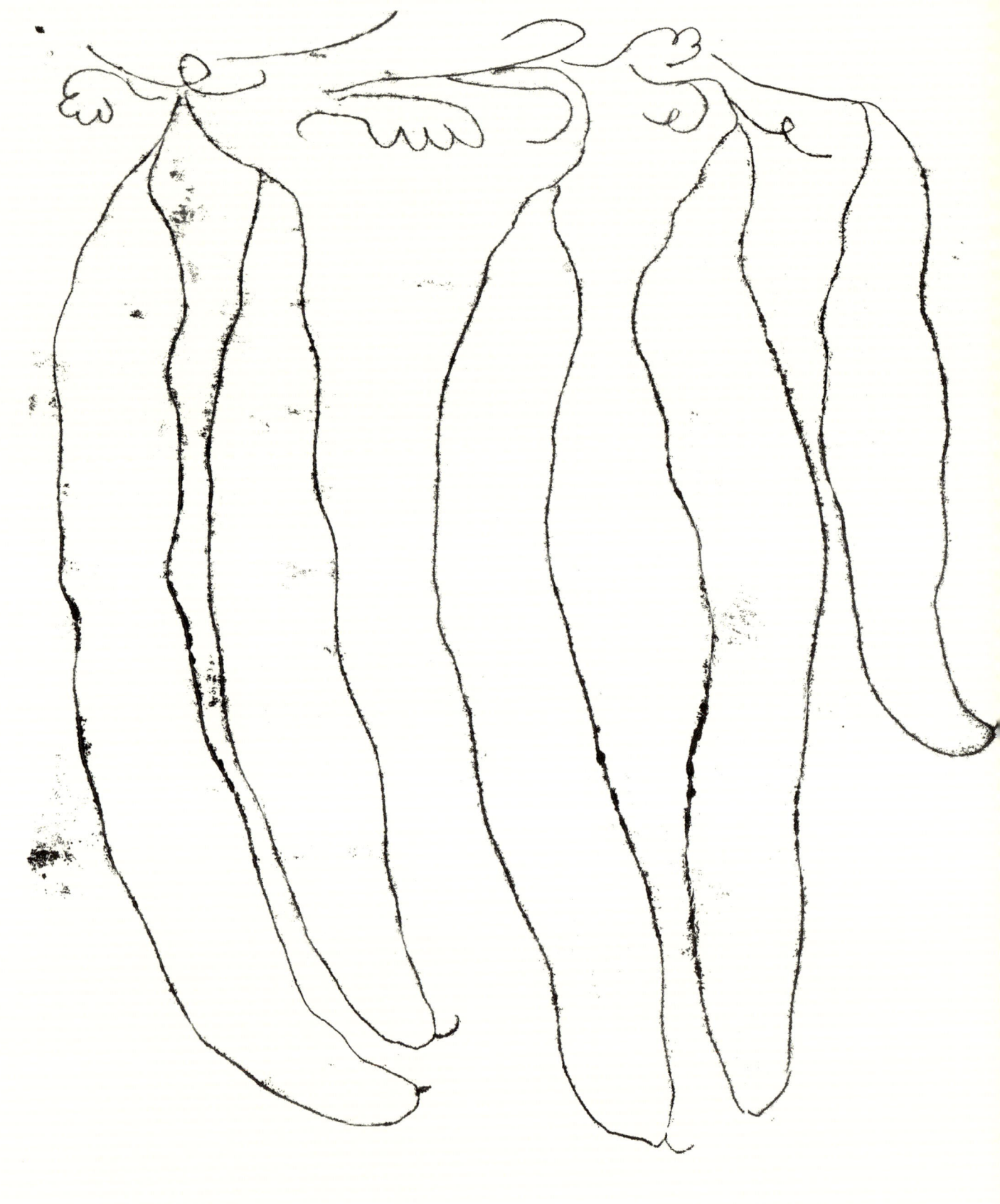

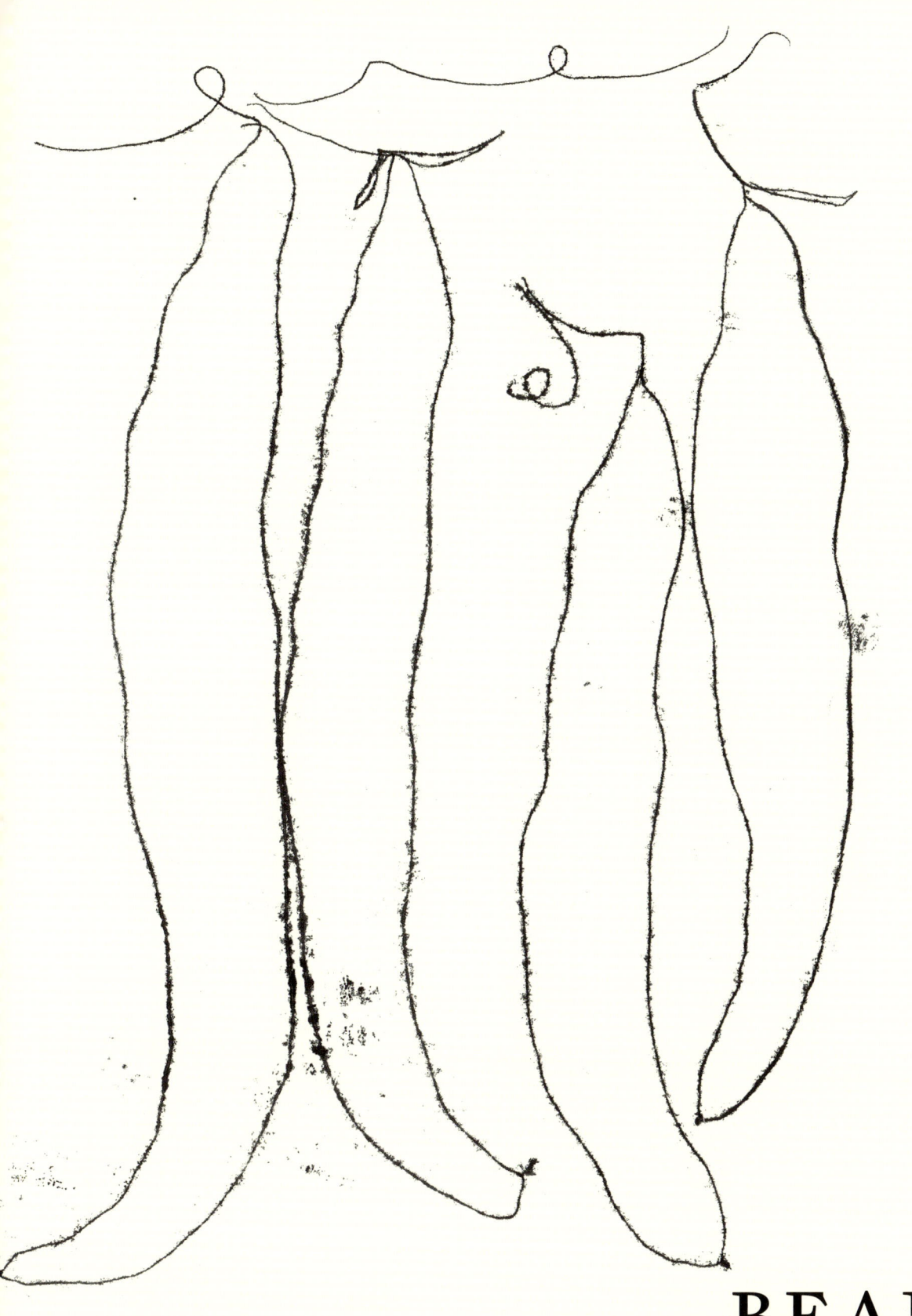

BEANS
and GRAINS

Beans and grains are my platonic ideals of pantry ingredients. These humble little legumes, pulses and the like bulk up soups and stews, they make a salad a meal, they turn a roast chicken into a spread. Each one is a shelf-stable blank canvas for carnivores and vegetarians alike, able to transform into something both casually rustic and surprisingly elegant.

I'm wary of recommending meat-free 'centrepieces' for those who do not eat meat (a whole roasted head of cauliflower will never replace a chicken), but I am confident that some of these (mostly vegetarian) recipes really do feel celebratory enough to pass as such. Baked or brothy, beans are visually impressive and hearty enough to serve as the main course on a table next to a big herby salad, perfect garlic bread and maybe a small wedge of soft, special cheese. Cooked until al dente and lightly fried in a shallow pool of olive oil, black lentils become the most important thing on the table next to a coil of spicy merguez sausage. And while I still struggle to cook the perfect pot of plain steamed rice (it's a journey, not a destination, etc.), somehow a gorgeous, buttery pilaf studded with plump dates and fried walnuts always delivers.

LONG-COOKED BROTHY CHICKPEAS with SHALLOT & CHILLI

SERVES 4–6

450 g (1 lb) dried chickpeas (garbanzos)

2–3 large shallots or 1 large red onion, sliced into rings about 5 mm (¼ inch) thick

½ bunch oregano, thyme, or rosemary

1 teaspoon finely crushed chilli flakes, such as Aleppo or gochugaru

kosher salt and freshly ground black pepper

90 ml (3 fl oz/⅓ cup) olive oil

a spoonful or two of Calabrian chilli (chopped, crushed or paste) or more chilli flakes (optional)

1 lemon, halved for squeezing over

NOTE
—
I am a realist and understand that not everyone has the time or desire to wait a small eternity to cook a dried chickpea, no matter how persuasive I may be. To make this recipe with tinned chickpeas, swap in 3 × 400 g (14 oz) cans, reduce the water to 480 ml (16 fl oz/ 2 cups), adjust the oven temp to 200°C/190°C fan/400°F (they don't need the low and slow), and pull them from the oven after 2-ish hours.

DO AHEAD
—
The chickpeas can be made 5 days ahead and refrigerated. They can also be frozen up to 3 months ahead. Rewarm in their broth before serving.

Even more so than a dried bean, a dried chickpea can really take forever to cook (regardless of soaking!), truly testing your patience for how long you can wait for a legume to become tender. But unlike beans, they're quite resilient, less likely to turn to mush no matter how long they cook. This is precisely why I have no anxiety about cooking them slowly in a super-low oven while I go about my business, perhaps even leaving the house to run a quick errand while they cook in my absence. They wind up intact yet (almost literally) bursting with flavour all the way to their core, with a golden-brown exterior and a specific tender-yet-chewy texture that could only come from cooking a tiny little legume from dried – no tinned chickpea can compare. (For more on cooking from dried versus tinned, page 171.)

The ingredients here are spare on purpose: The shallots do the lion's share of the work, going in raw and cooking down with the chickpeas, turning almost jammy, their telltale sweetness and savouriness melting into the broth. Ideal alongside any nicely braised, roasted, grilled or seared meat you're serving (especially Overnight Lamb, page 276), they're also amazing in a soup or stew. Or scoop them out of their liquid and use them as a blank canvas for any chickpea journey you're on: Sauté them in a skillet with some torn kale and serve under fried eggs or plop them into a food processor with a good spoonful of tahini and a squeeze of lemon for exquisite hummus.

1. Preheat the oven to 160°C/150°C fan/325°F.

2. Combine the dried chickpeas, shallots, herbs and chilli flakes in a large, oven-safe pot, preferably one with a lid. Season with salt (not quite salty like the sea, but a good amount) and pepper and pour the olive oil over. Fill the pot with about 1.9 litres (64 fl oz/8 cups) water. (The chickpeas should be covered by about 7.5 cm/3 inches.) Cover the pot (using foil if you don't have a lid) and place in the oven. Let cook (and don't touch) for 5–6 hours. (Chickpeas are especially flexible and resilient, so don't worry too much about overcooking here.)

3. Once cooked, the chickpeas will be perfectly tender, the shallots (or onion) will have all but melted into the chickpeas, and the broth will be well seasoned and luscious with olive oil. Transfer the chickpeas and some of that glorious broth to a large bowl, spoon over a bit of Calabrian chilli or more chilli flakes if you like, and add a nice squeeze of lemon.

CARAMELISED BEANS with TOMATO & CABBAGE

SERVES 4

4 tablespoons unsalted butter

4 tablespoons olive oil

½ small head (about 675 g/1½ lb) cabbage, cut into 2.5 cm (1-inch) wedges

kosher salt and freshly ground black pepper

1 large shallot, thinly sliced

2 × 400 g (14 oz) tins large white beans, such as butter (lima) beans, gigantes or cannellini, drained and rinsed

225 g (8 oz) tomatoes, preferably small, halved if small, quartered or chopped if large

1 tablespoon white wine vinegar, sherry vinegar or white distilled vinegar

a hunk of Parmesan cheese for grating on top, ricotta for spooning over or feta for crumbling (optional)

DO AHEAD

The beans can be made 2 days ahead, wrapped and refrigerated. Reheat in a 220°C/200°C fan/425°F oven, uncovered, until warmed through and bubbling once more, 20–30 minutes. Leftovers can also be scooped into a skillet and rewarmed on the stovetop.

EAT WITH

A hunk of sour, rustic bread, preferably made with hearty whole grains, for dipping and dunking (a modern 'brown bread' perhaps).

If the idea of having three baked bean recipes in one book doesn't thrill you beyond belief, we are not the same. They're all different, all special, all worthy of your time. This saucy, tangy recipe might be the closest of the three to traditional 'baked beans', but these are sweet not from brown sugar or molasses but rather from jammy tomatoes and browned cabbage. I understand that that probably sounds like when people describe dried fruit as 'nature's candy', but it's true: When caramelised and concentrated, both tomato and cabbage do become perceptibly sweeter and tangier, truly approximating that baked-bean feeling. While you could scatter a handful of olive oil-doused breadcrumbs on top to soak into the tomatoey broth and wrinkled cabbage leaves, I intentionally leave them out here, since they block the top bean-tomato-cabbage layer from caramelising – my favourite part, the reason we're all here.

1 Preheat the oven to 220°C/200°C fan/425°F.

2 Heat the butter and olive oil in a large skillet (preferably oven-safe) over a medium heat. Add the cabbage, cut-side down, and season with salt and pepper. Cook, without disturbing or peeking, until the cabbage is deeply golden brown on one side, 8–10 minutes. Using tongs or a fish spatula, carefully flip and repeat on the other side, another 8–10 minutes.

3 Once the cabbage is well browned on both sides, add the shallots and season with salt and pepper. Cook, stirring or shaking the skillet occasionally to make sure the shallots can make contact with the pan, until they are nicely browned and completely tender, 5–7 minutes.

4 Meanwhile, place the beans in a 1.4–1.9-litre (1½- to 2-quart) baking dish. Once the cabbage and shallots are nicely browned and tender, add them to the baking dish, along with the tomatoes, vinegar and 250 ml (8fl oz/1 cup) water. Season well with salt and pepper and rearrange, adjusting some of the wedges of cabbage and pieces of tomato so that they make their way to the top. (They will get so delicious in the oven.)

5 Place in the oven and bake until the liquid has reduced by quite a bit, everything is bubbling up the sides of the dish in a sticky, caramelised way, and the top is delightfully browned, bordering on crisp, 50–60 minutes.

6 Remove from the oven and let cool slightly. Serve with or without cheese.

CHILLI BEANS

SERVES 4–6

2 medium yellow onions, peeled
90 ml (3 fl oz/⅓ cup) olive oil
40 g (1½ oz) New Mexican or guajillo chillies (about 8), stems removed
8 garlic cloves, smashed
1½ tablespoons whole cumin seeds (or 2 teaspoons ground)
2 fresh or dried bay leaves or ½ bunch thyme
2 whole dried *chiles de árbol* or 1 teaspoon chilli flakes
450 g (1 lb) large dried beans, such as gigantes, butter (lima) or cannellini, or 4 × 400 g (14 oz) tins similarly sized beans, drained and rinsed
kosher salt
2 tablespoons white distilled vinegar, plus more to taste
1 handful coriander (cilantro), tender leaves and stems, finely chopped (optional)
60 g (2 oz/½ cup) crumbled *queso fresco* or other mild, fresh cheese (optional)

NOTE

This is best made with large dried beans, but I know not everyone takes pleasure in the long simmer, so I've adapted this for tinned as well.

DO AHEAD

The beans can be made 5 days ahead, stored in their liquid, covered and refrigerated.

EAT WITH

A spoonful of sour cream, your favourite tortillas and a fried egg.

This is not a recipe for chilli (you can find one on page 178) but rather for a pot of creamy beans swimming in an olive oil-slicked broth made from dried and toasted chillies with a bit of cumin. The resulting pot is ever-so-slightly reminiscent of chilli – dare I say the most elegant version you've ever had (and accidentally vegan!). As the beans cook, the dried chillies (which I prefer to keep whole for dramatic effect) hydrate and plump, nearly dissolving into the liquid, taking on an almost slippery texture and lovely sweetness, reminding you that they are, after all, little fruits. While it's nice to appreciate the beans and broth as is, ladled into a bowl and topped with a bit of sliced raw onion, coriander (cilantro) and *queso fresco*, I can also attest it's nice to cook them a bit further in a bit of olive oil or pork fat, until they're on the almost-mushy side, crushing them with a wooden spoon and treating them like refried beans.

1   Thinly slice half of one onion; set aside. (This is for finishing the beans.) Quarter the remaining onions.

2   Heat the oil in a large, heavy-bottomed pot over a medium-high heat. Add the New Mexican chillies, quartered onions (cut-side down) and garlic. Cook, turning each occasionally, letting them toast and fry in the oil until they've all got some colour on them, 3–4 minutes.

3   Add the cumin, bay leaves and *chiles de árbol* and swirl to toast for a minute in the hot oil. Add the beans and 2.35 litres (80 fl oz/10 cups) water if dried (950 ml/32 fl oz/4 cups if tinned) and season well with salt. Bring to a simmer and reduce the heat to medium-low. Continue to cook, uncovered, until the beans are tender and cooked through and the chillies are softened and nearly melted into the cooking liquid (turning it a pleasing red colour), 2–2½ hours for dried, 30–40 minutes for tinned. Throughout the simmer, adjust the heat as needed – you should see a few bubbles popping up every now and then, but decidedly never a boil.

4   Remove the beans from the heat and add the vinegar. Season with more salt and vinegar if you like (they shouldn't be too tangy, but nicely seasoned) and either store until ready to use or ladle into bowls or a large serving bowl. Top with the reserved sliced onion and, if you like, the chopped coriander and a dusting of *queso fresco*.

SPICED CHICKPEAS & GREENS

SERVES 4

60 ml (2 fl oz/¼ cup) olive oil plus 2 tablespoons, plus more to serve
1 bunch dark, leafy greens, such as collard greens, kale or Swiss chard
kosher salt and freshly ground black pepper
1 lemon, halved
1 large yellow or red onion, thinly sliced
2 × 400 g (14 oz) tins chickpeas (garbanzos), drained and rinsed
4 garlic cloves, thinly sliced
2 teaspoons Aleppo pepper and/or ½ teaspoon chilli flakes
2 teaspoons fennel seeds
1 teaspoon cumin seeds
250 g (9 oz/1 cup) full-fat Greek yoghurt or labneh
2 handfuls mixed herbs, such as dill, mint, chives, parsley or coriander (cilantro), coarsely chopped

DO AHEAD

The chickpeas can be made a few hours ahead and kept covered loosely at room temperature. Feel free to reheat in a skillet over a medium-high heat before serving, as they'll lose a bit of their crispness as they sit.

EAT WITH

Your friends who come over for Spicy Braised Short Ribs (page 278).

Chickpeas (or beans of any sort), fresh from the tin, are frankly not that appealing. But given some time with heat, lots of olive oil and plenty of salt, they are magnificent. Best of all is cooking them alongside onions or leeks as they caramelise, creating an exterior that can only be described as 'frizzled' – not quite fried, but more than sautéed. Sorry if I'm repeating myself, but it's still the best chickpea I know. Here, they're eaten over a good bit of tangy yoghurt, sautéed greens and a mess of herbs, easily served as a side to something grand, or eaten alone, as dinner in and of itself.

1. Heat 2 tablespoons of the olive oil in a large skillet over a medium-high heat. Tear up the greens with your hands (stems and all) and add them to the skillet. Season with salt and pepper and cook, stirring occasionally, until the greens are nicely wilted and tender, 3–5 minutes. Transfer the greens to a bowl, squeeze half of the lemon over top, and set aside.

2. Wipe out the skillet and heat the 60 ml (2 fl oz/¼ cup) of olive oil over a medium-high heat. Add the onion and season with salt and pepper. Cook, stirring occasionally, until the onion is just starting to brown, 5–8 minutes.

3. Add the chickpeas and garlic. Season with salt and pepper and toss to coat in the oily business. Continue to cook, shaking the skillet occasionally to make sure nothing is sticking and that the chickpeas are getting equal attention from the oil and heat, until the chickpeas are golden brown and appear fried around the edges and the onion is a deep golden brown and looks somewhere between fried and caramelised, a term we now call 'frizzled', 12–15 minutes. If the chickpeas are looking dry or sticking to the pan, drizzle a bit more olive oil into the skillet.

4. Once the chickpeas are nicely browned, add the Aleppo pepper, fennel seeds and cumin seeds. Cook for 2 minutes or so, to toast and bloom the spices. Taste a chickpea or two and make sure they're plenty seasoned, adding salt, pepper, and/or a pinch of chilli flakes, if you like things spicier. Remove from the heat and set aside.

5. Combine the yoghurt and the juice from the remaining lemon half in a small bowl and season with salt and pepper. Plop, spoon or swirl the yoghurt mixture onto the bottom of a serving bowl or plate. Top with the wilted greens, followed by the chickpeas to cover the greens and herbs to cover the chickpeas, giving everything a drizzle of olive oil to finish.

ALMOST CASSOULET

SERVES 4–6

This is not a real cassoulet; this is an almost cassoulet. The spirit and core remain intact: There are still wonderfully fatty meats (bacon and sausage) and beans, slowly melding together in the oven, becoming impossibly tender and wildly flavourful because of and for one another. But there's no duck confit, no obscure terrines or hard-to-find cuts of meat. And I use tinned beans for ease (remember, this is 'almost' cassoulet), but if you want to use beans cooked from dried, know that it will turn out perhaps even more delicious. I add fennel for a bit of sweetness and body; the rest of the ingredients, though, are what you'd expect. It still spends enough time in the oven to get fabulously browned on top with just enough of that telltale crust, but it doesn't require endless hours of cooking. It's my favourite thing to make when the weather is terrible and I need to pretend I live in a small cottage in a tiny French town. For it to work, you need to serve it with a big mustardy salad (dressing on page 149), turn off all electricity and eat by candlelight only – it's a truly transportive experience.

- 285 g (10 oz) slab bacon, cut into 2 cm (¾ inch) thick pieces (or the thickest-cut sliced bacon you can find)
- 900 g (2 lb) sausage (about 4 links), any type (pork, lamb, spicy, sweet), pierced a few times with a fork or knife
- 6 garlic cloves, crushed
- 2 medium leeks, thinly sliced
- 1 large fennel bulb, thinly sliced
- kosher salt and freshly ground black pepper
- a few sprigs of thyme
- 360 ml (12 fl oz/1½ cups) dry white wine
- 4 × 400 g (14 oz) tins of white beans, such as Great Northern, cannellini or haricot (navy), drained and rinsed
- 480 ml (16 fl oz/2 cups) chicken, beef or vegetable stock (or water plus Better Than Bouillon, see page 58)
- whole-grain mustard, for serving (optional)
- cornichons, for serving (optional)

DO AHEAD

Cassoulet can be made 2 days ahead, wrapped and refrigerated. To reheat, place the foil-wrapped baking dish in a 200°C/190°C fan/400°F oven until bubbling at the edges, 30–40 minutes.

EAT WITH

Greens dressed in mustard vinaigrette (page 149), a large jar of mustard.

1. Preheat the oven to 220°C/200°C fan/425°F.

2. Heat a large skillet or pot over a medium heat. Add the bacon and cook, turning occasionally, until nicely browned and much of the fat has rendered, 8–12 minutes (the timing will depend on how thick the bacon is). Transfer the bacon to a plate and add the sausage to the skillet. Cook, turning occasionally, until the sausage is browned and mostly cooked through, 5–8 minutes. (It'll continue to cook in the oven – you just want it nicely browned here.) Transfer to the plate with the bacon, leaving the fat behind, and set aside.

3. Add the garlic, leeks and fennel to the skillet and season with salt and pepper. Cook, stirring occasionally, until the vegetables are very tender and starting to brown slightly at the edges (you don't want full caramelisation, just a bit of colour), 12–15 minutes. Add the thyme and wine and cook until the wine has all but evaporated, 3–4 minutes.

4   Remove from the heat and transfer the vegetables to a large bowl (easier and less messy for mixing). Add the beans and stock, season with salt and pepper, and toss everything together to evenly coat. Spoon some of the bean mixture into a 1.9- to 2.85-litre (2- to 3-quart) baking dish. Layer in some of the bacon and sausage, followed by more beans and their liquid. Repeat until all of the beans and meat are nicely tucked into the baking dish, making sure some of the meat ends up on top so it can continue to brown in the oven.

5   Bake, without disturbing, until the beans are bubbling, the meat is brown and there's a whisper of that telltale cassoulet crust on top, 75–90 minutes. (The beans might look soupy, and you may wonder if there's too much liquid: There isn't! The beans will settle, and the liquid will get absorbed as everything cools.) Remove from the oven and let cool slightly before eating alongside some nice mustard and a few cornichons if you like.

TINNED
VERSUS
DRIED BEANS

First and foremost, there's an equation I need to get out of the way: 450 g (1 lb) of dried beans makes about 1 kg (6 cups) of beans when cooked. To get the same amount from tinned beans, you'll need three or four 400 g (14 oz) tins (it's an imperfect equivalent, as it depends on the bean). Second, I don't soak my dried beans, and I don't think you need to, but if you want to, that's great. Third, and this is not at all crucial, but I need to say it anyway: I'm thrilled for beans' recent-ish surge in popularity – beans are incredible – although I'll admit it does kind of feel like watching a band you love hit it big when you used to go see them at the local dive bar for a $5 cover charge. Anyway, now that we've gotten those three key pieces of bean information out of the way, let's discuss tinned and dried beans, the difference between the two, and why you need both.

Tinned beans are great for convenience, a reliable workhorse, arriving fully cooked and ready to turn into whatever you please. That said, it's an unfortunate truth that an untouched bean straight from the tin is not all that great. To reach their full potential of deliciousness, they should be baked, sautéed or simmered, probably in plenty of olive oil with more salt and possibly some garlic, at the very least. Using them as the base of a soup or stew is an obvious choice (there's a whole soups and stews chapter that heavily features beans), but the real magic of a tin of beans happens on an even simpler level, say, from tossing them in some chicken fat left over from searing a few thighs or baking them with an abundance of sautéed mushrooms and grated Parmesan until bubbling and crisp.

Then we also have dried beans. Dried beans are less the supporting role and more so the lead, which is to say I'm not going to spend two hours making a gorgeous pot of beans only to turn them into something else. The broth the beans cook in, the vegetables cooked alongside: That's it, that's the dish. Simmered in a pot of water with a few aromatics, maybe finished with herbs, chilli paste or fresh lemon juice, they require so little to be so fabulous – no need to gussy them up.

Dried beans are not convenient – they take time, planning and more time. They will not be ready for dinner unless you start them in the afternoon, but if you make them tonight to eat tomorrow, hey, they just might trick you into thinking they're convenient. And yet, while I am a fan of things that are fast and easy, these inconvenient beans are undeniably unparallelled in flavour and texture. Delicious, tender, creamy and bespokely seasoned beans plus a rich, luscious broth for which to drink or to simply store said beans in: It's your kitchen's greatest two-for-one experience. I don't own an Instant Pot or pressure cooker, preferring instead to do a long simmer on the stove or in the oven, which makes my house smell wonderful and gives me a sense of accomplishment, knowing that even if I'm staring at my phone, if I have a pot of beans going, I'm 'doing something'. Among all the virtues I could extoll, it's the vast variety of dried beans that keeps me most excited after all these years. A bean I've never tried? Tell me more! Will it be creamy and soft? Toothsome and starchy? Good when cold for a salad or destined to fall apart in a stew? It's like the first time, every time.

BEANS & GRAINS

TINY WHITE BEANS IN GREEN BAGNA CAUDA

SERVES 4–6

If you aren't convinced that serving green bagna cauda with steamed artichokes and boiled potatoes (page 21) is the best way to eat this warm, buttery, herby anchovy sauce, allow me to present my other favourite approach: bagna cauda as a bath for tiny little starchy white beans. Served warm, they're an unassuming, intensely flavoured bowl of beans that are best alongside something else warm and unassuming: a pot of Overnight Lamb (page 276), Crisp, Hot Roast Chicken (page 262) or a plate of cooked sausage and a nice baguette for all that green, saucy anchovy butter.

FOR THE BAGNA CAUDA

120 ml (4 fl oz/½ cup) olive oil
8 tablespoons unsalted butter
10 garlic cloves (8 thinly sliced, 2 finely grated)
1 × 60 g (2 oz) tin anchovies, plus their oil
4 spring onions (scallions), green parts finely chopped, white parts reserved for another use (or 1 bunch chives, finely chopped)

FOR THE BEANS

2 × 400 g (14 oz) tins small white beans, such as haricot (navy), drained and rinsed
1 fresh or dried bay leaf (optional)
kosher salt and freshly ground black pepper
a few additional anchovy fillets (optional)
1 lemon, halved for squeezing over
10 g (½ oz/½ cup) parsley, tender leaves and stems, chopped (optional)

DO AHEAD

This bagna cauda can be made 5 days ahead, stored wrapped and refrigerated. Rewarm gently over a low heat before serving. The beans can be dressed in the bagna cauda a few days ahead, stored wrapped and refrigerated. Rewarm gently over low heat before serving.

EAT WITH

A few nice radishes, a hunk of sourdough bread for dunking and a glass of white wine.

1. Make the bagna cauda: Combine the olive oil, butter and sliced garlic in a small pot over a low heat. Cook until the garlic is completely soft and tender, 10–15 minutes, lowering the heat even further as needed to maintain a subtle simmer and prevent the garlic from browning. Add the anchovies (don't worry about chopping them – they're going to dissolve in the hot fat) and continue to simmer, stirring occasionally, until the anchovies are completely dissolved and have begun to fry lightly in the fat – they'll start to smell a little nutty and browned – 15–20 minutes.

2. Add the spring onion greens and grated garlic. Continue to cook until the onions are wilted and the garlic is fragrant, another minute or so. Remove from the heat and set aside.

3. Make the beans: Combine the beans and bagna cauda in a medium pot over a medium-low heat. Add the bay leaf (if using) and let simmer together for 20–30 minutes. Taste a bean or two – they should be garlicky and buttery, herby and salty with anchovy. Adjust with salt, pepper and maybe another few anchovies if you like (otherwise, save them for topping at the end).

4. To serve, pour into a large serving bowl and squeeze lemon over everything. Top with more anchovies, if you like, and maybe some parsley.

CRISPY BAKED BEANS with MUSHROOMS & PARMESAN

SERVES 4

4 tablespoons unsalted butter
4 tablespoons olive oil, plus more as needed
1 large onion or 2 leeks, thinly sliced
kosher salt and freshly ground black pepper
450 g (1 lb) mushrooms, such as maitake, oyster or chestnut (cremini), sliced, chopped or torn into bite-size pieces
4 sage, thyme or oregano sprigs, leaves removed
2 × 400 g (14 oz) tins white beans, such as cannellini or haricot (navy) or a mix of both, drained and rinsed
125 g (4½ oz/1½ cups) grated Parmesan or pecorino cheese
45 g (1½ oz/¾ cup) panko or other coarse breadcrumbs

DO AHEAD

The beans can be made and placed in their baking dish 2 days ahead, wrapped and refrigerated; when you're ready to eat, top with the breadcrumb mixture and bake.

EAT WITH

Reheat in a skillet, tuck into a pork-fat tortilla and top with a just-scrambled egg.

These beans are a fantastic option for those who yearn for a cassoulet experience but don't eat meat – they're meaty in spirit and will certainly fill the void. Even if you do eat meat, I can confidently say they are exquisite beans. They're substantial enough to be a main course alongside a bitter salad, or they could serve as a side next to a simple roast chicken or assortment of sausages. Since there aren't that many ingredients here, it's important to treat each one well to maximise what you get from it: Really fry those onions, really brown those mushrooms. These two steps (and the Parmesan, of course) are going to give you all the flavour you need.

1 Preheat the oven to 220°C/200°C fan/425°F.

2 Heat the butter and 2 tablespoons of the olive oil in a large skillet over a medium-high heat. Add the onions and season with salt and pepper. Cook, stirring occasionally, until they're tender and nicely browned, 8–10 minutes.

3 Add the mushrooms and half of the sage leaves and season with salt and pepper. Cook, stirring occasionally, until they've released most of their water and become very tender and deeply browned, another 10–12 minutes. Add 250 ml (8 fl oz/1 cup) water to the skillet and remove from the heat. Using a wooden spoon or tongs, scrape up the browned bits from the bottom of the skillet.

4 Either add the beans directly to the skillet (if it's large enough) or combine the mushrooms and beans together in a large bowl. Add two-thirds of the Parmesan, season with salt and lots of pepper, and mix well.

5 Transfer to a 1.9- to 2.85-litre (2- to 3-quart) baking dish and top with the remaining Parmesan, remaining sage leaves, more pepper and a good drizzle of olive oil. Combine the breadcrumbs and remaining 2 tablespoons olive oil in a medium bowl and mix with your hands until it looks like wet sand. Season with salt and pepper and scatter over the top of the beans.

6 Bake the beans, uncovered, until the edges are thick and bubbling and the top is deeply golden brown and crisped, 40–45 minutes.

BEANS & GRAINS

FRENCH ONION BEANS & GREENS

SERVES 8-10

2 tablespoons olive oil, plus more as needed
2 large yellow onions, thinly sliced
8 garlic cloves, very well crushed
kosher salt and freshly ground black pepper
½ bunch thyme or 2 fresh or dried bay leaves
2 tablespoons Worcestershire sauce
450 g (1 lb) dried beans, any sort, or 4 × 400 g (14 oz) tins beans, any sort, drained and rinsed
1 smoked ham hock or 1 ham bone
2 bunches dark, leafy greens, such as kale, collard greens or cime di rapa, thick stems removed, chopped
grated Gruyère or cheddar cheese (optional)
sliced bread, for toasting and rubbing with garlic (optional)

DO AHEAD

The beans can be made 5 days ahead, stored covered and refrigerated. They also can be frozen (greens included) a few months ahead.

EAT WITH

Garlic-rubbed toast, a wedge of Gruyère.

I originally made these rich, fatty beans using the leftover ham bone from one of my famous (to me) Ham Parties, and ever since, I've become attached to making a version of this on a regular schedule (even in the absence of a party with batched martinis). The type of pork you use here is negotiable and should be whatever is easiest for you to get your hands on, but I will say that fatty, smoked pieces of pork (leftover ham bone, ham hocks, etc.) will give you perhaps the most excellently flavoured beans possible. Including so many onions in the broth, which simmer with the beans as they cook, turning oh-so soft and sweet, was born from a desire to eat French onion soup but without the rigmarole of making caramelised onions – and I will say, these beans really get there.

1. Heat the olive oil in a large heavy-bottomed pot over a medium heat. Add the onions and crushed garlic to the pot and season with salt and pepper. Cook, stirring occasionally, until the onions are nicely browned and tender, 15–20 minutes. These will not be true caramelised onions, but they will approximate the texture and flavour of them, I promise.

2. Add the thyme and Worcestershire sauce to the pot, stirring to coat the onions. Add the beans, smoked pork and 2.35 litres (80 fl oz/10 cups) of water (1.4 litres/48 fl oz/6 cups if using tinned beans) to the pot. Season with salt and pepper and bring to the boil. Reduce the heat to medium-low and cook, uncovered, letting the beans gently simmer, stirring every so often until they're very tender and the broth is thickened and impossibly delicious, 1–2 hours (depending on size and age of the bean). If using tinned, this will take 45–60 minutes. (Tinned beans are obviously already cooked, but simmering will help them tenderise further and become even more flavourful.)

3. Add the greens to the pot, season with salt and pepper and make sure they are submerged in the liquid so they can properly stew and soften. Cook until the greens are tender to your liking, 10–20 minutes.

4. To serve, if the pork hasn't naturally started to shred or fall apart on its own, pull out the hunks and do that, then mix it back into the beans. Ladle into bowls and enjoy as is or top with a nice pile of cheese and serve with toast rubbed with garlic (or make cheesy toasts to serve on top) for a more French-onion-soup feel.

A CHILLI, BECAUSE YOU ASKED

SERVES 10

1.35–1.82 kg (3–4 lb) chuck roast, sirloin or brisket, cut into 4 cm (1½ inch) pieces
kosher salt and freshly ground black pepper
2 tablespoons neutral oil or olive oil
2 medium yellow onions, finely chopped
8–10 garlic cloves, finely chopped
1 × 175 g (6 oz) tin tomato purée (paste)
2 tablespoons cumin seeds or 1 tablespoon ground cumin
2 teaspoons smoked or sweet paprika
1½ teaspoons hot paprika (or more smoked or sweet)
1½ teaspoons chilli flakes, or to taste
2 × 330 ml (12 oz) tins beer (something light, like a lager) or 750 ml (25 fl oz/3 cups) water
2 × 400 g (14 oz) tins crushed tomatoes
450 g (1 lb) dried beans (a white, black or pinto bean, or use a mix)
toppings (you must): thinly sliced spring onions (scallions), fresh or pickled red onion, shredded cheddar cheese, full-fat sour cream, chopped coriander (cilantro), thinly sliced fresh or pickled jalapeños, crumbled tortilla chips, lime wedges, etc.

DO AHEAD
—
Like all great soups and stews, this chilli gets better with age. It can be made 5 days ahead and refrigerated, or 3 months ahead and frozen.

EAT WITH
—
Cornbread, a bag of tortilla chips, another beer.

Chilli means many different things depending on where you are. This version calls for tomatoes (Texas chilli purists may as well stop reading now), is well spiced but will not necessarily light your mouth on fire, uses hunks of meat that slowly braise and calls for beans cooked from dried to soak up all that beefy, spiced, tomatoey liquid. It takes a long time to cook, simmering at least 3 hours. Is it worth it? I really think it is. The way the liquid thickens from both the long braise of the beef and the starches releasing from the beans: It's gorgeous.

1. Season the beef with salt and pepper. Heat the oil in a large heavy-bottomed pot over a medium-high heat. Add the beef in one layer (don't worry too much about crowding) and cook until deeply browned on all sides, 15–18 minutes total. Transfer the beef to a large plate or bowl, leaving the fat behind; set aside. (I do not drain the fat, but you can.)

2. Add the onions and garlic to the pot, season with salt and pepper, and cook, stirring occasionally, until they're softened, 3–5 minutes. Add the tomato purée and cook until it caramelises a bit on the bottom of the pot, 2–3 minutes. Add the cumin, smoked paprika, hot paprika and chilli flakes and cook, stirring constantly for a minute or so to toast.

3. Add the beer and use a wooden spoon to scrape up the caramelised bits on the bottom of the pot. Add the tomatoes, beans, 1.4 litres (48 fl oz/6 cups) water and the beef plus any juices. Season with salt and pepper and bring to a strong simmer.

4. Reduce the heat to medium-low – you want a gentle simmer – and cover the pot about 90 per cent of the way. (Use a baking tray if you don't have a lid.) Cook, checking and stirring only occasionally, until the pot has thickened into a beautiful chilli and the beef and beans are completely tender and nearly falling apart, 3–3½ hours.

5. Remove from the heat and, using a wooden spoon, encourage the hunks of beef to break down into smaller shreddy bits by gently pressing them against the side of the pot. Stir so the meat is evenly distributed and season once more with salt, pepper and maybe chilli flakes.

6. To serve, set out all the toppings you want. Use every small bowl and precious tiny plate to display your shredded cheese, sour cream and pickled things. Do not top anyone's bowl for them but encourage them to go wild. There are always more toppings where those came from, you say.

OLIVE OIL-FRIED LENTILS with HARISSA & HERBS

SERVES 4

1 lemon, halved, seeded
280 g (10 oz/1½ cups) dried black (beluga) or French lentils
60 ml (2 fl oz/¼ cup) olive oil
4–6 garlic cloves, thinly sliced
2–3 tablespoons harissa
kosher salt and freshly ground black pepper
1 large handful of parsley, tender leaves and stems, coarsely chopped
1 large handful of coriander (cilantro), tender leaves and stems, coarsely chopped
20 g (¾ oz/½ cup) dill and/or mint leaves, coarsely chopped

DO AHEAD

These lentils are excellent at room temperature and can be made a few hours ahead of when you'd like to eat them (no need to refrigerate). Alternatively, make them 2 days ahead and store wrapped and refrigerated; toss in a skillet over medium heat to take the chill off before serving.

EAT WITH

Labneh with Caramelised Harissa (page 28), a coil of merguez sausage, a Leafy, Herby Salad (page 148).

These are the lentils I make when I want a salad but also a side, something with personality that still properly commingles with a variety of things on the table, a dish that feels casual without seeming like a half measure. Yes, these lentils 'do it all'. A brief stint in a skillet with olive oil and toasted slivers of garlic does a lot to make 'a boiled lentil' something worth getting excited about. (While I happen to enjoy the austerity of a bowl of unadorned boiled lentils, I realise that will go only so far for most of you.) Adding to the thrill here is a bit of smoky, spiced harissa paste fried alongside the lentils, which then get finished with finely chopped lemon and fresh herbs to keep things both perky and peppery (the mark of a good salad/side hybrid). If the harissa is not complementary to your dining experience for whatever reason, you can skip it, maybe adding a spoonful of grainy mustard or a splash of sherry vinegar at the end instead.

1 Finely chop half of the lemon (peel, pith and all – the whole thing!) and set aside.

2 Cook the lentils in a medium pot of salted boiling water until tender. (How long this takes will largely depend on which lentils you end up using, so best to go according to package instructions.) Drain and set aside.

3 Heat the olive oil in a large skillet over a medium-high heat. Add the garlic and cook, stirring occasionally, until it's nicely golden brown, 2–3 minutes. Add the harissa (it will sizzle a bit in the oil, so be careful) and stir to get it nicely caramelised in the skillet (not unlike tomato purée/paste), a minute or two.

4 Add the lentils and the reserved finely chopped lemon and toss to coat in the red-hot harissa oil. Cook, letting the lentils (and lemon) make contact with the skillet to sort of fry a bit before tossing every so often. The lentils should be lightly frizzled, starting to crisp up slightly, 5–8 minutes. (Feel free to reduce the heat to medium if things in the skillet seem to be getting too hot.)

5 Remove from the heat and transfer to a large serving bowl or platter. Stir in the herbs and squeeze the remaining half of lemon over everything before serving.

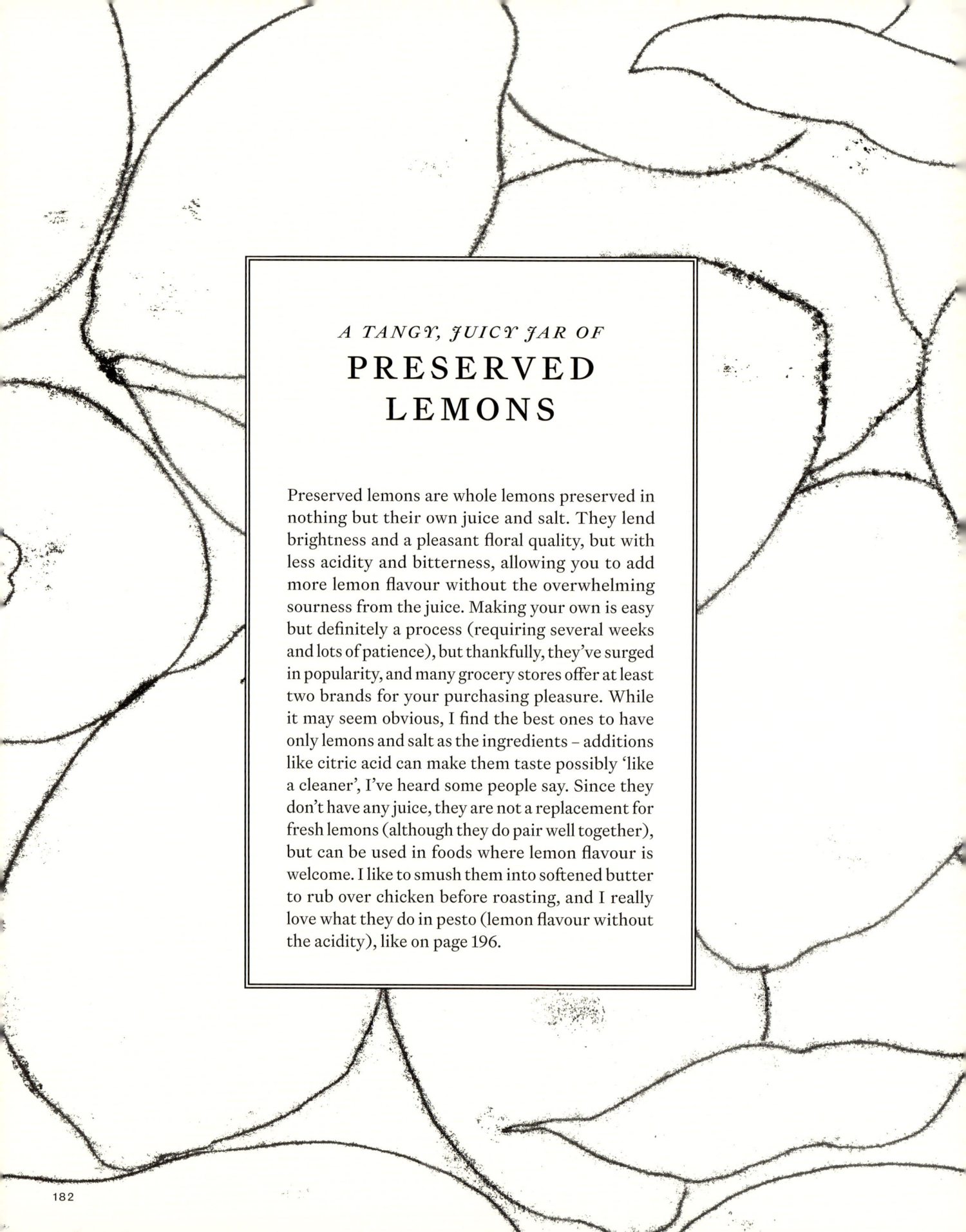

A TANGY, JUICY JAR OF
PRESERVED LEMONS

Preserved lemons are whole lemons preserved in nothing but their own juice and salt. They lend brightness and a pleasant floral quality, but with less acidity and bitterness, allowing you to add more lemon flavour without the overwhelming sourness from the juice. Making your own is easy but definitely a process (requiring several weeks and lots of patience), but thankfully, they've surged in popularity, and many grocery stores offer at least two brands for your purchasing pleasure. While it may seem obvious, I find the best ones to have only lemons and salt as the ingredients – additions like citric acid can make them taste possibly 'like a cleaner', I've heard some people say. Since they don't have any juice, they are not a replacement for fresh lemons (although they do pair well together), but can be used in foods where lemon flavour is welcome. I like to smush them into softened butter to rub over chicken before roasting, and I really love what they do in pesto (lemon flavour without the acidity), like on page 196.

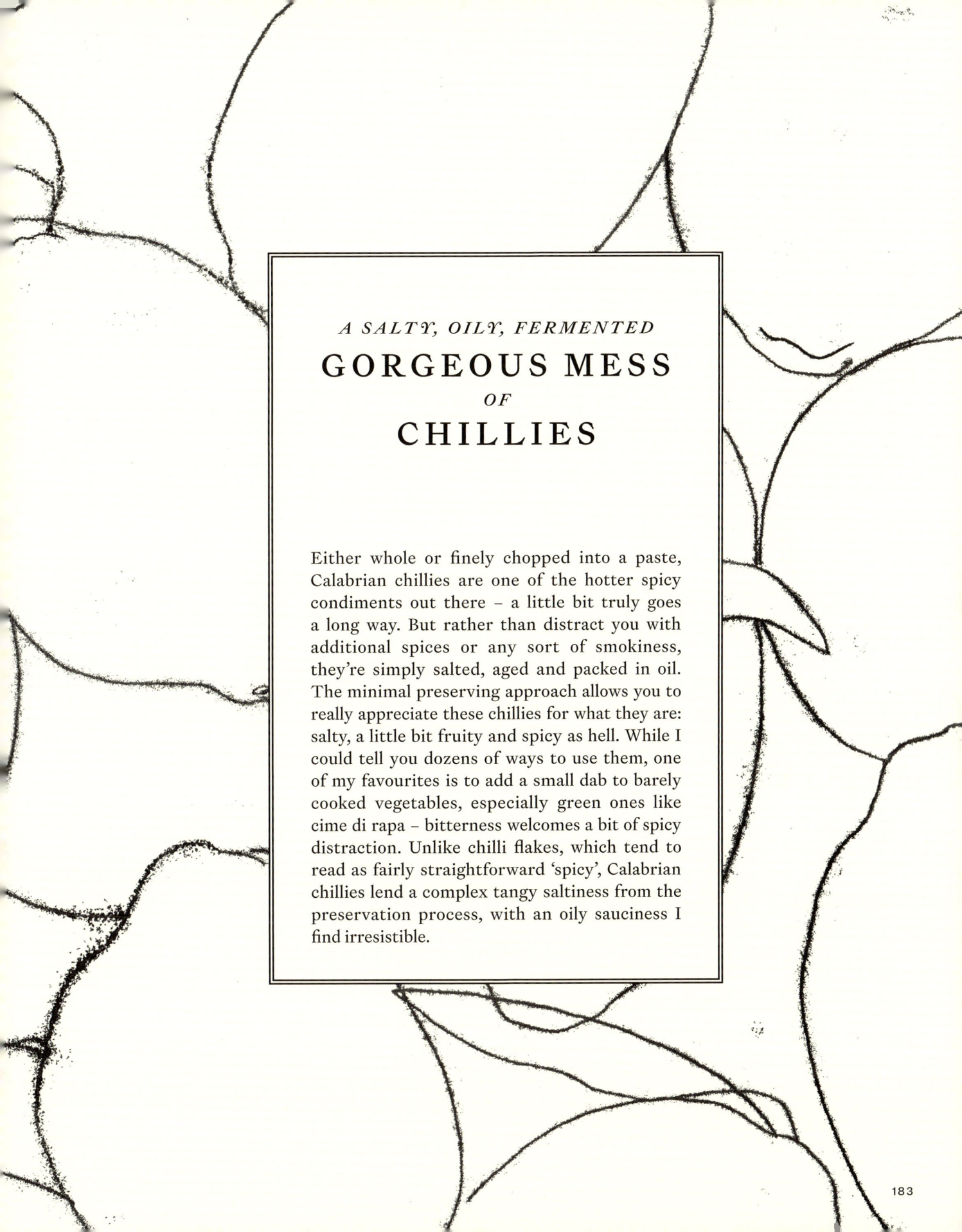

A SALTY, OILY, FERMENTED
GORGEOUS MESS
OF
CHILLIES

Either whole or finely chopped into a paste, Calabrian chillies are one of the hotter spicy condiments out there – a little bit truly goes a long way. But rather than distract you with additional spices or any sort of smokiness, they're simply salted, aged and packed in oil. The minimal preserving approach allows you to really appreciate these chillies for what they are: salty, a little bit fruity and spicy as hell. While I could tell you dozens of ways to use them, one of my favourites is to add a small dab to barely cooked vegetables, especially green ones like cime di rapa – bitterness welcomes a bit of spicy distraction. Unlike chilli flakes, which tend to read as fairly straightforward 'spicy', Calabrian chillies lend a complex tangy saltiness from the preservation process, with an oily sauciness I find irresistible.

SPELT with MUSHROOMS, FRIZZLED LEEKS & SOUR CREAM

SERVES 4

- 60 ml (2 fl oz/¼ cup) olive oil, plus more as needed
- 4 medium leeks, white and light green parts, thinly sliced
- 450 g (1 lb) mushrooms, such as maitake, oyster, chestnut (cremini) or chanterelle, torn into bite-size pieces
- kosher salt and freshly ground black pepper
- 385 g (13 oz/1¾ cups) pearled or semi-pearled spelt (farro) or barley
- 950 ml (32 fl oz/4 cups) vegetable stock, chicken stock or water plus Better Than Bouillon (see page 58)
- 25 g (1 oz/½ cup) finely chopped chives (from about 1 bunch)
- 40 g (1½ oz/1 cup) dill leaves, coarsely chopped
- 1 tablespoon finely grated lemon zest
- sour cream or full-fat Greek yoghurt, for serving
- lemon wedges, for squeezing over

EAT WITH

This one-stop shop doesn't need anything else, but if you wanted to serve it as part of a spread to make it 'more' of a meal, a simple dish of sautéed greens or some roasted sausages next to it would be nice.

This is one of several recipes in this book directly lifted from my experiences at Russian and Turkish bathhouses in New York, and at least partially informed by my Eastern European heritage. There is dill, there is sour cream, there are plump, savoury grains and there are browned, crisped mushrooms. Texturally similar to risotto (without the constant stirring), this dish is creamy, saucy and deeply cosy. Aside from boiling spelt (farro) like pasta and turning it into a salad (page 187), I think this 'cooked in broth until porridge-like' technique is the best celebration of this particular grain: The spelt sort of bursts as it cooks, releasing starch while still preserving its squeaky exterior, giving you chewiness and creaminess all at once. This is a lovely bed for nearly any vegetable, but meaty, golden-brown mushrooms and crisped, frizzled leeks to me are the dreamiest combination.

1. Heat the olive oil in a large, heavy-bottomed pot over a medium-high heat. Add half of the leeks and half of the mushrooms and season with salt and pepper. Cook, stirring occasionally, until browned and crisped, 12–15 minutes. (They will start giving off moisture before this happens.)

2. Using a slotted spoon, transfer the leeks and mushrooms to a medium bowl, leaving any olive oil behind. (They will absorb the oil at first and then release some of it back as they crisp.) Add a bit more olive oil so you're back to ¼ cup or so in the pot. Cook the remaining leeks and mushrooms, adding them to the bowl with the others.

3. Without wiping out the pot, add the spelt and season with salt and pepper. Cook over that same medium-high heat, stirring frequently, until the spelt is toasted on the outside (it will go from pale golden brown to a toastier golden brown), about 5 minutes. Add the stock and 480 ml (16 fl oz/2 cups) water and season with salt and pepper.

4. Bring to a simmer and reduce the heat to medium-low. Simmer gently, stirring occasionally, until the spelt is fully cooked and most (but not all) of the liquid has been absorbed, 20–25 minutes. It should still look a bit loose, like risotto. Remove from the heat and add half of the chives.

5. Toss the dill, remaining chives and lemon zest together in a small bowl. To serve, season the spelt with salt and pepper and ladle into bowls. Top with a good spoonful of sour cream, the mushrooms and leeks and the dill mixture. Serve with more sour cream and lemon wedges alongside.

SPELT & PEA SALAD with PRESERVED LEMON

SERVES 4

300 g (10½ oz/2 cups) shelled garden peas (fresh or frozen)

450 g (1 lb/2 cups) pearled or semi-pearled spelt (farro), wheatberries or barley

2 garlic cloves, finely grated

25 g (1 oz/½ cup) finely chopped chives

4 tablespoons fresh lemon juice, plus more as needed

2 teaspoons fish sauce, plus more as needed (optional)

kosher salt and freshly ground black pepper

225 g (8 oz) sugar snap peas, halved lengthways

2 handfuls of pea shoots, dill or parsley, tender leaves and stems

2 tablespoons olive oil, plus more for drizzling

185 g (6½ oz/¾ cup) full-fat Greek yoghurt or labneh

½ preserved lemon, seeded, finely chopped

DO AHEAD

The spelt can be dressed (sans peas and pea shoots) 2 days ahead, stored wrapped and refrigerated. Preserved lemon yoghurt can be made 5 days ahead, stored wrapped and refrigerated.

EAT WITH

Bring on a picnic and eat for lunch with a few tins of fish. Or have for dinner next to Slow-Roasted Salmon with Preserved Lemon & Sesame (page 303), Saucy, Wine-Roasted Chicken with Mushrooms (page 269) or Steak Like Tartare (page 293).

I am guilty of giving more attention to beans and grains in the winter months, combining them with warming broth, lots of cheese and other things that make me say the word 'cosy'. One major exception to this is my love for perfectly cooked, lightly chewy, still-a-little-squeaky spelt, brightly dressed and mixed with the vague-but-evocative category of 'spring vegetables': perky green things like peas, thinly sliced asparagus or tiny tender little sprouts and shoots. This salad is fresh and vibrant, a reminder that grains (and beans) also love to be seen alongside tins of fish or poached chicken for what could only be called 'a sensible lunch' (great phrase), enjoyed with an iced tea on a little patch of grass in the sun.

Buried beneath the pile of grains, there's a gorgeous dollop of preserved lemon yoghurt, which is good on a number of things, lending rich fattiness and refreshing tanginess. Yoghurt, especially when bolstered by a good bit of salty preserved lemon, really does it all.

1. Bring a large pot of salted water to the boil. Add the peas and cook until tender and bright green, 1–3 minutes. Using a slotted spoon or small strainer, transfer the peas to a large bowl to cool, leaving the water behind (you'll use it to cook the grains); set aside.

2. Add the spelt to the pot and boil until tender and cooked through (cook according to package instructions). Drain the spelt, running it under cool water for a minute or so before adding to the peas.

3. Add the garlic, chives, 3 tablespoons of the lemon juice and the fish sauce (if using) to the grains. Season with salt and pepper and toss to coat everything evenly. Taste and season with more lemon juice, salt, pepper or fish sauce as needed to make sure the grains taste adequately flavourful – garlicky, lemony, salty.

4. Add the sliced snap peas, pea shoots and olive oil and toss to coat; set aside.

5. Combine the yoghurt, preserved lemon and the remaining 1 tablespoon lemon juice in a small bowl; season with salt and pepper. Spoon into the bottom of a large serving bowl or platter, spreading a bit to create a sort of base layer of yoghurt on which to place the salad. Top with the spelt salad, making sure some of the peas and pea shoots get on top (we eat with our eyes!). Drizzle with a little more olive oil before serving.

BUTTERED POLENTA with FRESH CORN

SERVES 4–6

225 g (8 oz/1½ cups) coarsely ground polenta
6 tablespoons unsalted butter
15 g (½ oz/¼ cup) grated Parmesan or pecorino cheese, plus more as needed
kosher salt and freshly ground black pepper
400 g (14 oz/2 cups) corn kernels (from 2–3 ears corn) or frozen kernels
¼ teaspoon hot or smoked paprika
pinch of chilli flakes

DO AHEAD
—
Polenta and sautéed corn can both be made a few hours ahead. (You may need to add water to the polenta upon reheating – it tends to stiffen up as it sits.)

EAT WITH
—
Pork chops, a tomato salad, a plate of grilled sausages. Without the corn topping, it's also one of my preferred companions for Goodbye Meatballs (page 288).

This is really just a recipe for a perfect bowl of polenta, which, if you're starting with high-quality polenta (polenta is the name for both the cooked thing and the dried, coarsely ground corn from which it comes) and whisk in enough good butter, can be one of life's greatest pleasures. It's a pot of something everyone should have in near-constant rotation as their carb of choice for dinner, especially in the colder months when the thought of another potato or bag of pasta is simply too much to bear. That said, it's great in the summer months as well: corn with corn, corn on corn . . . (Can you imagine a more pleasing phrase than 'corn on corn'?) Close your eyes, and you can see it now: a bowl of perfectly tender, creamy polenta with plenty of black pepper and just the right amount of Parmesan, generously topped with lightly spiced, just-cooked corn. It's a starch, it's a carb, it's a vegetable, it's celebrating both peak summer produce and reliable pantry staples, it's everything! A summer dream if there ever was one.

1   Bring 1.4 litres (48 fl oz/6 cups) of salted water to the boil in a large pot. Reduce the heat to low and whisk in the polenta. Cook, whisking occasionally to prevent it from clumping or sticking to the bottom of the pot, until cooked through, 15–20 minutes. Once the polenta is fully cooked, remove from the heat, whisk in 4 tablespoons of the butter and the Parmesan, and season with salt and pepper. Season with more salt, pepper and Parmesan as you like.

2   Meanwhile, heat the remaining 2 tablespoons butter in a medium skillet over a medium heat. Add the corn kernels and season with salt and lots of pepper. Add the paprika and a pinch of chilli flakes and cook, stirring occasionally, just to take the raw edge off the corn and bring out the sweetness, 2–3 minutes.

3   Spoon the polenta into a large serving bowl and top with the corn, more pepper or chilli flakes, and Parmesan.

TOASTED RICE PILAF
with CRUSHED WALNUTS & DATES

SERVES 4–6

6 tablespoons olive oil, plus more as needed

75 g (2½ oz/¾ cup) walnuts, crushed or finely chopped

kosher salt and freshly ground black pepper

1 garlic clove, finely chopped or grated

4–6 dates, preferably Medjool, pitted and chopped

200 g (7 oz/1 cup) basmati or jasmine rice

4 tablespoons unsalted butter

2 large shallots or 1 medium onion, finely chopped

1 lemon, thinly sliced, seeded, or ½ preserved lemon, finely chopped

small pinch of ground turmeric (optional)

300 ml (10 fl oz/1¼ cups) chicken or vegetable stock, or water

EAT WITH
—

Some flatbread and a plate of pickles with a bowl of Labneh with Caramelised Harissa (page 28), a whole grilled trout or branzino, or Crisp, Hot Roast Chicken with Leeks (page 262).

The fact that I still struggle to simply steam rice successfully deterred me from making my own rice pilaf for years, but eventually the siren song of grains of rice toasted in butter, cooked until tender and perfectly hydrated in a flavourful broth was too much to ignore. After more trial and error than I'd like to admit, I finally figured out what worked for me: a straightforward ratio, basic instructions, less fear, more ignoring (overly fussed-with rice pilaf is prone to disaster). While butter and rice is an undeniably perfect combination, the additions at the end here really do make this pilaf, adding textural contrast, sweetness, saltiness and savouriness: Plump dates and toasted walnuts tossed with raw garlic get spooned over the rice, left to soften during that important final rest. While this is very much a celebration of the simplicity of pantry cooking, it is hard to deny how good this would be with fresh herbs or a generous bowl of salted yoghurt on the side, too.

1. Heat 2 tablespoons of the olive oil in a medium pot (wider than tall, if there's the option – you'll use it to cook your rice after) over a medium heat. Add the walnuts, season with salt and pepper, and cook, stirring often, until well toasted, about 4 minutes. Transfer the walnuts (and oil) to a small bowl and add the garlic, dates and an additional 2 tablespoons of the olive oil. Season with salt and pepper and set aside. Using paper towels, wipe out any walnut bits from the pot.

2. Rinse the rice very well in cold water, changing the water each time until it runs clear (this will take a few minutes and multiple changes); set aside.

3. Heat the butter and the remaining 2 tablespoons olive oil in that same pot over a medium-high heat. Add the shallots and season with salt and pepper. Cook, stirring occasionally, until nicely tender but without too much colour, 8–10 minutes.

4. Add the lemon, rice and turmeric (if using), stirring constantly to toast the rice in the butter mixture, until the grains have turned a light golden-brown colour, 5–8 minutes. Add the stock, season with salt and pepper and bring to a simmer. Reduce the heat to low, cover and cook until all the liquid has evaporated and the rice is fluffy and tender, 15–18 minutes.

5. Remove from the heat, fluff with a fork or spoon, and spoon the garlicky date mixture over the top, giving it a good (but gentle) toss to incorporate. Cover to rest another 5–10 minutes before serving.

PASTAS and NOODLES

If you've bought this book and flipped straight to this chapter, I am you and you are me. Sure, it's not very imaginative to say pasta is your favourite food, but, alas, pasta is, undeniably, my favourite food. On any given weeknight, you're likely to find me sidestepping a more ambitious kitchen project in favour of caramelising shallots, melting a tin of anchovies and opening a tub of tomato purée (paste) to make a perfect sauce for which to dress an already-opened bag of bucatini (a very special something from nothing if ever a thing did exist).

While I could write a whole book of recipes featuring pasta and the like, I wanted to whittle down a collection of some of my personal essentials. Here, they range from the herby and salad-y to the red saucy and cheesy, even including one aubergine (eggplant) Parmesan, since, despite not containing any pasta, it really felt like it belonged in this chapter.

WALNUT PESTO PASTA

SERVES 4 / MAKES ABOUT 480 ML (16 FL OZ/2 CUPS) PESTO

50 g (1¾ oz/½ cup) walnuts or almonds
4 garlic cloves, smashed
kosher salt and freshly ground black pepper
2 bunches parsley, tender leaves and stems
1 large bunch chives, finely chopped
½ preserved lemon, seeds removed, chopped (optional)
250 ml (8 fl oz/1 cup) olive oil, plus more as needed
350–450 g (12 oz–1 lb) dried pasta (any shape)
1 lemon, halved for squeezing over
Parmesan or pecorino cheese, finely grated for serving

NOTE

This pesto is also a nice place for those obscure spring things like wild garlic or garlic scapes.

DO AHEAD

This is best eaten on day of making (one of those things that does not get better with age), but the pesto can be made 2 days ahead and stored in a resealable container in the refrigerator or frozen for up to 2 months (probably more).

EAT WITH

Spaghetti is unbeatable in its simplicity for this pesto, but this is a good sauce for underneath roasted vegetables or tossed with simply cooked grains or lentils and a nice six-minute egg (page 144).

I'm calling this pesto because I believe it to be, but you'll quickly find out that there is no basil here and the cheese is on the side. There are also no pine nuts, although that might scandalise you less. Does that still make this a pesto? Is a hot dog a sandwich? Let's not do that here.

This pesto is garlicky, it's green as hell, and you don't have to blanch anything. While the bulk of the sauce is fresh herbs, I'd still argue that the prominent flavour and texture of walnuts makes this a certified pantry recipe. (You can swap in almonds, but the walnuts grind to such a gorgeous texture, with a perfect tannic flavour unmatched in other nuts.) This is one of the few recipes that requires 'special equipment', like a food processor or mortar and pestle, but if you have a sharp knife, you can combine all these ingredients and dress your pasta with it and it would be wonderful (if a little less 'pesto'). While the cheese is not included in the pesto itself, I do think it should go on top of your pasta for serving. Adding the cheese separately keeps the pesto saucier and fresher feeling – one woman's opinion!

1. Preheat the oven to 180°C/160°C fan/350°F. Toast the walnuts on a baking tray until lightly golden brown, 8–10 minutes. (Alternatively, use a toaster oven.) Let cool completely.

2. Place the cooled walnuts and garlic in a food processor and season with salt and pepper. Process until the walnuts are well ground, like a chunky paste. Add the parsley, chives and preserved lemon (if using) and process until the herbs are very finely chopped. Add the olive oil and pulse to combine. Season again with salt and pepper, adding more olive oil as needed to get the texture you like.

3. Bring a large pot of salted water to the boil. Cook the pasta until al dente. Save at least 250 ml (8 fl oz/1 cup) of pasta water, then drain the pasta. Transfer the pasta to a large bowl and add half of the pesto, along with 120 ml (4 fl oz/½ cup) pasta water. Give it a good toss and keep tossing until the pasta looks nice and glossy, almost thickened. (It should also turn a brighter green – adding the hot pasta water is almost like blanching the parsley.) Add more pesto and pasta water as needed to make sure each piece of pasta is nicely coated and it feels saucy – never stiff or gloopy. Season with salt and pepper.

4. To serve, divide the pasta among bowls, and give each a squeeze of lemon, a showering of cheese, a bit more pepper and a drizzle of olive oil.

LEMON PEPPER PASTA with BROWNED BUTTER

SERVES 4

350–450 g (12 oz–1 lb) dried pasta (a long noodle works best here)
6 tablespoons unsalted butter
½ teaspoon chilli flakes, plus more to taste
kosher salt and freshly ground black pepper (lots of it)
1 lemon, zested and juiced
30 g (1 oz/½ cup) finely grated Parmesan cheese, plus more to serve

NOTE

If this sounds too simple to be spectacular, I encourage you to just try it as is, because it really does dazzle. That said, feel free to add a little thinly sliced preserved lemon or maybe a finely grated clove of garlic to the skillet, or toss in a handful of leafy greens at the end if you're still craving more.

EAT WITH

Yes, this is a very tangy, lemon-forward pasta, but it's also a rich, creamy pasta that definitely wants – nay, needs – something bright and acidic to cut through it. I like a good crunchy salad (Salty Celery Salad with Anchovy, page 134) or simple blanched broccoli doused with lemon juice.

This high-low pasta tastes enough like an excellent boxed macaroni and cheese to hit many of the same pleasure receptors, with the texture of an elegant cacio e pepe. Unfortunately, it does require a bit more technique (the simplest things often do), as the sauce is created with only browned butter, finely grated Parmesan, pasta water and... not much else. If this isn't something you've done before, wow, are you in for a treat. But also, be patient: The al dente pasta does take a bit of time to fully cook in the skillet and create a thick-enough sauce. It's the ultimate 'I can't believe this came from only that' – my favourite way to cook.

1 Bring a large pot of salted water to the boil. Cook the pasta until just before al dente (it'll finish cooking in the sauce). Save 480 ml (16 fl oz/ 2 cups) of pasta water, then drain the pasta, setting both aside.

2 Meanwhile, melt the butter in a large skillet over a medium heat. Use a whisk to scrape up all the browned bits as they form – this will give you a nice, evenly browned butter. Cook, continuing to whisk occasionally until the foam has subsided, the butter is evenly browned and it all smells incredible, 3–4 minutes.

3 Add the chilli flakes, lots of freshly ground black pepper (about two to three times more than you'd usually use) and the lemon zest. Add the pasta, along with the Parmesan and 120 ml (4 fl oz/½ cup) of the pasta water. Season with salt and increase the heat to medium-high. Cook, tossing frequently (I like to use tongs), until the liquid starts to thicken and evaporate, 3–4 minutes or so. Add another 120 ml (4 fl oz/½ cup) of pasta water to the skillet and continue to cook, tossing, tossing, tossing... until the liquid starts to thicken and evaporate, 2–3 minutes.

4 Add another 120 ml (4 fl oz/½ cup) of pasta water and continue to cook until the sauce appears thickened, glossy, starchy and luscious. Taste a noodle: It should be fully cooked (but not mushy). If you think the pasta or sauce needs it, give it another splash of pasta water to get it where you want it to be.

5 Remove from the heat and add half of the lemon juice. Season with salt and maybe more pepper or chilli flakes. Taste another noodle and add the remaining lemon juice if 'very lemony' is what you're after. (It's what I'm after.) Divide among bowls, making sure each has a nice pool of sauce. Top with more pepper and Parmesan if you like.

PASTAS & NOODLES

SAUCY ROASTED AUBERGINE PASTA

SERVES 4–6

2 large globe aubergines (eggplants) (about 900 g/2 lb), sliced 5 mm–1 cm (¼–½ inch) thick
kosher salt and freshly ground black pepper
175 ml (6 fl oz/¾ cup) olive oil
60 g (2 oz/1 cup) panko breadcrumbs
15 g (½ oz/¼ cup) Parmesan or pecorino cheese, plus more for grating
15 g (½ oz/½ cup) chopped parsley, basil, or both
4 garlic cloves, thinly sliced
225 g (8 oz) Sungold or cherry tomatoes, halved if large
1–2 tablespoons tomato purée (paste), harissa or gochujang
chilli flakes (optional)
350–450 g (12 oz–1 lb) dried pasta, such as calamarata, rigatoni, ziti, paccheri or any short, tube shape

DO AHEAD
—
This pasta is shockingly good the next day, cold out of the fridge (it can also be reheated).

Something very magical happens when you add water to deeply roasted, well-browned aubergine (eggplant) in a skillet. The mixture becomes thick, luscious, almost creamy in texture. In other words, a perfect sauce for pasta. Assisted by just-burst tomatoes and finished with breadcrumbs, this pasta tastes like an excellent version of aubergine Parmesan, a compliment of the highest order.

1   Preheat the oven to 220°C/200°C fan/425°F. Arrange the aubergine in an even layer on a sheet pan, season with salt and pepper and drizzle with 120 ml (4 fl oz/½ cup) of the olive oil. Roast for 45–50 minutes, flipping the aubergine halfway through, until deeply browned on both sides.

2   Meanwhile, heat 3 tablespoons of the olive oil in a large skillet over a medium heat. Add the breadcrumbs and season with salt and pepper. Cook, tossing occasionally, until the breadcrumbs are golden brown, 4–6 minutes. Add the Parmesan and toss to coat, letting it melt into the crumbs. Remove from the heat and transfer to a small bowl. Add a tablespoon or two of the chopped herbs, toss, and set aside.

3   Wipe out any crumbs from the skillet and add the remaining 2 tablespoons olive oil. Add the garlic and cook over a medium-high heat, stirring occasionally, until softened and nicely toasted, 3–5 minutes. Add the tomatoes, tomato purée and chilli flakes (if using). Season with salt and pepper and cook, stirring occasionally, until the tomatoes burst, another 3–5 minutes, then remove from the heat.

4   Once your aubergine is where you want it, add it all to the skillet, stirring it in so it melts into the tomatoes. It will look a little dry at first but you're going to add lots of pasta water, which will give you more of a 'sauce'.

5   Meanwhile, bring a large pot of salted water to the boil. Cook the pasta until just before al dente. Save 480 ml (16 fl oz/2 cups) of pasta water, then drain the pasta.

6   Add the pasta and 360 ml (12 fl oz/1½ cups) of the pasta water to the skillet and cook over a medium heat until the sauce becomes thick and almost creamy, 3–5 minutes. Each piece of pasta should be coated – add more pasta water if needed. Season with salt and pepper as you go.

7   Divide the pasta among bowls and top with the breadcrumbs, remaining herbs and more cheese to serve.

CREAMY CAULIFLOWER PASTA with PECORINO BREADCRUMBS

SERVES 4

6 tablespoons olive oil

60 g (2 oz/¾ cup) fresh, coarse or panko breadcrumbs

kosher salt and freshly ground black pepper

30 g (1 oz/½ cup) finely grated pecorino cheese, plus more to serve

225 g (8 oz) dried rigatoni, ziti or campanelle

1 large shallot, finely chopped

1 medium head cauliflower (about 900 g/2 lb), sliced about 1 cm (½ inch) thick (I like to include the leaves and stem, but that is optional)

250 ml (8 fl oz/1 cup) double (heavy) cream

1 tablespoon finely grated lemon zest, plus more to serve

25 g (1 oz/½ cup) finely chopped chives

chilli flakes (optional)

EAT WITH
—
Like all heavier, creamier pastas, this is especially nice with a brightly dressed Leafy, Herby Salad (page 148).

This recipe is wonderful for many reasons: A whole head of cauliflower caramelises in a skillet before being simmered with cream, black pepper, pecorino cheese and a bit of lemon zest, breaking down into a special (and yes, decadent) sauce to coat the pasta shape of your choosing. It's all very dreamy. But really, it's the pecorino breadcrumbs we're here for, and that's okay – they're magnificent. A crunchy, oily, salty vehicle for more cheese and much-needed texture, they're the ideal finish to a saucy pasta such as this, but don't stop there. Use them as tiny croutons to finish a Caesar salad (page 150) or scatter them over the top of a pot of saucy beans (page 177). Once they're in your life, you'll never want to be without them.

1. Heat 3 tablespoons of the olive oil in a large skillet over a medium heat. Add the breadcrumbs and season with salt and pepper. Stir to coat evenly in the oil and cook, tossing occasionally, until they're evenly toasted and golden brown, 4–6 minutes. Add half of the pecorino and toss to coat, letting the cheese melt and clump among the breadcrumbs (think granola-like clusters). Remove from the heat and transfer to a small bowl or plate; set aside.

2. Meanwhile, bring a large pot of salted water to the boil. Cook the pasta until al dente; save about 250 ml (8 fl oz/1 cup) of pasta water, then drain.

3. Wipe out any crumbs from the skillet and heat the remaining 3 tablespoons olive oil over a medium heat. Add the shallot and cauliflower and season with salt and plenty of pepper. Cook, tossing occasionally, until the cauliflower has completely softened and both the cauliflower and shallots are beginning to caramelise and brown, 12–15 minutes.

4. Add the cream and lemon zest and bring to a simmer, then let the cream reduce and thicken, 2–4 minutes. Season with salt and plenty of pepper.

5. Add the pasta to the cauliflower along with the remaining pecorino and 175 ml (6 fl oz/¾ cup) of the pasta water. Cook, tossing to coat the pasta and thicken the sauce, until it's thick and glossy and almost resembles macaroni and cheese, adding more pasta water by the tablespoon as needed, 4–6 minutes.

6. Remove from the heat. Divide the pasta among bowls and top with pecorino breadcrumbs, chives, more lemon zest, chilli flakes (if using) and more cheese if you like.

WINTER SQUASH PASTA with CHILLI & TOASTED GARLIC

SERVES 4

4 tablespoons unsalted butter (or more olive oil)

2 tablespoons olive oil

6–8 garlic cloves, thinly sliced or chopped

1 teaspoon chilli flakes, plus more to taste

a few leaves of sage, thyme, rosemary or oregano (optional)

1 small winter squash, such as kabocha, acorn or butternut, peeled, seeded and chopped (about 350 g/12 oz/2 cups of cut-up squash)

kosher salt and freshly ground black pepper

350–450 g (12 oz–1 lb) dried pasta, smaller, tube shapes preferred

1 teaspoon sherry vinegar or white wine vinegar, plus more to taste

Parmesan or pecorino cheese, for grating, or ricotta or burrata, for dolloping

NOTE
—
Your choice of cheese will come down to personal preference. I will always want the salty, hard cheese that leans savoury over the soft, creamy cheese that embraces the sweet. But to thine own self be true!

EAT WITH
—
Some sort of autumnal salad full of chicories and sliced tree fruits, like the one on page 137.

One of the more wonderful parts of squash is its ability to turn into utter mush with little to no effort. Impossibly hard when raw, it becomes effortlessly soft with just a bit of heat and time. No blender or food processor required. Magical. Although I'm not usually a fan of squash, I make an exception here because it turns into such a gorgeous sauce with which to coat little pieces of pasta that it would be a shame not to take advantage. While the squash will very clearly start to fall apart as it cooks, it'll still rely on the addition of (quite a bit of) pasta water to turn it into a sauce loose enough to coat, so be prepared to add more water than you'd expect. While it can be made a little fancier with a dollop of burrata, ricotta or a handful of toasted nuts, feel free to resist: It's tough to beat the delight of something so fabulous made with so few ingredients.

1 Heat the butter in a large, heavy-bottomed pot (or a large skillet) over a medium heat. Let it melt, then sizzle, until it's all foamy and browned, 3–4 minutes. Add the olive oil, then add the garlic and chilli flakes, plus any herbs. Cook, stirring, until the garlic is nicely toasted, browned and crisped, 3–4 minutes. Using a spoon, transfer all the garlic and about half of the fat in the skillet to a small bowl; set aside.

2 With the heat still on medium, add the squash to the pot and season with salt and pepper. Cook, stirring occasionally, until the squash is completely softened and tender, while also nicely browned and caramelised in spots, 12–15 minutes. You should be able to easily smash a piece of squash with a spoon; if it's still a little hard, keep cooking.

3 Meanwhile, bring a large pot of salted water to the boil. Cook your pasta until it's al dente (really al dente – you'll finish cooking the pasta in the squash sauce). Save 480 ml (16 fl oz/2 cups) of pasta water, then drain the pasta. Once the squash is so soft you can easily smush it, add the pasta and 250 ml (8 fl oz/1 cup) of pasta water. Cook, stirring constantly, until the squash has melted into a thick purée, starting to coat the pasta. Add more pasta water, 60 ml (2 fl oz/¼ cup) at a time, until it's decidedly sauce-like and the pasta is fully cooked, a few minutes.

4 Add the vinegar and season the pasta with more salt, pepper, vinegar and chilli flakes if you like. Grate the Parmesan (if using) directly onto the pasta, and divide among bowls or plates. Grate a bit more cheese or dollop your soft, creamy cheese on top (if using). Regardless, end with a spoonful of the crispy garlic chilli oil and another grind of pepper.

CARBONARA FOR TWO

SERVES 2

1 tablespoon olive oil

60 g (2 oz) guanciale or pancetta (if you want to use bacon, okay), cut into 5 mm (¼ inch) pieces

1 large egg

1 large egg yolk

1 garlic clove, finely grated (optional, but it is my preference)

about 30 g (1 oz/½ cup) finely grated Parmesan and/or pecorino cheese, plus more to serve

kosher salt and freshly ground black pepper (lots of it)

2 large palmfuls of dried spaghetti (175–225 g/6–8 oz)

EAT WITH
—
Someone you love.

I am in no way saying this is the definitive way to make spaghetti carbonara. It might not even be 'the right way'. (There's garlic, a divisive but important addition.) But: This is the way I make it. It makes sense to me, it feels right, I'm impressed with its foolproof-ness and, frankly, it's as close to Rome as I can get without leaving my house. This recipe, with the short, humble ingredient list and simple yet precise technique, feels like the truest meaning of 'something from nothing'.

1. Heat the olive oil and guanciale in a medium skillet over a medium heat and cook, stirring occasionally, until most of the fat has rendered out and the meat starts to brown, 8–10 minutes. Remove from the heat and transfer the meat to a small bowl, leaving the fat behind.

2. Whisk the egg, egg yolk, garlic (if using) and Parmesan in a medium bowl. Season with salt and LOTS of black pepper. Set aside.

3. Meanwhile, bring a large pot of salted water to the boil. Cook the pasta about halfway through – it should be malleable but not quite al dente.

4. Return the skillet with the fat to a medium heat and, using tongs, transfer the pasta to the skillet. (This way I don't have worry about 'reserving' the pasta water – it just stays in the pot.) Add about 120 ml (4 fl oz/½ cup) of pasta water, swirling to scrape up all the sticky, porky bits, and cook for a minute or so.

5. Whisk 175 ml (6 fl oz/¾ cup) pasta water into the egg-cheese mixture and then add the pasta to that bowl, using your tongs to toss, toss, toss.

6. Return the pasta and all the sauce to the skillet. (It will look watery and soupy and not all that great – just wait!) Cook the pasta over medium heat and continue to toss, moving the skillet and the pasta and letting the sauce come together and become totally emulsified and creamy. If you notice any bits of scrambled eggs, your heat is too high – remove the pan from the heat and let it cool before continuing.

7. Just before the sauce looks thick enough, remove the skillet from the heat, and keep tossing. Add more pasta water if it's looking a bit dry. (This pasta goes from saucy to sticky very quickly.)

8. Transfer the pasta to a bowl or eating vessel of your choice. Top with more pepper, Parmesan and a sprinkle of the meaty crispy bits.

CARAMELISED SHALLOT PASTA

SERVES 4

60 ml (2 fl oz/¼ cup) olive oil
6 large shallots (about 350 g/12 oz), very thinly sliced
5 garlic cloves (4 thinly sliced, 1 finely chopped)
kosher salt and freshly ground black pepper
1 teaspoon chilli flakes, plus more to serve
1 × 60 g (2 oz) tin anchovy fillets (about 12), drained
125–185 g (4½–6½ oz/½–¾ cup) tomato purée (paste) (equivalent to 1 whole tube or tin, see page 214)
350–450 g (12 oz–1 lb) dried pasta, preferably a long, thin noodle like bucatini or spaghetti
1 handful of parsley, tender leaves and stems, finely chopped
flaky sea salt

DO AHEAD

The shallot paste can be made 1 month ahead, stored sealed and refrigerated.

To say this recipe changed my life might be a bit dramatic, but it also might be true. I'm grateful so many people love a little skillet of caramelised shallots, a tin of anchovies and a whole lot of tomato purée (paste) as much as I do.

1 Heat the olive oil in a large skillet or casserole (Dutch oven) over a medium-high heat. Add the shallots and sliced garlic and season with salt and pepper. Cook, stirring occasionally, until the shallots have become completely softened and caramelised with golden-brown fried edges, 15–20 minutes.

2 Add the chilli flakes and anchovies. (No need to chop the anchovies; they will dissolve on their own.) Stir to melt the anchovies into the shallots, about 2 minutes.

3 Add the tomato purée and season with salt and pepper. Cook, stirring constantly to prevent any scorching, until the tomato purée has started to cook in the oil a bit, caramelising at the edges and going from bright red to a deeper brick-red colour, about 2 minutes. Remove from the heat and transfer about half of the mixture to a resealable container, leaving the rest behind. (These are your leftovers to be used elsewhere: in another batch of pasta, smeared onto roasted vegetables, spooned over fried eggs or spread underneath crispy chicken thighs.)

4 Bring a large pot of salted water to the boil. Cook the pasta until very al dente (perhaps more al dente than usual). Save 480 ml (16 fl oz/2 cups) of pasta water, then drain the pasta. Transfer the pasta to the pot with the remaining shallot mixture (or a skillet if you are using the leftover portion) and 250 ml (8 fl oz/1 cup) of pasta water. Cook over a medium-high heat, swirling the skillet to coat each piece of pasta and using a wooden spoon or spatula to scrape up any bits on the bottom, until the sauce is reduced and a little sticky, perfectly coating each strand of pasta, 3–5 minutes (you can always add a splash or two more pasta water if you need it).

5 Combine the parsley and the finely chopped garlic in a small bowl and season with flaky salt and pepper. Divide the pasta among bowls or transfer to one large serving bowl and top with the parsley mixture and a few more chilli flakes if you like.

SHALLOT PASTE

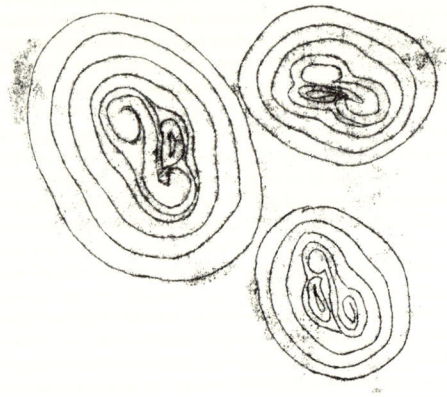

The recipe for the caramelised shallot pasta was born one Christmas Eve from accidentally ordering too many shallots and needing to make use of them for a dish eligible for my Feast of the Seven Fishes menu. But what a happy accident it was! The recipe for the paste itself is almost too simple: many shallots and a few cloves of garlic cooked in a good amount of olive oil until deeply caramelised (you must really caramelise – it's in the name), followed by the addition of a tin of anchovies and one tube of tomato purée (paste), which get melted and caramelised, respectively. I think this recipe became so popular because people either really love anchovies or they really love using the whole tin of tomato purée.

You might notice the recipe for the shallot paste makes enough for a double batch of pasta (not a mistake). It's because I never want you to be left with half a tin of tomato purée, which I find almost always gets buried in the back of the fridge, never to be seen, heard from or used again. The shallot paste, however, will be front of mind, surely. It keeps in your fridge for up to a month, but I've heard reports that it rarely lasts that long. People have been dazzling me with new ways to use it for years, including but not limited to: thinning out with water for shakshuka, smearing over chicken thighs before roasting in the oven, and spreading onto toast or an English muffin and topping with a jammy egg for breakfast.

SECRET INGREDIENT PASTA SALAD

SERVES 6–8

450 g (1 lb) dried pasta (I like a short tube shape like campanelle, radiatori or rigatoni for this)

½ small red onion, sliced (not too thin)

2 tablespoons red wine vinegar

kosher salt and freshly ground black pepper

60 ml (2 fl oz / ¼ cup) olive oil, plus more as needed

4 garlic cloves, thinly sliced

chilli flakes, harissa or hot sauce – anything spicy

450–675 g (1–1½ lb) any type of tomatoes (I like the smaller ones on the vine), quartered

80–160 g (2¾–5¾ oz / ½–1 cup) sun-dried tomatoes (!), chopped, sliced, whatever

2 tablespoons capers, drained (optional)

60–120 g (2–4 oz) coarsely chopped pecorino or Parmesan cheese (about ½ cup) (optional)

NOTE

I like using sun-dried tomatoes packed in oil (the oil is delicious and can be used to cook with), but the dry sun-dried tomatoes also work. There's no need to replump or rehydrate them before using; they'll do their thing in the skillet.

DO AHEAD

The pasta salad can be made up to 5 days ahead and refrigerated.

EAT WITH

Spicy sausages, hot dogs and mustard, celery sticks dipped in ranch, beer on ice, cold red wine.

This pasta salad kind of has a 'cold Amatriciana' feel to it, which, if you've ever eaten cold, leftover Amatriciana, you know is a very good thing. (Amatriciana is a classic Roman-as-in-Rome pasta, made with cured pork, tomato and sometimes onion and pecorino.) You can eat it immediately, but it's truly better after a few hours, either cold or at room temp, a textbook example of a great 'eat directly out of a container' food. As always, she is flexible – skip the capers if you like, make it spicy or not, go cheeseless if you dare, use shallots instead of red onion – but resist the urge to throw in everything under the sun. This salad should be composed, elegant and focused, tasting of jammy tomatoes, summertime and secrets (sun-dried tomatoes).

1. Bring a large pot of salted water to the boil. Cook the pasta until just past al dente (it's not getting cooked again, so it should be as tender as you want it in the end), drain and set aside. (The pasta should still be warm when you dress it, so don't do this too far in advance.)

2. Meanwhile, combine the onion and vinegar in a small bowl, season with salt and pepper, and set aside. (The onions are marinating rather than pickling, which feels like an important distinction to make!)

3. Heat the olive oil in a large skillet over a medium heat. Add the garlic and season with salt and pepper. Cook, swirling the skillet occasionally, until the garlic is tender and just starting to brown, 3–4 minutes. Add your spicy something of choice (a sprinkle of chilli flakes, a dab of harissa, a few dashes of hot sauce), the fresh and sun-dried tomatoes, and the capers (if using) and season with salt and pepper.

4. Cook, tossing and crushing occasionally, until the fresh tomatoes are just bursting and juicy, 5–8 minutes.

5. Combine the pasta and tomato mixture in a large bowl. Add your onions, drizzle with more olive oil, and season again with salt, pepper and more of your spicy something. Toss, toss, toss, until every piece of pasta is evenly coated. Let it sit for 10 minutes or so and toss again. Think of it as marinated pasta, knowing that the flavour will change a bit as it sits.

6. Top with lots of cheese, if you like, before eating, paired with a cold and effervescent drink.

PASTA SALAD with COURGETTE, LEMON & WALNUTS

SERVES 4

60 ml (2 fl oz/¼ cup) olive oil, plus more if you like

60 g (2 oz/½ cup) walnut pieces or almonds, coarsely chopped

kosher salt

2 bunches spring onions (scallions)

freshly ground black pepper

½ teaspoon chilli flakes, plus more to taste (optional)

450 g (1 lb) courgettes (zucchini) (about 2 medium), thinly sliced

1 × 60–85 g (2–3 oz) jar capers, drained

225 g (8 oz) dried pasta, such as rigatoni or another short tube shape

2–3 garlic cloves, finely grated

2 tablespoons fresh lemon juice or white wine vinegar, plus more to taste

60–85 g (2–3 oz) hunk of Parmesan cheese, coarsely chopped or crumbled (about ½ cup)

2 handfuls fresh herbs, such as parsley, coriander (cilantro), dill and/or mint (a mix is great)

DO AHEAD

This pasta salad truly gets better with time, and it's best when the salad has had a chance to sit at room temperature for a while before serving (low maintenance at its finest). Otherwise, it can be made 3 days ahead, wrapped and refrigerated.

Pasta salad, as a concept, is a thrill, and yet in practice, it's nearly always a bore. This one, however, truly delivers. There's brilliant tanginess from tons of capers and lemon, plus a delightful mix of textures: jammy pieces of courgette (zucchini), frizzled bits of spring onion (scallion), salty nuggets of Parmesan, crunchy walnuts and perfectly cooked pasta.

1. Heat the olive oil in a large skillet over a medium heat. Add the walnuts and fry until deeply golden brown and smelling almost like popcorn, 2–3 minutes. Using a slotted spoon, remove the nuts (leaving the oil behind) and transfer them to a small bowl. Season with salt and set aside.

2. Thinly slice about one-third of the spring onions; set aside. Coarsely chop the remaining spring onions (the whole thing) and add to the skillet with the oil. Season with salt and pepper and cook over a medium-high heat until they're lightly browned at the edges, bordering on 'melty', 8–10 minutes.

3. Add the chilli flakes (if using) and half of the courgettes, season with salt and pepper and cook down until tender and translucent, 10–15 minutes. Once there, add the remaining courgettes (you should have more space in your skillet now) and additional olive oil, if needed. Season again with salt and pepper. Add the capers and cook for another 8–10 minutes: The ideal pasta salad will have some courgette that's very soft and tender and some that's got a touch more bite.

4. Meanwhile, bring a large pot of salted water to the boil. Cook the pasta until just past al dente. (You aren't cooking it again, so it should be fully cooked but not mushy.) Drain and rinse under cold water; set aside.

5. Transfer the courgette mixture to a large bowl and add the garlic, lemon juice and reserved thinly sliced spring onions; season everything with salt and pepper. Add the pasta and gently toss to coat. (I don't even use a spoon here – just some casual bowl tossing.) Season again with more chilli flakes and lemon juice if you think it needs it.

6. Add half of the Parmesan, half of the fried walnuts and half of the herbs and toss to coat. Transfer to a serving bowl (or serve out of the bowl you just made it in) and top with the remaining Parmesan, walnuts and herbs.

BROTHY VINEGAR NOODLES with MUSHROOMS & SESAME

SERVES 4

3 tablespoons olive oil

675 g (1½ lb) mushrooms, such as oyster, chestnut (cremini), shiitake, maitake, etc., torn or cut into bite-size pieces

kosher salt and freshly ground black pepper

225 g (8 oz) Chinese broccoli, broccolini, baby pak choi (bok choi), or other leafy greens of your choosing, for serving (optional)

225–280 g (8–10 oz) dried udon or soba noodles

4 garlic cloves, thinly sliced

120 ml (4 fl oz/½ cup) soy sauce or tamari, plus more to taste

90 ml (3 fl oz/⅓ cup) white distilled vinegar, plus more to taste

1–2 tablespoons toasted sesame oil

2.5 cm (1 inch) piece of fresh ginger, finely chopped or grated

40 g (1½ oz/¼ cup) toasted sesame seeds (optional)

25 g (1 oz/½ cup) finely chopped garlic chives, spring onions (scallions) or chives

DO AHEAD

These noodles are best made and eaten in one go, although if they are al dente enough, they can be dressed and chilled a few hours ahead.

For me, one of life's greatest pleasures is a bowl of perfectly cooked, slippery udon or soba noodles in a shallow pool of something salty and vinegary, eaten alone on a brief but well-deserved lunch break. These noodles are an homage to the countless delightful solo lunches I've had at a variety of wonderful Japanese restaurants. While the restaurant versions are undoubtedly more complex and skilfully made, I find it still deeply satisfying to make a proxy, using just a handful of pantry ingredients in a relatively short amount of time.

Keep in mind that while the brothy sauce (or saucy broth?) is designed to pool generously at the bottom of your bowl, this is certainly not a soup, and there shouldn't be enough of it to drink – only to generously dress your noodles. It's intense in the best way, and hopefully there's a bit left at the end to dip your lightly blanched greens into (only a suggestion, but a good one).

1. Heat the olive oil in a large, heavy-bottomed pot over a medium-high heat. Add the mushrooms and season with salt and pepper. Cook, stirring occasionally, until they're all evenly and nicely browned, 12–18 minutes. (Mushrooms tend to really range in how long they take to cook. Be patient and keep cooking if they aren't browned at the 18-minute mark.)

2. Meanwhile, bring a medium pot of salted water to the boil. If using greens, quickly blanch them (1½–2 minutes for thick-stemmed ones like Chinese broccoli or pak choi, about 1 minute for leafy greens like kale). Remove using tongs or a slotted spoon and set aside (no need for an ice bath).

3. Add your noodles and boil until cooked through. (Each noodle will vary – follow the package instructions.) Drain and rinse under cold water.

4. Once the mushrooms are nicely browned and cooked through, add the garlic and stir to cook for a minute or two. Add the soy sauce, vinegar and 750 ml (25 fl oz/3 cups) water, bring to a simmer and remove from the heat. Add the sesame oil and ginger. Taste the sauce and adjust with more salt, soy or vinegar.

5. To serve, divide the noodles among bowls. Ladle broth into each bowl, topping with mushrooms. Scatter the sesame seeds (if using) and chives over. Serve with your greens alongside for dipping.

CHICKEN NOODLE SALAD with SPICY LIME DRESSING

SERVES 4

FOR THE DRESSING

2 tablespoons lime zest (from 2–3 limes)
120 ml (4 fl oz/½ cup) fresh lime juice (from about 4 limes), plus more to taste
2 teaspoons fish sauce, plus more to taste
1 teaspoon honey or light brown sugar (optional)
2–4 garlic cloves, finely grated or finely chopped
1 jalapeño, finely grated or finely chopped
3 tablespoons olive oil or neutral oil
kosher salt and freshly ground black pepper

FOR THE SALAD

225–280 g (8–10 oz) rice noodles or soba noodles
280 g (10 oz/2 cups) cooked chicken meat, from leftover roasted, rotisserie or poached chicken
crunchy lettuce leaves, such as romaine, butterhead or Little Gem (can also use shredded cabbage)
4 spring onions (scallions), cut into 7.5 cm (3 inch) pieces
2 small to medium cucumbers, thinly sliced
sprigs of coriander (cilantro), mint and/or basil, for serving

DO AHEAD

The dressing can be made a few days ahead and refrigerated.

I love a cold noodle salad so much that, more often than not, I barely wait for the noodles to become actually cold, happily settling for a room-temperature noodle salad. The name doesn't have the same appeal (although in Vietnam, the noodles are often served at a more ambient temperature, and I'll take their lead, since no place does it better).

This dressing is acidic, a little spicy – much punchier than your average 'salad dressing' – and has the necessary amount of fish sauce and garlic to properly influence a bowl of neutral noodles. The rest of the salad can kind of have whatever you want, but I'd say it should be full of herbs and a lot of crunchy green things like cucumber and tiny lettuces. I like to include chicken (especially cold, poached chicken, but leftover roast/rotisserie/grilled is great, too) to make it feel like an actual meal, although I sometimes skip it and double down on the noodles. Speaking of, rice noodles (I love the mid-size flat variety) are ideal for this sort of thing (I keep them in my pantry for this exact purpose), but I also love a cold buckwheat soba. Spaghetti works in a pinch but always sort of feels like leftovers.

1 Make the dressing: Combine the lime zest and juice, fish sauce, honey (if using), garlic and jalapeño in a small bowl. Whisk in the oil and season with salt, pepper and more lime juice and fish sauce as needed.

2 Make the salad: Cook the noodles according to the package instructions; drain and rinse with cool water.

3 Place the noodles and chicken in a large bowl, spooning half of the dressing over and tossing to coat; taste a noodle and add more dressing if you want, serving any remainder alongside for spooning as needed. (Rice noodles especially will really soak up the dressing as they sit, so it's best to dress them as soon as you're ready to eat.)

4 Place a few pieces of lettuce in each bowl and divide the dressed noodles and chicken among them. Scatter with the spring onions, cucumbers and herbs and spoon a bit of dressing over the naked toppings before serving.

SHRIMP SCAMPI

SERVES 4

900 g (2 lb) large prawns (shrimp), peeled and deveined

kosher salt and freshly ground black pepper

350 g (12 oz) dried pasta, like shells, rigatoni, linguine, etc.

8 tablespoons unsalted butter

2 tablespoons olive oil, plus more as needed

1 medium red onion, finely chopped

8–10 garlic cloves, thinly sliced

½ thinly sliced fresh chilli, such as jalapeño, or ½ teaspoon chilli flakes (optional)

250 ml (8 fl oz/1 cup) dry white wine

1 teaspoon fish sauce, plus more as needed (optional)

2 handfuls parsley, tender leaves and stems, finely chopped

25 g (1 oz/½ cup) finely chopped chives

2 lemons, halved for squeezing over

NOTE
—
Most 'fresh' prawns have been previously frozen, so never feel shame about opting for frozen. I prefer large or jumbo prawns (wild, if available). Head-on prawns would be an incredible choice, if you don't mind the tearing of shells and heads among the pasta (I don't). The opposite is also lovely: small, sweet, tender, tailless bay prawns.

EAT WITH
—
Shrimp scampi feels like something you want to eat with a cold martini (extra olives) and a Caesar salad (page 150). The prawns are also great *sans* pasta, over wilted greens or on top of olive oil–fried toast.

Shrimp scampi: fun to say, more fun to eat. It's a true classic, bright red prawns (shrimp) cooked in an ever-so-brothy wine-laced sauce full of garlic and butter. There's hardly anything new here, but you might find this recipe above-average delicious thanks to the above-average amounts of things like wine, butter and garlic. Plus, a little touch of fish sauce takes it to just this side of salty, herbs add perkiness and lemon is mandatory for squeezing over. While I've eaten versions of this pasta at any restaurant that'll serve it to me, I can honestly say this is still the best I've ever had.

1. Season the prawns with salt and pepper; set aside. (Do not skip this step.)

2. Bring a large pot of salted water to a boil. Cook the pasta until al dente. Drain and toss with a healthy drizzle of olive oil so it doesn't stick together; set aside. (Usually, I'd have you do this after your pasta ingredients are cooked, but everything happens very quickly and you want the pasta to be ready.)

3. Heat the butter and olive oil in a large skillet over a medium-high heat until the butter is melted and foamy, about 2 minutes. Add the onion and garlic and season with salt and pepper. Cook, stirring occasionally, until the onion has softened and is starting to brown on the edges and the garlic is completely softened, 4–6 minutes. If you want a spicy scampi, add the sliced chilli or chilli flakes.

4. Add the prawns and toss in the hot fat until bright pink on the outside and starting to curl up (cute!), about a minute or so. Add the wine and fish sauce (if using), season again with salt and pepper and let the liquid simmer around the prawns, gently steaming and cooking them all the way through, reducing into something that could only be described as a very good sauce.

5. Toss the prawns and all the fantastic sauce with the parsley, chives and cooked pasta. (Do this in a bowl, do this in the skillet – wherever you have space.) Toss, toss, toss! The whole thing should be saucy and glossy: two words that always belong together.

6. Squeeze lemon over everything before serving and scatter with more herbs if you like.

LINGUINE & CLAMS with SPICY BREADCRUMBS

SERVES 4–6

2 × 225 g (8 oz) tins whole clams, plus their juices, clams coarsely chopped or left whole (or 1.8–2.25 kg/4–5 lb small fresh clams, such as littlenecks or cockles)

kosher salt

90 ml (3 fl oz/⅓ cup) olive oil, plus more for drizzling

45 g (1½ oz/¾ cup) panko breadcrumbs

freshly ground black pepper

chilli flakes

12 garlic cloves (10 thinly sliced, 2 grated)

2 lemons, peels removed with a peeler then finely chopped, then halved for juicing

480 ml (16 fl oz/2 cups) dry white wine, such as verdejo or pinot grigio

450 g (1 lb) dried linguine, fettuccine, or spaghetti

1 handful finely chopped parsley and/or chives (I like to mix)

EAT WITH
—
The rest of that white wine.

If linguine and clams have one fan, it's me. I'll order it anytime it's on the menu (any menu), even if I know that the version about to land in front of me might be a little bland, lacking salt, sauciness or the number of clams I'd prefer. This version doesn't suffer from any of that: It has so much flavour, by way of chopped fresh lemon peel, toasted slivers of garlic, and no shortage of clams in every salty, saucy twirlful of pasta.

A great linguine and clams is only as good as the brothy, garlicky wine sauce you build. It should be delicious enough to drink on its own before adding even one single clam or your extremely al dente pasta. Fresh clams are of course magnificent (and you should use them if you can), but tinned clams are also wonderful (and underused!) – should you find yourself in a place without fresh seafood, they're a true luxury.

Whether you stick to this recipe or go off on your own journey (add a chopped fennel bulb, maybe brown some sausage with the garlic), just remember that fresh clams must be rinsed to the best of your ability (can't pick sand out of pasta). Oh, and you may notice there's no pasta water reserved: Congratulations, you don't need it! There should be more than enough clam juice in the pot to do the job.

1. If you're using fresh clams: With the water gently running, use a clean kitchen sponge or scrubber to scrub the clams, focusing on the hinge (not the opening) and ridges of the shell, where most of the grit and sand live. If the clams are very fresh or look especially dirty, you can place them in a large bowl of cold water and let them soak for an hour or two so they can filter out the sand and sediment (not always necessary, but I like to if I can think to plan ahead).

2. Bring a large pot of salted water to the boil.

3. Meanwhile, heat half of the olive oil in another large pot (or skillet) over a medium-high heat. Add the breadcrumbs and season with salt and pepper. Stir to coat evenly in the oil and cook, tossing occasionally, until they're well toasted and evenly browned, 3–5 minutes. Add as many chilli flakes as you'd like (I'd start with a generous pinch) and remove from the heat. Transfer the breadcrumbs to a small bowl and set aside.

4   Wipe out any crumbs from the pot or skillet, then heat the remaining olive oil over a medium-high heat. Add the sliced garlic and cook, stirring occasionally, until lightly browned, 2–3 minutes. Add the chopped lemon peel and let it fry in the garlic oil for about 30 seconds. Add the white wine and clams, season with a little salt, and bring to a simmer. If using tinned clams, cook, uncovered, shaking the pot occasionally until the clams are warmed through and the sauce has reduced by about half, 5–8 minutes. If using fresh clams, cook, uncovered, only shaking the pot occasionally, letting the clams steam open inside, 5–8 minutes (this may take longer with larger or thicker-shelled clams).

5   If using fresh clams, use a slotted spoon to transfer the clams to a large bowl, leaving any liquid behind (any clams that came out of the shells can stay behind, too).

6   Meanwhile, boil the pasta until just before al dente. (This is important! The pasta should be not quite cooked through because you'll continue to cook it in the clam broth you've just made.)

7   Drain the pasta (or simply lift the pasta from the pot using tongs). Add the pasta to the clam liquid and bring to a simmer. Cook for 4–6 minutes, tossing occasionally with your tongs to make sure all the pasta is getting even attention from the liquid and to encourage the sauce to thicken.

8   Taste a pasta strand and make sure it's well seasoned and cooked through, adding more salt and pepper as needed. Add the grated garlic to the pot and stir to combine. If using fresh clams, add them back to the pot along with half of the herbs and toss to coat. Transfer to a serving bowl and top with the remaining herbs, a drizzle of olive oil and the juice from the halved lemons. Serve with spicy breadcrumbs sprinkled over.

SNAIL BUTTER PASTA
(SNAILS OPTIONAL)

SERVES 4

---

kosher salt

350–450 g (12 oz–1 lb) dried pasta, preferably a long, thin noodle like spaghetti or linguine

4 tablespoons olive oil

120 g (4 oz) unsalted butter

1 large shallot, finely chopped

6 garlic cloves, finely chopped

freshly ground black pepper

250 ml (8 fl oz/1 cup) dry white wine

2 × 90–135 g (3–5 oz) tins snails, coarsely chopped or left whole

1 bunch parsley, tender leaves and stems, very finely chopped (yes, it's a lot of parsley)

2 tablespoons finely chopped tarragon leaves (optional)

NOTE
—
Not to give you an out, but this recipe would also be wonderful with tinned clams, mussels or even sardines.

EAT WITH
—
This Parisian-inspired meal wants a carafe of wine (or use a mason jar), a nice tablecloth and many, many candles.

My husband is what you'd call a picky eater. But he inexplicably loves . . . snails. The word 'escargot' on a menu is met with glee by a man who 'doesn't love' olives. I share this only to encourage anyone who thinks of themselves as open-minded and yet still can't get past 'snail': If Max can do it, you can do it. If I had to describe the flavour and texture of snails, I would put them somewhere between a chestnut (cremini) mushroom and a clam. Earthy yet water-adjacent? Meaty yet chewy? They're honestly wonderful, and I think in a few years, they'll really have a moment. (But wouldn't it feel nice to be ahead of the curve?)

Anyway, this pasta is modelled after the iconic *escargots à la Bourguignonne* and has all the same ingredients – butter, garlic, parsley – which makes it very approachable and easy to love. But also, snails! I get it! Try them out – you might surprise yourself by discovering your new favourite pantry protein is a tin of snails.

1. Bring a large pot of salted water to the boil. Cook the pasta until al dente; save 480 ml (16 fl oz/2 cups) of pasta water, then drain the pasta.

2. Meanwhile, heat the olive oil and butter in a large skillet over a medium-high heat. Add the shallot and garlic and season with salt and pepper. Cook, stirring occasionally, until the shallots are tender and translucent, 5–7 minutes.

3. Add the wine and cook until it's reduced by a little more than half (should be saucy but not taste 'winey'). Add the snails, season with salt and pepper, and toss to coat in the sauce.

4. Add the cooked pasta and 250 ml (8 fl oz/1 cup) of pasta water. Cook over a medium heat, tossing frequently (preferably using tongs), until the pasta is past al dente and perfectly cooked through and the sauce is nicely thickened and glossy. Add most of the parsley and tarragon, seasoning again with salt and pepper.

5. Divide the pasta among bowls and top with the remaining herbs.

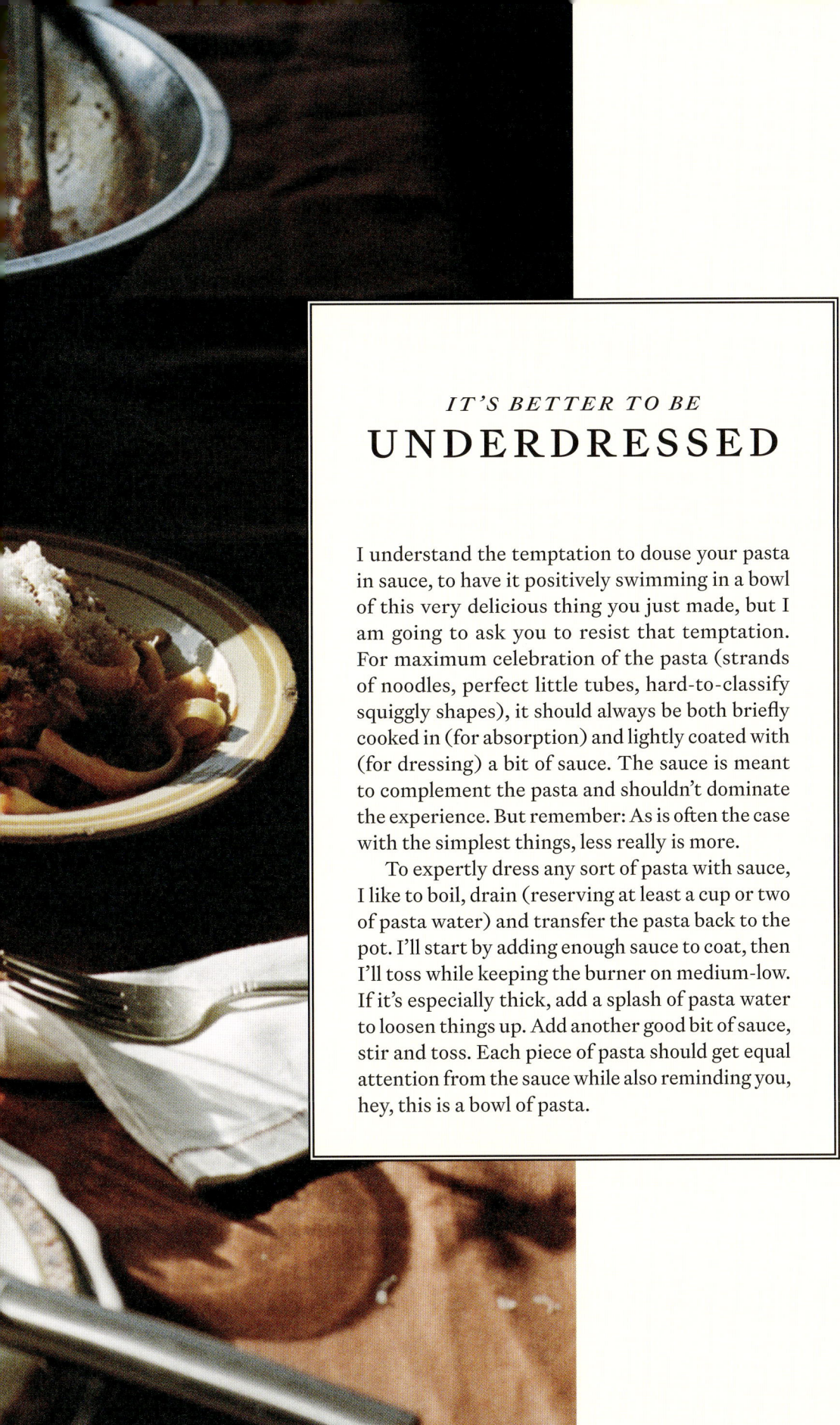

IT'S BETTER TO BE UNDERDRESSED

I understand the temptation to douse your pasta in sauce, to have it positively swimming in a bowl of this very delicious thing you just made, but I am going to ask you to resist that temptation. For maximum celebration of the pasta (strands of noodles, perfect little tubes, hard-to-classify squiggly shapes), it should always be both briefly cooked in (for absorption) and lightly coated with (for dressing) a bit of sauce. The sauce is meant to complement the pasta and shouldn't dominate the experience. But remember: As is often the case with the simplest things, less really is more.

To expertly dress any sort of pasta with sauce, I like to boil, drain (reserving at least a cup or two of pasta water) and transfer the pasta back to the pot. I'll start by adding enough sauce to coat, then I'll toss while keeping the burner on medium-low. If it's especially thick, add a splash of pasta water to loosen things up. Add another good bit of sauce, stir and toss. Each piece of pasta should get equal attention from the sauce while also reminding you, hey, this is a bowl of pasta.

A VERY GOOD TOMATO SAUCE

SERVES 6–8

90 ml (3 fl oz/⅓ cup) olive oil

2 large onions (about 450 g/1 lb), finely chopped

8–10 garlic cloves, thinly sliced

kosher salt and freshly ground black pepper

2 × 400 g (14 oz) tins whole peeled tomatoes

2 × 400 g (14 oz) tins crushed tomatoes

½–1 teaspoon chilli flakes, plus more to taste (optional)

DO AHEAD
—
The tomato sauce can be made 5 days ahead and refrigerated, or months ahead and frozen.

This is my gold standard, simple, basic, very good tomato sauce. It's the recipe I use in a baked pasta (page 239) or lasagne, to start meatballs or as the backbone of a classic ragù. My all-time favourite usage, though, is this: tossed with just al dente pasta and showered with hard, salty cheese. It's a level up from 'noodles with butter' but feels as at home on the kids' menu as it does at an elegant Italian-inspired dinner party. Do not confuse uncomplicated with boring: A very good tomato sauce can be transcendent. Aside from using both whole and crushed tomatoes for the perfect combination of chunky texture and smooth body, the key is to really and properly sweat the onions and garlic to tame their sharpness and bring out their sweetness. Plus, make sure you're using the full amount of olive oil (nothing scandalous, but tomatoes really need fat in order to cut their acidity and truly shine) and plenty of salt. Seasoning as you go is always important, but I find myself tending to a pot of simmering tomato sauce, affectionately adding pinches of salt, more often than with anything else I've got on the stove.

1 Heat the olive oil in a large, heavy-bottomed pot over a medium-high heat. Add the onions and garlic and season with salt and pepper. Cook, stirring occasionally, until the onions are softened and translucent (without letting them brown, turning down the heat if needed), 8–10 minutes.

2 Crush the whole tomatoes by hand and add them (including the juice) and the crushed tomatoes to the pot, stirring to scrape up any bits from the bottom of the pot. Fill one of the empty tins about halfway with water, swirling to get any excess tomato hanging around, and add it to the sauce. Season with salt and pepper and add the chilli flakes (if using). Bring to a simmer, then reduce the heat to medium-low (or low, depending on your stove).

3 Cook, uncovered, stirring occasionally and letting it bubble gently, until the tomato sauce has thickened and the flavours have come together, at least 30 minutes and up to 90 minutes. (The longer the better, although you might want to reduce the heat if planning on going the full 90 minutes.)

4 Once the sauce is tasting how you'd like and is thickened nicely, season it again with salt, pepper and more chilli flakes if needed. Simmer it for a minute or two, then remove it from the heat.

BAKED (BUT NOT STUFFED) SHELLS

SERVES 6-8

225 g (8 oz/1 cup) whole-milk ricotta
3 tablespoons double (heavy) cream
2 garlic cloves, finely grated
kosher salt and freshly ground black pepper
450 g (1 lb) large pasta shells, rigatoni, ziti or any tube-shaped pasta
1.4 litres (48 fl oz/6 cups) A Very Good Tomato Sauce (page 237)
1 × 225 g (8 oz) ball fresh mozzarella, roughly torn by hand or grated on a box grater
45 g (1½ oz/¾ cup) finely grated Parmesan cheese, plus more as needed

DO AHEAD
—
This dish can be assembled and baked several days ahead, kept wrapped and refrigerated. To reheat from cold, simply bake again per the instructions at right. It can also be assembled and frozen up to 2 months ahead. To reheat from frozen, keep wrapped in foil and bake at 160°C/150°C fan/325°F until totally thawed and bubbly (60-ish minutes), remove the foil, increase the temperature to 220°C/200°C fan/425°F, and bake until golden brown, 20 minutes or so.

EAT WITH
—
A giant, gorgeous salad. This baked pasta needs nothing more, really.

While I do think it's nice and cheeky to make a version of baked shells that you don't have to individually stuff, other shapes, like (one lucky) rigatoni or classic ziti, would work well here, too. (Personally, I can't stand penne. It's a prejudice I will never overcome.) For the sauce, it's my gold standard, basic and perfect tomato sauce, which you'll find on page 237. The cheese is dollops of ricotta plus double (heavy) cream for luxuriousness (cream prevents that weird grainy baked ricotta texture), torn pieces of mozzarella for stretchy pulls and a good grating of Parmesan for an edge of saltiness. Baked shells are a classic for a reason, and I wouldn't tinker too much with it (no, I don't think it's the time to add sausage or anchovies). After you pull this perfect dish from the oven, all bubbling and saucy, red and white with crispy browned edges, I think you'll be glad you didn't.

1 Preheat the oven to 220°C/200°C fan/425°F. Combine the ricotta, cream and garlic in a medium bowl. Season with salt and pepper and set aside.

2 Bring a large pot of salted water to the boil. Cook the pasta until it's nearly al dente, then drain. Return the pasta to the pot and add 480 ml (16 fl oz/2 cups) of the tomato sauce, tossing to make sure the sauce gets in all the nooks and crannies and nicely coats the pasta.

3 Time to assemble! What joy. Try not to fuss too much over the measurements when layering – just be mindful that you want to end up with a good amount of cheese and sauce on the top to give you a bubbly, browned top. Spoon a bit of the remaining sauce in the bottom of a 2.85-litre (3-quart) baking dish, then add one-third of the pasta. Spoon a little sauce on top, then dollop with ricotta, dot with mozzarella and sprinkle with about a third of the Parmesan. Add another third of the pasta, followed by more sauce, more ricotta, mozzarella and Parmesan. Add the rest of the pasta, more sauce, then the rest of the ricotta, mozzarella and Parmesan, finishing with a few grinds of pepper.

4 Place the baking dish on a foil-lined baking tray and loosely cover the baking dish with foil. Bake for about 20 minutes, then remove the foil and continue to bake until it's nicely browned and bubbling, another 20-ish minutes. Let cool at least 5 minutes or so before eating – it will stay VERY hot for a while, so don't worry about it cooling down too much.

A LITTLE AUBERGINE PARM

SERVES 2

1 large globe aubergine (eggplant) (about 450 g/1 lb), sliced 1–2 cm (½–¾ inch) thick
120 ml (4 fl oz/½ cup) olive oil
kosher salt and freshly ground black pepper
1 small onion, thinly sliced
4 garlic cloves, thinly sliced
chilli flakes (optional)
4 anchovy fillets, plus more if you want (optional)
2 × 400 g (14 oz) tins whole peeled tomatoes
45 g (1½ oz/¾ cup) panko breadcrumbs
20 g (¾ oz/⅓ cup) grated Parmesan cheese
10 g (½ oz/⅓ cup) coarsely chopped parsley
2–3 tablespoons capers, drained, coarsely chopped
2 tablespoons chopped fresh oregano or marjoram (you can skip, or use half the amount of dried)
225 g (8 oz) fresh mozzarella, thinly sliced or torn

As much as I love the idea of a 'Parmesan' dish – cutlets or aubergine (eggplant) slices, breaded and fried, smothered in tomato sauce and topped with a nicely browned slab of mozzarella – I tend to find aubergine Parmesan too saucy, too messy, too heavy. Plus, almost nothing annoys me more than the idea of going through the effort of making something crispy, just to make it soggy.

And yet! The undeniable appeal of tender, custardy slices of aubergine coupled with a tangy little tomato sauce and some milky, stretchy cheese calls to even the hardest of hearts (mine). So, I made a version even I could love: aubergine roasted until deeply browned and caramelised, tender in all the right places, slightly crisped in others, layered judiciously with a light tomato sauce, maybe some fresh herbs, a lot of Parmesan (suspiciously absent from 'Parmesan' dishes?) and just enough mozzarella to excite you.

No, the aubergine does not need to be salted; no, we will not be frying the aubergine. Yes, it is still aubergine Parmesan but lighter, fresher, tangier, crunchier. If you don't care for capers or anchovies, you can skip them – just know that you are, in fact, missing out.

Unless you are doubling this recipe (which you can easily do – just bake it in a larger 1.9-litre/2-quart vessel), you are only using half of the tomato sauce here. Save the rest by freezing it, or just pop it in the fridge to eat over pasta later in the week.

1 Preheat the oven to 230°C/220°C fan/450°F.

2 Place the aubergine on a rimmed baking tray and drizzle with about half of the olive oil; season with salt and pepper. Roast, turning the aubergine halfway through (I use tongs or a fork), until it's as tender as custard and both sides are as browned as if they were fried, 25–30 minutes. A lot of the flavour in this dish will come from the aubergine being very, very browned, so please don't be scared to 'take it there', so to speak. Please take it there. Take it very there.

3 Meanwhile, make the sauce. Heat 2 tablespoons of the olive oil in a medium pot over a medium-high heat. Add the onion and garlic and season with salt and pepper. Cook, stirring every now and then, until the onions and garlic are tender and starting to brown, 8–10 minutes.

DO AHEAD

—

Every component can be made 2 or 3 days in advance. Keep everything except the breadcrumbs (store those at room temperature) wrapped and refrigerated until you're ready to assemble and bake. This is ideal eaten right out of the oven, but it's also really great as leftovers (cold, room temperature, or reheated at 200°C/190°C fan/400°F until bubbling again).

EAT WITH

—

The only thing this needs is an acidic salad with lots of shallot or garlic in the dressing. I would go for iceberg and pickled shallots, maybe some olives. But something mustardy with some raw grated garlic would also be fun.

4   If using, add the chilli flakes and anchovies and stir, letting both melt into the onions. Pour the juices from the tomatoes into the pot and, one by one, crush the tomatoes with your hands into the pot. (I like to keep the tomatoes on the chunkier side for more texture in the finished dish.) Season again with salt and pepper and let it simmer gently until some but not all of the liquid is evaporated, 15–30 minutes. Once it tastes very good and feels nicely thickened, remove it from the heat. Set half aside and freeze or refrigerate the rest.

5   The last annoying thing to do here is to toast the breadcrumbs (less annoying than frying, though, right?). Heat the remaining 2 tablespoons olive oil in a medium skillet over a medium heat. Add the breadcrumbs and season with salt and pepper. Stir to coat evenly in the oil and cook, tossing occasionally, until all the breadcrumbs are the colour of your morning toast, 5–7 minutes. Remove from the heat.

6   Okay, it's time to assemble this thing! How thrilling. There's not a ton of technique here, but here's how I do it to most closely mimic the classico aubergine Parm. Spoon about half of the tomato sauce on the bottom of a 950 ml (1-quart) baking dish or 15-cm (6-inch) cast-iron skillet. (Cake pans, terracotta baking dishes, glass Pyrexes . . . you can use pretty much anything that holds about 950 ml (32 fl oz/4 cups) of volume. The shape doesn't matter, as long as it's heatproof.)

7   Top with half of the aubergine (a little overlap is fine, so are gaps – don't fuss!), followed by half of the Parmesan, half of the parsley, half of the capers and half of the oregano (and, if you love anchovies, layer in a few fillets here as well). Scatter half of the breadcrumbs in a nice even layer on top of all that, followed by half of the mozzarella. Repeat all the layers, ending with the mozzarella. Add a little more Parmesan if you feel like it and maybe some pepper.

8   Now, bake it. Pop it into the same 230°C/220°C fan/450°F oven and bake until the cheese is browned and everything is bubbling around the edges, 15–20 minutes. Remove from the oven, finishing with some more parsley if you've got it stuck to your cutting board, and let it cool ever so slightly before eating. I like to just serve it by scooping with a spoon – it's not really meant to be sliced.

WEEKNIGHT LAMB RAGÙ with ANCHOVY

SERVES 4–6

2 tablespoons olive oil
1 medium yellow onion, finely chopped
4 garlic cloves, finely chopped
kosher salt and freshly ground black pepper
pinch of chilli flakes (optional)
2 anchovy fillets or ½ teaspoon fish sauce
2 tablespoons tomato purée (paste)
450 g (1 lb) minced (ground) lamb
2 × 400 g (14 oz) tins crushed tomatoes
350 g (12 oz) dried pasta (noodles or tubes), for serving
a good hunk of Parmesan or pecorino cheese, for serving
a small handful of marjoram, oregano, or thyme leaves, for serving (optional)

DO AHEAD

The ragù can be made 3 days ahead, stored wrapped and refrigerated, or up to 2 months ahead, wrapped and frozen.

EAT WITH

A bowl of fresh figs and melon and a large hunk of Parmesan cheese, for nibbling. Lots of wine.

This ragù is unapologetically lamb forward. If that terrifies you because of a preconceived aversion to lamb, I'll ask you to give it a try: Tomatoes (and, yes, anchovies) have a way of softening the lambiness, and this could very well be a gateway to your new life as a person who enjoys lamb. You could also use pork, beef or a mix, and it will turn out great – this recipe is really just a Trojan horse to inspire you to add anchovies or fish sauce to a quick ragù. These pantry staples deepen the flavours, suggesting complexity that's usually achieved only through time. Either ingredient is simultaneously virtually undetectable and paramount to success: Barely anyone will notice they're there, except to remark on how above-average fantastic this ragù is.

1 Heat the olive oil in a large heavy-bottomed pot over a medium heat. Add the onion and garlic and season with salt and pepper. Cook, stirring occasionally, until the onions are translucent and softened, 5–8 minutes. Add a pinch of chilli flakes (if using) and the anchovies and cook for a minute or two to toast the pepper and melt the anchovies.

2 Add the tomato purée (paste) and continue to cook, stirring occasionally, so it has a chance to stick to the bottom of the pot and caramelise a bit, 2–3 minutes.

3 Add the lamb and season with salt and pepper. Using a wooden spoon or a spatula, stir until the fat starts to soften and the meat begins to break down. Continue to cook, stirring rather frequently, until the lamb begins to brown and sizzle in its own fat, 8–10 minutes.

4 Add the crushed tomatoes, stirring to scrape up any bits on the bottom of the pot. Fill the empty tin halfway with water, swirling to get any excess tomato hanging around, and add to the sauce. Season with salt and pepper and bring to a simmer. Reduce the heat to medium-low and continue to cook until the sauce is thickened and insanely flavourful, 25–30 minutes.

5 Meanwhile, bring a large pot of salted water to the boil and cook the pasta until just before al dente, reserving 250 ml (8 fl oz/1 cup) of the pasta water. Drain and transfer the pasta back to the pot.

6 To serve, toss the sauce into the pasta along with 120 ml (4 fl oz/½ cup) of pasta water. Cook over medium heat until the pasta is perfectly cooked and nicely dressed, 2–3 minutes. Remove from the heat and divide among bowls, topping with plenty of cheese. Scatter with marjoram if you like.

BOLOGNESE with FENNEL

SERVES 8–10

2 tablespoons olive oil
450 g (1 lb) minced (ground) beef
450 g (1 lb) minced (ground) pork
kosher salt and freshly ground black pepper
6 garlic cloves, thinly sliced
2 medium yellow onions, finely chopped
1 fennel bulb, finely chopped
2 tablespoons fennel seeds
pinch of chilli flakes, plus more as needed (optional)
250 ml (8 fl oz/1 cup) dry white wine
2 × 400 g (14 oz) tins crushed tomatoes (or whole peeled tomatoes, crushed by hand)
750 ml (25 fl oz/3 cups) chicken, vegetable or beef stock, or water (or water plus Better Than Bouillon, see page 58), plus more if needed
480 ml (16 fl oz/2 cups) whole milk
2 tablespoons unsalted butter (optional)
450 g (1 lb) dried pasta (long, flat noodles or short, fat tubes)
cheese (hard and salty, such as Parmesan or pecorino), for serving

NOTE

The wine you use should be acidic and not too fancy but still something you'd love to drink. To make this without alcohol, use water and a good splash of white wine vinegar.

This is my bolognese, emphasis on the 'my'. Will it be for the purists? Not likely. At its core, it still plays by the rules: fatty meat, tomato, wine, milk and a long, slow, gentle simmer. There are no carrots or celery here, but there is a fennel bulb (sweet like carrots, vegetal like celery), and to double down on the blasphemy, a bit of fennel seed. This version might be a touch more tomatoey than a classic bolognese, but that's how I prefer it, almost splitting the difference between ragù and bolognese. I'm not wedded to the classic mythology of chopping the meat by hand, so feel free to mix your own blend of ground pork, beef, veal or – because someone is going to ask – sure, turkey (but it's virtually fat-free, so don't expect that rich, creamy emulsification, no matter how long you simmer).

This bolognese will make more than you need to adequately sauce 450 g (1 lb) of pasta, and that's great. It's a sauce that requires a bit of time and effort, so you may as well make the most of it.

1. Heat the olive oil in a large casserole (Dutch oven) or heavy-bottomed pot over a medium-high heat. Add the beef and pork and season with salt and pepper. Using a wooden spoon or spatula, break up the meat as it browns. (The goal is for the meat to effectively melt into the sauce, so you want it in smaller pieces from the get-go.)

2. Continue cooking the meat until it's about 80 per cent browned to your liking (this should take 10–15 minutes, at least), then add the garlic, onions and fennel. Season again with salt and pepper and continue cooking until the meat is browned 100 per cent to your liking and the onions and fennel are softened nicely but without much colour themselves, another 10–15 minutes.

3. Add the fennel seed and chilli flakes (if using), stirring to bloom the spices in the fat. (If you're leaving out the chilli flakes: Are you some sort of purist? Honestly, I respect that.)

4. Add the wine and let it cook down until it's barely there, 3–5 minutes, then add the tomatoes, stock and milk. (The milk may separate a bit or look grainy at this point – don't worry; the sauce will meld as it simmers.) Bring to a strong simmer, then reduce the heat to medium-low (or low if you have an especially powerful range). Let this sauce gently simmer and lightly bubble for at least 2 hours, uncovered, stirring occasionally,

DO AHEAD
—
If you find yourself with more sauce than you can eat tonight, well, don't worry: This sauce freezes beautifully – I would know, I almost always have a container of it in my freezer, which, when run under warm water to loosen from the container and reheated in a saucepot over medium heat, passes for freshly made bolognese at a moment's notice. Future self thanks you!

tasting as you go because it already smells so good and you can't believe you have to wait that long.

5 You do not want this sauce to boil or you'll risk messing up its eventual emulsification (meaning, it'll stay soupy and grainy rather than silky and creamy). If it seems very thick after 1 hour, add more stock and consider reducing your heat – it's likely too high. Alternatively, you can pop your (oven-safe) pot into a 150°C/140°C fan/300°F oven for the same amount of time, but then it becomes more difficult to taste as you go, my favourite part.

6 Around the 2-hour mark, the sauce should be thickened considerably, the meat melting into the tomatoes, everything tasting slightly sweet, a little tangy, and deeply meaty. If it still looks soupy or like the meat is not fully incorporated into the sauce, it needs more time. And if it needs more time, it needs more time! Keep simmering. Once the sauce is to your liking, stir in the butter (if using), letting it melt as the perfect finishing touch.

7 When your sauce is almost ready, bring a large pot of salted water to the boil. Cook your pasta until pleasantly chewy and al dente. Save 480 ml (16 fl oz/2 cups) of pasta water, then drain the pasta. Transfer the pasta to a large bowl or pot. From there, take out the cheese and your grater or Microplane. Pour some wine. Make a little salad if you want. Get ready for the whole experience: It's almost time for bolognese.

8 When it's time to add the sauce, I know you're going to do what you want, but let me say this: Pasta should be lightly dressed with bolognese, not doused. This sauce is rich and fatty and needs to be treated almost like a condiment. Remember: You can always add more, but you can't take it away. Start by adding the sauce to the pasta (never the other way around) a cupful at a time. Individual preferences will vary, but for 450 g (1 lb) of pasta, I find about 950 ml (32 fl oz/4 cups) of sauce does the trick.

9 Place the pasta on the table, perfectly dressed and gingerly tossed. Serve next to a hunk of cheese for grating and a dish of chilli flakes for sprinkling. Sadly, and you'll almost never hear me say this, this isn't the time or place for parsley or any other herbs.

PASTAS & NOODLES

MEATS *and* FISHES

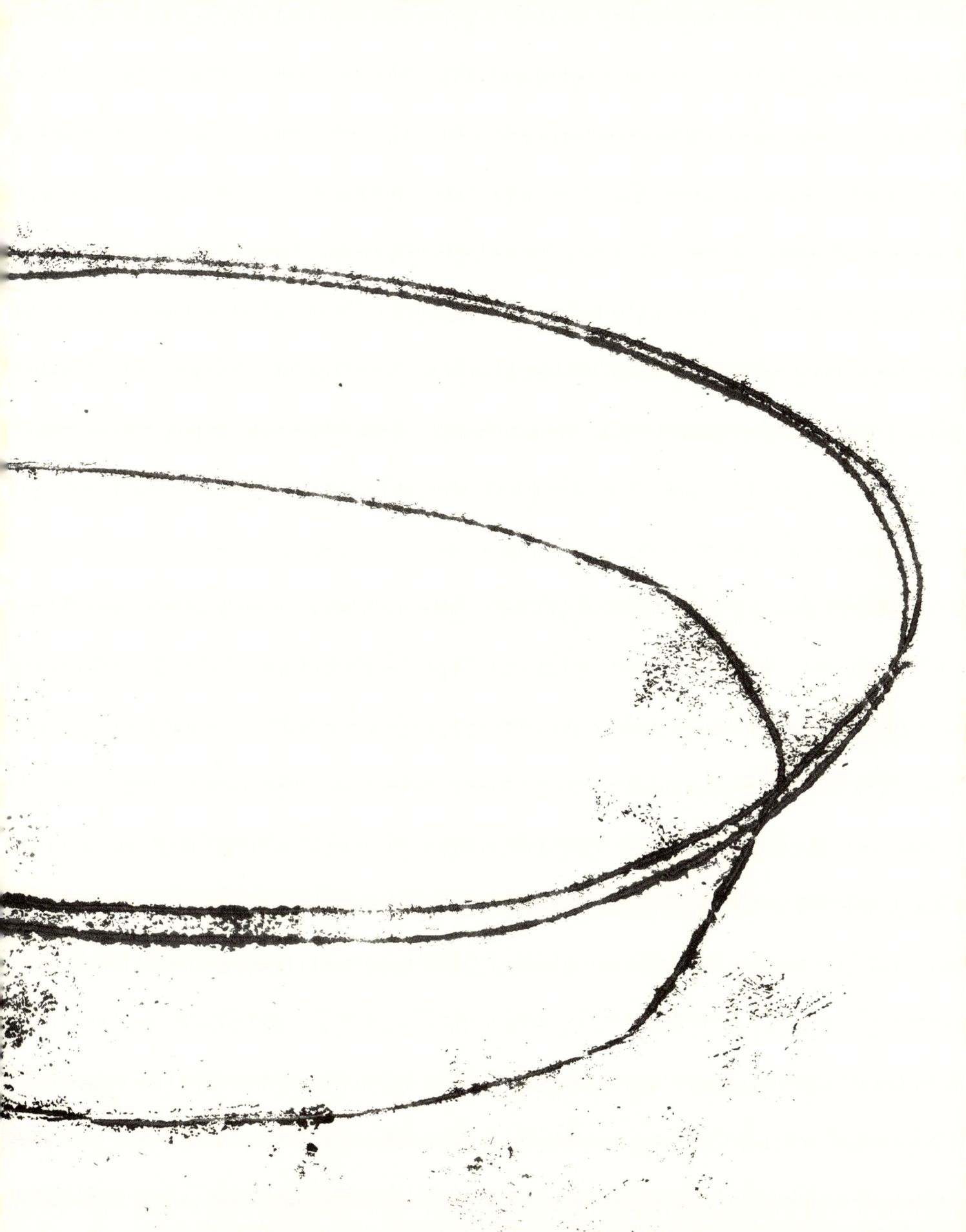

To cook and eat meat and fish is a luxury, and like with most luxurious things, I believe less is more. I need nothing but a salt-and-pepper seasoning on a roast chicken, a medium-rare steak served with only a perfect baguette, a nice piece of salmon slow-cooked in olive oil and just a squeeze of lemon. In this chapter you'll find those things, and then some (otherwise, it would be a very short chapter), but the spirit remains: simple preparations augmented with a few of your favourite pantry items, like olives, preserved lemon and breadcrumbs.

It's also my hope that you might start to think of the freezer as an extension of your pantry – an arsenal of things that are waiting to be (carefully) thawed and prepared as if you had gotten to the butcher that day (you didn't). I personally find unusual delight in digging something out of the too-small frozen drawers – pork chops nestled together, a bag of wild prawns (shrimp), a pound of chicken legs – and combining whatever I find with, say, a handful of tomatoes and a box of orzo, and ending up with a truly spectacular dinner.

OLIVE OIL-ROASTED CHICKEN & CHICKPEAS

SERVES 4

900 g–1.15 kg (2–2½ lb) whole chicken legs, or bone-in, skin-on drumsticks or thighs
kosher salt and freshly ground black pepper
2 garlic heads, unpeeled, halved widthways
1 × 400 g (14 oz) tin chickpeas (garbanzos), drained and rinsed
1 lemon, thinly sliced, seeds removed
½ bunch oregano, plus more leaves for garnish
1 bunch small, thin carrots, halved lengthways (quartered if large)
250 ml (8 fl oz/1 cup) olive oil

NOTE
—
In place of the carrots, you can use 1 medium fennel bulb, thinly sliced, or ½ winter squash, peeled and thinly sliced, or 1 bunch baby turnips, greens removed and halved.

DO AHEAD
—
Actually one of the best make-ahead dinners (for company or just yourself). The chicken and chickpeas can be cooked 3 days ahead, stored in the baking dish and fat they're roasted in, covered, and refrigerated. Reheat the whole dish a 160°C/150°C fan/325°F oven until warmed through, 20–25 minutes.

EAT WITH
—
Greens dressed in mustard vinaigrette, Salty Celery Salad with Anchovy (page 134).

This is an infinitely adaptable base recipe for one of my favourite combinations (and not just because it's fun to say): chicken and chickpeas (garbanzos). Specifically, chicken and chickpeas covered in olive oil, slow-roasted together until tender and browned and crisped in all the right places. Not quite a true confit, but the spirit is there; the chicken nearly falls off the bone while the chickpeas turn into rich little orbs, creamy on the inside, lightly frizzled on the outside.

While the basic chicken and chickpea combination is impossibly delicious on its own, any number of fabulous items can be added to roast and sizzle alongside them: vegetables (carrots or fennel are nice); spices (chilli flakes, fennel seeds, cumin); a dab of something like tomato purée (paste), harissa or gochujang; or various herbs. No matter what, there's always lemon (never forget the lemon!). The chewy, caramelised little slices add so much bright acidity, sweetness and texture, which you'll definitely want after eating something bathed in all that olive oil and chicken fat.

1. Preheat the oven to 160°C/150°C fan/325°F.

2. Season the chicken with salt and pepper. Arrange the chicken in a large shallow baking dish or shallow braising pot (2.35–2.85 litres/2½–3 quarts) so that the legs are snug and lying flat. Scatter the garlic head halves, chickpeas, lemon slices and oregano sprigs among the chicken, nestling everything in there.

3. Add your vegetables (carrots, fennel, squash, turnips, etc.), letting them poke out a bit – they'll get the most colour by not being submerged. Pour the olive oil over the chicken, chickpeas and vegetables. Season again with salt and pepper.

4. Roast, uncovered, until the chicken is so tender it nearly falls off the bone and the vegetables and lemons are nicely caramelised, 90–110 minutes.

5. Remove from the oven and let cool slightly. Divide the chicken, chickpeas, vegetables and lemons among plates (or serve straight from the dish it was cooked in). Scatter with more oregano before eating. Reserve the leftover, schmaltzy olive oil in the baking dish for another purpose. (It can be strained, stored in an airtight container and refrigerated for up to 1 month. Use it to fry eggs, roast vegetables or make breadcrumbs.)

SPICY VINEGAR CHICKEN OVER TOMATOES

SERVES 4

---

1 × 1.8–2 kg (4–4½ lb) chicken, cut into pieces (or 1.6–1.8 kg/3½–4 lb bone-in, skin-on chicken parts, such as legs and thighs, all thighs, etc.)

kosher salt and freshly ground black pepper

2 tablespoons olive oil, plus more as needed

4 garlic cloves, crushed

¾ teaspoon chilli flakes or 1 tablespoon Calabrian chilli paste, plus more as needed

1 medium red or yellow onion, thinly sliced

450 g (1 lb) tomatoes, thinly sliced or halved if small

120 ml (4 fl oz/½ cup) white distilled vinegar, plus more as needed

375 g (13 oz/2 cups) cooked orzo, pearl couscous or rice (optional)

flaky sea salt

NOTE
—

Use any combination of chicken pieces; I like to cut mine from a whole chicken so I can save the backbone for soup or stock, but a package of thighs or breasts or any combo would be perfect – just be sure they're bone-in, skin-on. The flavour from both pays dividends to the sauce, which I love to say is 'better than it ought to be' given the limited number of ingredients.

DO AHEAD
—

The chicken can be made a few hours in advance – I wouldn't even reheat it. Also, the leftovers make VERY good soup: Basically, pull the chicken from the bones, add water or broth and finish with herbs.

While chicken and tomatoes love to be treated simply and basically left alone (who among us doesn't?), they really do sing together. Here the chicken gently braises alongside tomatoes that burst and become saucy, then raw tomatoes come in at the end, lending tanginess, sweetness and more juiciness. This pot of perfection needs nothing more. That said, I can tell you it's a very good idea to add your choice of cooked orzo, pearl couscous or rice to the pot of schmaltzy, vinegary liquid you're left with. To leave it behind would be a true missed opportunity.

1. Season the chicken with salt and pepper. Heat the olive oil in a large pot over a medium-high heat. Working in batches, add the chicken, skin-side down, and cook until deeply golden brown, 8–10 minutes. Flip and continue to cook until browned on both sides, 3–4 minutes.

2. Transfer the chicken to a large plate and repeat with the remaining chicken, turning the heat down during the second batch if needed.

3. Add the garlic and chilli flakes to the pot, letting it all sizzle in the chicken fat for a minute or two. Add three-quarters of the sliced onions and stir, scraping up any bits from the bottom of the pot. Cook, stirring occasionally, until they start to soften and brown at the edges, 4–6 minutes. Add half of the tomatoes and season with salt and pepper. Cook, stirring occasionally, until they start to burst, 3–5 minutes.

4. Return the chicken to the pot, skin-side up, nestling everything in there nice and tight. Add the vinegar and 120 ml (4 fl oz/½ cup) of water. Season with salt and pepper and drizzle with a bit more olive oil. Bring to a simmer, then reduce the heat to medium-low and cook, uncovered, until the chicken is cooked through and the sauce is slightly thickened, 12–15 minutes.

5. To serve, scatter the remaining tomatoes and sliced onion on a large serving platter or your largest dinner plate and season with salt.

6. Once the chicken is cooked through, using tongs or two forks, place the chicken on top of the tomatoes, leaving the braising liquid behind. If using, add the cooked orzo, couscous or rice to the pot, stirring to coat in the sauce, and season with salt, pepper and more vinegar. Spoon all the orzo and sauce next to and around the chicken and tomatoes, finishing with a drizzle of olive oil, some flaky salt and pepper.

BRAISED CHICKEN PICCATA

SERVES 4

1.15–1.35 kg (2½–3 lb) bone-in, skin-on chicken parts, such as breasts, legs or thighs
kosher salt and freshly ground black pepper
2 tablespoons neutral oil or olive oil
2 tablespoons unsalted butter
6–8 garlic cloves, thinly sliced
2 tablespoons capers, drained
1 lemon, very thinly sliced, seeds removed
½ teaspoon chilli flakes, plus more to taste
360 ml (12 fl oz/1½ cups) dry white wine, such as pinot grigio
small handful of parsley, tender leaves and stems, coarsely chopped

DO AHEAD
—
The chicken can be braised 3 days ahead, covered and refrigerated. It can be reheated gently on the stovetop, or in a 160°C/150°C fan/325°F oven for 30 or so minutes, or until warmed through.

EAT WITH
—
Personally, I can't imagine anything better than a bowl of pearl couscous or pot of egg noodles to soak up all that sauce, but it's really a choose-your-own-carbohydrate adventure, as so many would be good here: crusty baguette, pool of buttery polenta, a tangle of long al dente noodles...

While I resent the question, my answer to 'If you were a food, what would you be?' would almost certainly be chicken piccata. It's saucy, full of capers and loves white wine: Same! This chicken piccata does not require you to pound out cutlets or dredge the breasts in flour. Here, it's bone-in, skin-on chicken parts that brown nicely in the pan, giving you lots of bits and bobs to scrape up with white wine. This forms the start of a wonderful braising liquid for the chicken to swim in, becoming so tender it nearly falls apart. There's also, of course, lots of butter, crisped-up garlic and capers, and (whole) lemon slices, simmered in the white winey sauce until soft and jammy and scattered in at the end for a jolt of perky bitterness. Classique.

1 Season the chicken with salt and pepper; set aside. Heat the oil in a large, heavy-bottomed pot or high-sided skillet over a medium-high heat. Add the chicken, skin-side down, to the skillet, pressing lightly with tongs to ensure even contact. Cook until deeply golden brown, 8–10 minutes. Flip and cook until browned on both sides, for an additional 4–6 minutes.

2 Transfer the chicken to a plate. Without wiping out the pot, reduce the heat to medium and add the butter, garlic and capers. Using a wooden spoon, tongs or a fish spatula, do your best to scrape up the browned bits (more will come up when you add the wine). Cook, swirling occasionally, until the garlic and capers are golden brown and crispy, about 2 minutes. Transfer half of the garlic and capers to a small bowl; set aside.

3 Add half of the sliced lemon and the chilli flakes to the pot, stirring to lightly toast the chilli flakes and soften the lemon. Add the wine and 360 ml (12 fl oz/1½ cups) water and season with salt and pepper. Add the chicken back to the pot, skin-side up, nestling it in to partially submerge.

4 Bring the sauce to a gentle simmer, then reduce the heat to medium-low. Simmer gently, uncovered, until the chicken is tender and the sauce has reduced from watery wine to buttery, tangy, salty and a little spicy, 30–35 minutes. (It should remain brothy!) Taste the sauce and give it a final season of salt, pepper and more chilli flakes if you like.

5 Transfer the chicken to a serving platter or divide among plates. Spoon the magic sauce over everything. Scatter with the remaining lemon slices, reserved crispy garlic mixture, parsley and chilli flakes.

CRISP, HOT ROAST CHICKEN with LEEKS

SERVES 2–4

1 × 1.6–2 kg (3½–4½ lb) chicken
kosher salt and freshly ground black pepper
½ lemon, optional (see step 2 for alternatives)
1 large leek (or 2 smaller leeks)
60 ml (2 fl oz/¼ cup) olive oil, plus more as needed
½ bunch chives, finely chopped
1 bunch parsley, tender leaves and stems, finely chopped
4 anchovy fillets or 2 tablespoons capers, drained, finely chopped
2 garlic cloves, finely grated
1–2 tablespoons white wine vinegar or white distilled vinegar or fresh lemon juice, plus more

OPTIONAL BUT RECOMMENDED FOR THE EXPERIENCE
—
small potatoes, boiled until tender
asparagus or green beans, blanched until al dente
radishes, snap peas, crunchy lettuces or sliced fennel, raw
a whole or half tin of anchovies
Aioli (page 45)

NOTE
—
This is also a nice opportunity to use the fun spring alliums, like green garlic, wild garlic or garlic scapes.

DO AHEAD
—
Leek salsa verde can be made a day ahead, stored wrapped and refrigerated.

While there are a million ways to roast a bird, many of them wonderful, I find the '220°C/200°C fan/425°F for about an hour' technique produces the best version for nearly all my needs: golden-brown skin, crispy bits of chicken and still-juicy, tender breasts. There is no patting dry of the skin, no overnight seasoning, no wire rack required. It's pretty bare-bones, straightforward and wonderful: a near-perfect one-skillet situation.

The beauty of a roast chicken – and how I have come to think of it as a 'pantry meal' – is that you can (and I will!) add anything you have on hand to the skillet to roast alongside it. Potatoes, mushrooms, torn pieces of bread that become croutons: I've done it all. But it's the long, elegant leek that excites me most. While roasting alongside the chicken, leeks become all at once softened and braised, crunchy and crackly – perhaps tasting better than the chicken itself. While you could stop here, serving this with a garlicky aioli, leek salsa verde (made from the tops of the leeks) and an assortment of whatever vegetables you can find makes this whole thing feel like a true event, a chicken worthy of your finest company or sweetest date night.

1. Preheat the oven to 220°C/200°C fan/425°F.

2. Place the chicken on a baking tray or in a large cast-iron skillet. Season with salt and lots of pepper. If you happen to have a half a lemon, a halved head of garlic, a quartered onion or some rogue sprigs of herbs, you can stuff the cavity with those things, but if you don't, I wouldn't sweat it. Tie (or don't tie) your chicken legs together in a casual truss.

3. Remove the darkest green part of the leek. (Set aside – we're going to eat it.) Quarter the remaining white and light-green parts lengthways and give them a rinse. (If you're using small leeks, just halve them lengthways.) Lay the leeks beside the chicken, encouraging the layers to separate – if they're feeling long or large, simply bend them to curve around the chicken and skillet to make them fit. Drizzle the whole thing (leeks, chicken) with the olive oil and season with salt and pepper.

4. Place the chicken into the oven and don't look at it for at least 35 minutes. No peeking, no touching, no basting, no turning, no fussing.

5   After 35 minutes, you can peek – it should not be 'there' yet. You can baste or rotate the pan if you like, but keep roasting for another 20–25 minutes. You're looking for deeply browned chicken skin and a combination of entirely tender, almost silky braised leeks coupled with crispy, dark, frizzled leeks. I like mine almost burned, zero regrets. (If you're nervous about them getting a little dark before the chicken is ready, well, maybe this is not the chicken dish for you.)

6   While the chicken is roasting and the leeks are almost burning, make use of the other part of the leek, the part we typically throw away (unless you're making Potato Leek Soup, page 73). Finely chop the dark-green part of the leek and place it in a small bowl. Add the chives, parsley, anchovies and garlic. Season with salt and pepper, the vinegar or fresh lemon juice, and enough olive oil to make it saucy and spoonable. This should taste oniony, briny, bright, and extremely GREEN. Let it sit while your chicken finishes roasting.

7   Once your chicken is roasted to perfection, so golden brown you can hardly stand it, remove it from the oven and let it hang out on your counter in the vessel it was roasted in for 5–10 minutes.

8   When it's time to eat, place all your vegetables (the blanched, the boiled, the raw, the sliced) onto a large plate. If you opened a tin of anchovies for the sauce, place the tin on or next to the plate, too.

9   Here's a fun chicken tip: Before carving the chicken, tilt the bird upright in whatever vessel it was roasted in to catch all the juices (so they don't run all over your cutting board). Then, slice the legs away from the body of the bird, to catch even more juices. *Then* transfer the chicken to a cutting board to carve. Once carved, transfer to a large plate or serving platter, top with your fantastic leeks and spoon any chicken drippings/juice over the whole thing.

10 Serve with your leek salsa verde, aioli and whatever vegetables of your choosing. Dip the chicken into both sauces, followed by a perfect little boiled potato. Place an anchovy on a radish; dip that in the aioli. Snack on a lettuce. Drag a slice of chicken through the juices that have pooled on the bottom of the plate. Have a sip of wine, wish you had an artichoke, feel full and happy and grateful for all the things you have, but today, especially for that chicken.

HOW TO
ROAST A CHICKEN

Probably one of the most asked questions in the world of home cooking is: How do I make a great roast chicken? Well, you'll be both pleased to know that I have an answer and perhaps less pleased to know that it's one you may be frustrated by. Perfectly roasting a chicken is a meditation, a practice, a lifelong pursuit. Each time I do it, I'm trying to best myself, and even if I don't, I end up with something pretty remarkable. This is the attitude I wish for you to have. 'Perfection is not the goal' is what I want you to repeat as the bird slides into the oven. 'It's the journey, not the destination,' you'll say as you smell the chicken fat dripping off, the skin browning alongside something wonderful like skinny leeks or cloves of smashed garlic, already so pleased with yourself (and your chicken).

Now, practically speaking, there are two kernels of wisdom I can lend that will lead you closer to a truly excellent roast chicken (brown skin, tender legs and thighs, juicy breasts, crispy wings, well-seasoned drippings).

One: Please make sure your chicken has enough salt. If you aren't confident enough in your culinary prowess to know what's 'enough', then go ahead and measure out 1 teaspoon (I use Diamond Crystal kosher) per 450 g (1 lb) to make sure. As for 'what else', I can confidently say I don't know a better chicken than one that's been well dusted with kosher salt and freshly ground black pepper, stuffed with an old onion and half a lemon, and drizzled with plenty of olive oil. Resist the urge to gussy up your bird before you've tasted the bliss of one that's been simply and perfectly seasoned.

Two: Roast your chicken longer than you think. An under-roasted chicken is pale, flabby and – perhaps counterintuitively – tough, not tender. Not unlike baking a cake, the biggest hurdle in writing a recipe for a roast chicken is knowing that every oven is different. Does yours heat from the bottom or the top? Is it gas or electric? Does it run hot, cool or sometimes both? While I can't write personalised recipes for each oven, I can tell you what works for me, my oven and a 1.8–2 kg (4–4½ lb) chicken: 220°C/200°C fan/425°F for approximately 1 hour. The 'approximately' is doing a lot of work here, so here's what to look for: If the skin isn't as brown as a perfect piece of toast, if the wingtip isn't crispy enough to nibble like a chip, if the leg isn't tender enough to pull the bone clean out, then the chicken needs more time. Please, give it more time.

CRUSHED-OLIVE CHICKEN with TURMERIC

SERVES 4

1.6–1.8 kg (3½–4 lb) bone-in, skin-on chicken parts
1 teaspoon ground turmeric
6 tablespoons olive oil
kosher salt and freshly ground black pepper
120 ml (4 fl oz/½ cup) white wine vinegar or 90 ml (3 fl oz/⅓) cup white distilled vinegar
360 ml (12 fl oz/1½ cups) Castelvetrano or other mild, green olive, crushed and pitted
2 garlic cloves, finely grated
1 handful of parsley, tender leaves and stems, chopped

EAT WITH
—
Toasted Rice Pilaf with Crushed Walnuts & Dates (page 191), a bowl of small boiled potatoes.

This chicken has far too few ingredients to be as complexly flavoured as it is, but that is the magic of vinegar, crushed briny olives, fresh garlic and lots of chicken fat. Given how simple this whole thing is (classic 'roasting tray dinner'), my one plea is to really roast your chicken until it's deeply browned – the success of this recipe depends on it. I know that may seem obvious, but different ovens function differently, so I want you to ask yourself before removing the chicken: 'Could this chicken be browner?' If you hedge even a little, the answer might be yes. Keep roasting. Colour equals flavour, which is why this (maybe very scary) recipe asks you to turn your oven to 230°C/220°C fan/450°F, pushing at least one person reading this beyond their comfort zone. But the result when cooking chicken this way is browned skin, juicy meat and fantastically golden, schmaltzy bits left behind, which get deglazed with garlic, crushed olives and a bit of water for dressing your chicken. A true pan sauce, done in a roasting tray, all tangy and stained with turmeric, good enough to drink.

1 Preheat the oven to 230°C/220°C fan/450°F.

2 Place the chicken on a roasting tray, toss with the turmeric and 2 tablespoons of the olive oil, and season with salt and pepper. Make sure the chicken is in one layer, skin-side up, then pour the vinegar over and around the chicken and place the tray in the oven.

3 Bake the chicken, without flipping, until it's cooked through and deeply browned all over, 25–30 minutes.

4 Meanwhile, combine the olives, garlic, parsley, the remaining 4 tablespoons olive oil and 2 tablespoons water in a small bowl; season with salt and pepper.

5 Once the chicken is cooked, remove the roasting tray from the oven and transfer the chicken to a large serving platter, leaving behind any of the juices and bits stuck to the tray.

6 Make sure the tray is on a sturdy surface (the stovetop, a counter), then pour the olive mixture into it. Using a spatula or wooden spoon, gently scrape up all the bits the chicken left behind, letting the olive mixture mingle with the rendered fat and get increasingly saucy. Pour the olive mixture over the chicken, then serve.

SAUCY, WINE-ROASTED CHICKEN WITH MUSHROOMS

SERVES 4

1 × 1.8–2 kg (4–4½ lb) chicken
kosher salt and freshly ground black pepper
1 large yellow onion, quartered
4 tablespoons olive oil
350–450 g (12 oz–1 lb) mushrooms, such as oyster, maitake, chanterelle, trumpet or chestnut (cremini), cut or torn into bite-size pieces
2 garlic heads, unpeeled, halved widthways
½ bunch thyme, sage, savory, oregano or rosemary
2 tablespoons unsalted butter
480 ml (16 fl oz/2 cups) dry white wine

EAT WITH
—
A wheel of soft, bloomy-rind cheese and someone you love.

I am not a rule-follower, but I do love and respect tradition – a real juxtaposition. Coq au vin, one of the more 'classic' French dishes that Americans learn about and maybe feel an affinity for, is typically made with red wine, tiny pearl onions (no thanks) and mushrooms. This chicken here came about because one evening I thought, 'Wouldn't it be nice to cook a whole chicken in lots of white wine with some soft, tender mushrooms and a bit of butter?' and then realised, 'Oh, that's effectively a white coq au vin.' Who said there are no new ideas?

1   Preheat the oven to 160°C/150°C fan/325°F.

2   Season the chicken with salt and pepper and stuff the cavity with the onion.

3   Heat 2 tablespoons of the olive oil in a large, oven-safe pot with a lid over a medium heat. Add the chicken, breast-side up (so the backbone is making contact with the pot). Cook, without disturbing the chicken, until it's golden brown and chicken fat has started to render, 12–15 minutes.

4   Using tongs or two large forks, carefully remove the chicken from the pot, letting it rest on a plate or baking tray while you cook the mushrooms (they won't all fit with the chicken in there). Add the mushrooms, garlic, thyme and butter and season with salt and pepper. Toss to evenly coat and cook, tossing occasionally, until they start to see some colour, 8–10 minutes. Return the chicken to the pot, nestling it into the mushrooms.

5   Add the wine and season again with salt and pepper. Bring to a simmer, place the lid on the pot, and transfer it to the oven. Roast, undisturbed, for 45–50 minutes, at which point the chicken will be cooked through but pale.

6   Remove the lid and increase the oven temperature to 220°C/200°C fan/425°F. Carefully spoon a bit of the pooled sauce over the chicken and continue to roast, undisturbed, until the top of the chicken is nicely browned, 25–30 minutes. (If it's not brown enough, give it a little more time.)

7   Remove the chicken from the oven and let cool slightly before carving and serving. (I like to carve the chicken in the pot so the juices escape into the mushroom sauce.)

CHICKEN POT PIE

(A REAL CLASSIC)

SERVES 4–6

900 g (2 lb) bone-in, skin-on chicken breasts or thighs (smaller work better here)

kosher salt and freshly ground black pepper

2 tablespoons olive oil

1 medium onion, thinly sliced

6 garlic cloves, finely chopped

4 celery stalks, thinly sliced

120 ml (4 fl oz/½ cup) white wine

30 g (1 oz/¼ cup) plain (all-purpose) flour

750 ml (25 fl oz/3 cups) low-sodium chicken broth or stock (or water plus Better Than Bouillon, see page 58)

80 g (2¾ oz/½ cup) frozen peas (sadly, a whole bag is too many peas for me)

10 g (½ oz/¼ cup) finely chopped parsley, plus more as needed

15 g (½ oz/¼ cup) finely chopped chives

2 tablespoons finely chopped tarragon (optional)

1 × 350–400 g (12–14 oz) sheet (or two 240 g/8½ oz sheets pressed together at the edges) frozen puff pastry, thawed

1 large egg

EAT WITH

—

A large spoon, a bowl of parsley dressed with lemon and salt.

Having made many versions of pot pie – some with pie crust, others with puff pastry, some with mushrooms or an intense dose of leafy greens – I've come to determine that my favourite pot pie is the most classic. There's shredded chicken, vegetables (celery, peas, but no carrots) and herbs swimming in a savoury, brothy, lightly white-winey sauce. It tastes how you think it might, only better. This is the pot pie for you if stuffing is your favourite part of Thanksgiving and you enjoy things baked beneath a buttery crust. If you don't like peas, use fennel or carrots instead (you still need a touch of sweetness). Want to make it vegetarian? Use mushrooms as you would the chicken, browned in plenty of fat before proceeding with the recipe. Don't have good puff pastry? Use shortcrust (pie crust). This recipe, while appearing fussy, is actually extremely flexible (I can relate) and shockingly pantry-friendly.

I am confident that this recipe is foolproof, but as someone who's made close to a hundred pot pies in her life, I will still offer two pieces of wisdom for success: First, counterintuitively, your mixture will actually thin out slightly when baking beneath whatever crust you place on top, so you want the chicken mixture to be on the thicker side before it goes into the oven. Second, a well-baked crust should be deeply golden brown, feel hard when you tap on it, and be shatteringly flaky when broken into.

1. Preheat the oven to 220°C/200°C fan/425°F. Line a baking tray with baking paper.

2. Season the chicken with salt and pepper. Heat the olive oil in a large (20–25 cm/8–10 inch) skillet (preferably cast iron or another heavy-bottomed skillet) over a medium heat. Sear the chicken, skin-side down, until deeply golden brown and most of the fat has begun to render out, 5–8 minutes. Flip and continue to cook until the chicken is evenly browned and cooked through on the other side, an additional 8–10 minutes. Transfer to a plate or cutting board, leaving the drippings behind in the skillet.

3. Add the onion and garlic to the skillet, season with salt and pepper, and cook, stirring occasionally, until mostly softened with a bit of caramelisation at the edges, 3–5 minutes. Add the celery, season with salt and pepper and cook, stirring occasionally, until the celery is tender

and just cooked through, 5–8 minutes. Add the wine and cook, stirring constantly, until it is mostly evaporated, a minute or so.

4 Add the flour on top of the vegetables and stir to coat them all. Cook, stirring constantly, until the flour has started to turn a light golden brown with no white, floury bits left, 3–4 minutes. (You're toasting the flour here, but because of the vegetables, it might take longer than a usual roux.)

5 Slowly add the chicken broth or stock, 120 ml (4 fl oz/½ cup) at a time, using a wooden spoon to blend and scrape up any browned bits on the bottom of the skillet. Do not worry about lumps or it looking too thick – it'll smooth out, promise. Once all the broth or stock is added, bring to a simmer and remove from the heat.

6 Remove any bones and cartilage-y bits (discard or compost them) from the chicken and shred the meat and skin into bite-size pieces. (Alternatively, use a knife and fork to cut into bite-size pieces.) Add the picked chicken, peas, parsley, chives and tarragon (if using) and stir to combine. Season one final time (lots of seasoning in this recipe) with salt and pepper.

7 Carefully unfold the puff pastry and, if you feel like it needs it, smooth it out using a rolling pin (or your hands). For extra credit, you can roll it into more of a circle shape (approximately 30 cm/12 inches in diameter), but don't stress too much about this. Working quickly, place it on top of the skillet, letting some of the dough hang off the sides (this will keep it from shrinking too much).

8 Whisk the egg with 1 teaspoon water in a small bowl and brush it onto the top of the puff pastry. Cut three 6 cm (2½ inch) slits, about 2.5 cm (1 inch) apart. Sprinkle the top with salt and pepper, maybe a few parsley leaves for superfluous yet delightful décor. Place the skillet on the prepared baking tray to catch any drips as it bakes.

9 Bake until the puff pastry is deeply golden brown, cooked through all the way, and the filling has started to bubble out of the top, 35–40 minutes. Remove from the heat and let cool slightly before eating.

THE IMPORTANCE OF A
HEAVY-BOTTOMED POT

Just like my belief in a minimal but well-stocked pantry, I don't think you need much in the way of equipment to get you to the promised land of wonderful food. But there are a few bigger-ticket items that are worth the larger investments – and will last you a lifetime. Generational cookware, if you will. Many sources will promise the same quality at half the price, but in my experience, when it comes to cookware (and a lot of other things), half the price nearly always means half the quality. Frankly, I'd rather buy something once and never think about it again versus replacing a cheaper version every few years.

This leads me to one of my most well-loved and often-used pieces of cookware: a heavy-bottomed pot (preferably with a lid). A casserole dish (Dutch oven) is the most popular example of one of these pots (although not all heavy-bottomed pots are casseroles). It's something that you'll find yourself using repeatedly throughout this book, but also, if you just simply cook a lot, you really should own one. You can braise in it, roast in it, soup and stew in it. It can be in the oven overnight (helpful for the lamb on the next page) or on the stove for 30 minutes for your weeknight ragù (page 244). It can withstand 25 minutes of searing a large piece of brisket (page 284) and is also large enough to fit a whole, gently simmering chicken for a batch of broth (page 51).

Casserole or not, the description 'heavy-bottomed pot' is not open to interpretation: It should feel nearly indestructible and truly heavy, which means almost certainly made from cast iron. The interior can be coated with enamel or not – I own and use both types. (The enamel coating can be helpful for seeing the food more clearly – to get a sense for whether things are properly browned or caramelised.)

This type of pot is invaluable and will almost certainly become one of your most used kitchen tools. With any luck, the bottom will become splattered with all sorts of mysterious splotches from years of long oven braises and stovetop flames licking the sides, getting uglier with each use. These pots aren't meant to be pristine and spotless; they should show their age, proudly wear their patina. 'I really cook,' they declare, all imperfect, clearly worn and so very well loved.

OVERNIGHT LAMB & POTATOES IN WHITE WINE

SERVES 6–8

1 × 1.8–2.25 kg (4–5 lb) bone-in (or 1.35–1.8 kg/3–4 lb boneless) shoulder or leg of lamb, untied
kosher salt and freshly ground black pepper
900 g (2 lb) waxy potatoes, such as King Edward, peeled or unpeeled, left whole or halved
2 garlic heads, unpeeled, halved widthways
2 lemons, halved widthways
1 bunch fresh oregano, marjoram or thyme, plus more as needed
1 × 750 ml (25 fl oz) bottle dry white wine
olive oil, for drizzling
1–2 handfuls of tender herbs, such as parsley, dill, chives and/or mint, for serving (optional)

NOTE

Boneless lamb is easier to find, but I promise the bone-in cut is worth seeking out. The bone holds the meat together and seasons the cooking liquid even more deeply – plus, the drama!

DO AHEAD

This lamb can be made 3–4 days ahead, covered and refrigerated. Reheat in a 140°C/120°C fan/275°F oven until the lamb and potatoes are warmed through, 35–40 minutes.

EAT WITH

This lamb loves a party, so feel free to centre a holiday or any big-ticket celebration around it. It welcomes an abundance of sides, several bottles of cold wine and an appreciation for large hunks of meat.

This lamb is for people who don't like lamb, for those who are scared to cook (and potentially ruin) large hunks of meat, and for anyone who yearns to feel like they are on vacation in Greece. Inspired by a dinner I had while on a very short trip to Athens (a story for another time), the lamb (leg or shoulder, preferably bone-in) is cooked in a heavy pot in little else than an entire bottle of white wine and its own gorgeous rendered fat. After many hours, the lamb falls off the bone, melting into itself, and becomes exquisitely browned on top and lightly crisped in all the right places, with ample sauce left behind to spoon over the shredded meat that's miraculously still pink and impossibly tender.

The most important part of this recipe is to not overthink it. The technique happens in the oven, not before and not after, requiring so little actual cooking from you that you might feel guilty for the praise you'll receive once it's served. Trust the process, the process being: It goes into the oven and, 12 hours later, it comes out. No, you don't need more liquid. No, it won't burn. Yes, it really can go overnight. And yes, this recipe takes a long (slow) time. Plan ahead.

1. Season the lamb with salt and pepper. (About 1 teaspoon of Diamond Crystal kosher salt per 450 g/1 lb of meat; use half that for Morton kosher salt.) Leave in the fridge for 12–24 hours if you're able.

2. Preheat the oven to 140°C/120°C fan/275°F. Place the lamb in a large casserole (Dutch oven). (The pot you use really needs to be heavy bottomed, preferably with a lid.) Scatter the potatoes, garlic, lemons and oregano around the lamb and pour the wine over everything. Give it a good glug of olive oil so that a nice, thick layer of it is floating on top. Cover the pot with the lid (or, wrap very tightly with foil if you don't have a lid).

3. Place in the oven and do not look or peek at it. Do not touch, poke or prod it for at least 10 hours, closer to 12 if your lamb is on the larger side, closer to 8 if boneless. If it goes a little longer, that's okay. This lamb is resilient. You'll know the lamb is done when it's golden brown and shreds easily.

4. Remove from the oven and let cool slightly. To serve, transfer the lamb to a large platter (or leave it in the pot) and pull the lamb apart into largish hunks. Spoon all the sauce, potatoes and bits of garlic over the lamb. Top with fresh herbs (if using) and another good pour of olive oil.

SPICY BRAISED SHORT RIBS
with GARLIC & LEMON

SERVES 8–10

2.25 kg (5 lb) bone-in short ribs, at least 3 cm (1½ inches) thick, cut into single-bone portions (or 1.6–1.8 kg/3½–4 lb boneless, at least 3 cm/1½ inches thick)
kosher salt and freshly ground black pepper
4 tablespoons neutral oil, such as grapeseed or rapeseed (canola)
4 lemons, halved
2 large yellow onions, unpeeled, quartered
2 garlic heads, unpeeled, halved widthways, plus 4 cloves, finely chopped
2 teaspoons chilli flakes or 1–2 tablespoons Calabrian chilli paste, plus more to taste
2 tablespoons honey
120 ml (4 fl oz/½ cup) sherry vinegar, apple cider vinegar or white wine vinegar
120 ml (4 fl oz/½ cup) soy sauce or tamari
4 thyme sprigs
1 handful of parsley and/or coriander (cilantro), tender leaves and stems, finely chopped
1 bunch chives, finely chopped
flaky sea salt

NOTE

While my preference is almost always bone-in for any cut of meat, this recipe will work with boneless short ribs, too. And it also works for brisket – just add an additional hour or so to the cooking time for a 1.8 kg (4 lb) brisket.

I feel like many people are always in search of a steady, reliable short-rib recipe: not too basic or boring but not so loud it couldn't happily mingle with anything else on the table. Something satisfying, with a foolproof technique that yields perfectly tender, shreddable, fall-off-the-bone meat in a pool of well-seasoned sauce (which I'm tempted to describe as 'beefy'), without being too heavy. Short ribs that can be made with ingredients you've already got on hand, cooked ahead of time, reheated with ease.

These are those short ribs, the answer to 'What is your favourite basic-but-delicious short rib recipe?' There's no tomato purée (paste) or finely chopped vegetables, no bottle of Barolo – just a pot of gorgeous short ribs bathed in a sauce that's equal parts tangy and salty, sweet and savoury. They are simultaneously so complex and so beautifully basic, you might wonder whether they are the platonic ideal of a braised short rib. (I think they are.)

1 Season the short ribs with salt and pepper at least 1 hour (at room temperature) and as much as 48 hours (covered and refrigerated) in advance.

2 Preheat the oven to 150°C/140°C fan/300°F.

3 Heat 2 tablespoons of the oil in a large casserole (Dutch oven) over a medium-high heat. Working in batches, sear as many short ribs as will comfortably fit in the pot until deeply golden brown on both large flat sides, 4–6 minutes per side. Transfer the browned short ribs to a large plate or cutting board and drain all but about 2 tablespoons fat from the pot; repeat with the remaining short ribs. Once you've seared all the short ribs, remove and discard all the fat from the pot and carefully wipe it out. (There's no need to wash the pot; just get rid of any scorched bits.)

4 In the same pot over a medium-high heat, heat the remaining 2 tablespoons oil and add 2 of the lemons, the onions and halved heads of garlic. Cook, stirring occasionally, until the lemons, onions and garlic get a bit of colour, 5–7 minutes. Add the chilli flakes or chilli paste and cook for a minute or two. Add the honey and cook, stirring, until it starts to bubble furiously and turn a few shades darker, 2–3 minutes. (Caramelising the honey a bit gives you a more 'mature' flavour rather than just 'sweet', which will do the braising liquid many favours.)

DO AHEAD
—

You can remove the short ribs from the oven after step 6, let them cool at room temperature, and place them in the fridge overnight. When ready to serve, remove them from the fridge and, using a spoon, scrape off the solidified fat on the top layer. Return the short ribs, covered, to a 160°C/150°C fan/325°F oven until totally warmed through, 30–40 minutes. Remove the lid, increase the temperature to 220°C/200°C fan/425°F and continue to cook, uncovered, to let the short ribs brown a bit on top and reduce the braising liquid, another 35–45 minutes.

EAT WITH
—

A bowl of delightfully creamy polenta (page 189), a pile of lemony potatoes (page 98) or crusty bread for sopping. If you're lucky enough to have leftovers, shred them and fold them into tomato sauce (page 237) for a gorgeous little ragù.

5   Add the vinegar, soy sauce, thyme and 950 ml (32 fl oz/4 cups) water (careful, it'll bubble considerably). Using a wooden spoon or spatula, scrape up the bits on the bottom of the pot and bring to a strong simmer. Season with salt and pepper and add the short ribs back in, bone-side up (you want the meat to be as submerged in the liquid as possible). Cover the pot and place it in the oven. Do not look at it or remove the lid for 3 hours. (Nothing bad will happen, promise.)

6   After 3 hours, check the short ribs. They should be extremely tender and nearly falling apart, almost having the jiggly texture of a baked custard or jelly. (If not, continue roasting another 20–30 minutes.) Remove from the oven.

7   At this stage – and this is optional! – you can remove the lid and, using a spoon, carefully skim off as much of the top layer of fat as possible (the short ribs might seem a little greasy without skimming, but worse things have happened). Increase the oven temperature to 220°C/200°C fan/425°F and return the pot to the oven, uncovered, to let the short ribs brown on top and thicken the braising liquid a bit, another 35–45 minutes.

8   Meanwhile, combine the parsley and chives in a small bowl and season with flaky salt; set aside.

9   Once the short ribs are nicely browned, the sauce is slightly reduced, and you're ready to serve, remove the short ribs from the oven. Add the chopped garlic to the pot and squeeze the remaining lemons over, letting the raw garlic and fresh lemon juice season the braising liquid. Serve straight from the pot or transfer the ribs to a shallow bowl or plate with high sides, spooning the braising liquid over. Sprinkle with the herb mixture before serving.

SOMETHING FROM NOTHING

BRAISED PORK STEW
with CABBAGE, OLIVES & LEMON

SERVES 6-8

1.35 g (3 lb) boneless pork shoulder, cut into 3–5 cm (1½–2 inch) pieces

kosher salt and freshly ground black pepper

1 tablespoon neutral oil or olive oil

1 large onion, thinly sliced

6 garlic cloves, thinly sliced

2 tablespoons tomato purée (paste)

1 tablespoon smoked or sweet paprika

1 teaspoon chilli flakes, plus more as needed

120 ml (4 fl oz/½ cup) white distilled vinegar, plus more as needed

1 medium or ½ large head cabbage (about 570 g/1¼ lb), chopped or torn into large pieces

225–350 g (8–12 oz) kielbasa, sliced (not too thin)

150 g (5½ oz/1 cup) pitted mild green olives (Castelvetrano, Cerignola or Gordal), thinly sliced

1 lemon, thinly sliced, seeds removed

60 g (2 oz/1½ cups) dill, finely chopped

DO AHEAD

It can be made 5 days ahead, stored in a resealable container and refrigerated, or frozen for up to 1 month.

EAT WITH

This stew *almost* wants potatoes simmered in it (which you could do), but it's also nice served over Long-Cooked Potatoes, Garlic & Lemon (page 98) or any simple roasted, steamed or boiled potato.

I like to go to the Russian baths as often as I can. Part of the pleasure (and it is all about pleasure) is that in between sweating it out in any number of ways, you also have access to some very, very good Russian and Eastern European food: *pelmeni*, **chopped salads with the good feta and lots of wonderful soups, stews and braise-y meats. One of my favourites,** *solyanka* **(once listed as 'pickle soup' and had sliced hot dogs in it) is something I've aspired to and failed to re-create in my own home, but the pursuit did lead me here: a brothy bowl of sour cabbage and fatty smoked pork, studded with fresh lemon and green olives, finished with a fistful of dill. I'm going to call this one supremely elegant (not the usual term used to describe pork stews) – something you might be inspired to serve 'for company', alongside either a dish of slow-cooked potatoes or perhaps nothing at all.**

1   Season the pork with salt and pepper. Heat the oil in a large pot over a medium-high heat. Add the pork – the pot might be a little crowded at first, but the meat will shrink as it cooks. Cook, turning occasionally, until each side is nicely browned, 15–20 minutes. Transfer the pork to a plate or bowl while you build the rest of the stew. (If your pork was especially fatty, you might want to pour off some of the fat from the pot.)

2   With the heat still on medium-high, add the onion and garlic to the pot and season with salt and pepper. Cook until the onions get a bit of colour, 5–8 minutes. Add the tomato purée and cook for a minute or two. Add the paprika and chilli flakes and cook for a minute or two to toast the spices.

3   Add the vinegar, 1.9 litres (64 fl oz/8 cups) water, the cabbage and the reserved pork (plus any juices that have accumulated). Season with salt and pepper and bring to a simmer. Reduce the heat until just barely bubbling and simmer gently, uncovered, until the pork is impossibly tender – after 3–3½ hours, it should nearly fall apart when prodded with a fork or knife. At this point, the broth should also taste very good and the cabbage will be translucent and almost melty in texture. If the pork doesn't quite want to fall apart just yet, be patient and keep simmering.

4   Once the stew is in a good place, add the kielbasa and olives, letting them simmer together for 10–15 minutes. Taste the stew and adjust with salt, pepper and more vinegar if you feel like it needs it. Finally, remove the pot from the heat and add the lemon slices and dill, swirling to evenly distribute. Ladle into bowls and serve.

MEATS & FISHES

TANGY BRAISED BRISKET with SHALLOTS & HORSERADISH

SERVES 8–10

2–2.25 kg (4½–5 lb) brisket, preferably cut from the fatty end
kosher salt and freshly ground black pepper
2 tablespoons rapeseed (canola) oil
2 garlic heads, unpeeled, halved widthways
450 g (1 lb) (6–8) shallots, halved lengthways, quartered if large
950 ml (32 fl oz/4 cups) beef or chicken broth (or water plus Better Than Bouillon, see page 58)
250 ml (8 fl oz/1 cup) white distilled vinegar or white wine vinegar, plus more to taste
90 ml (3 fl oz/⅓ cup) Worcestershire sauce, soy sauce or tamari, plus more to taste
60 g (2 oz/¼ cup) freshly grated horseradish, or 3 tablespoons prepared horseradish, plus more to taste
2 fresh or dried bay leaves, or ½ bunch thyme
flaky sea salt
parsley, tender leaves and stems, to finish (optional)

NOTE
—
I don't peel the shallots – I like the way the peel holds them together, getting all wrinkled and papery as they slow-cook. But you can peel them if you like.

I consider brisket a celebratory piece of meat. Celebratory in the sense that the large size is ideal for big gatherings for special occasions, but also in that its hands-off nature and minimal ingredients list make it a true celebration of the magic of simple cooking (earnest but true). Aside from a massive hunk of meat, the key components of this recipe are really just two humble pantry standbys: white distilled vinegar and Worcestershire sauce. The tangy, salty, beefy liquid created with those ingredients and a good bit of time is nothing short of magnificent. But of course, there's more: shallots for sweetness, horseradish for gentle, earthy spiciness, bay leaves for a 'certain something' that, yes, I'm sure exists. While I strongly suggest you keep the braising liquid as written, you can really customise the rest however you like: adding onions instead of shallots, throwing in a few carrots or celery stalks or leaving out the horseradish if that's not your thing.

1 Season the brisket with salt and pepper. (If you're measuring, this is at least 1 teaspoon of kosher salt per 450 g (1 lb) of meat. I use Diamond Crystal; halve it if you're using Morton salt.) Do this a few hours (up to 24) in advance, if you're able, and keep it uncovered in the fridge. It's also fine just to season and go ahead and braise it right away, too.

2 Preheat the oven to 140°C/120°C fan/275°F.

3 Heat the oil in a large (at least 5 litres/5½ quarts), heavy-bottomed pot over a medium heat. (If you don't have a large, heavy-bottomed pot or casserole/Dutch oven, you can sear the brisket, shallots and garlic in a large skillet, then transfer them to a roasting pan or baking dish. Pour the liquid over everything and cover tightly with foil before putting in the oven.)

4 Sear the brisket fat-side down first. Use tongs (or any implement of your choosing) to press the meat to encourage as much contact with the pot as possible for the most even browning. Cook the brisket, without moving, until deeply browned, 10–12 minutes. (Doing this over medium heat rather than medium-high will take longer but will reduce the risk of burning the rendered fat.)

DO AHEAD

—

This brisket can be made 3 days ahead, stored in the braising liquid, covered and refrigerated. To reheat, place in a 140°C/120°C fan/275°F oven for 30–40 minutes, or until the brisket is warmed through.

EAT WITH

—

Fruit Salad with Chives & Sticky Walnuts (page 137), Long-Cooked Potatoes, Garlic & Lemon (page 98), Forever-Roasted Squash with Browned Butter Dates (page 104).

5   Using tongs or two large spoons, flip the brisket to brown on the other side, another 10–12 minutes. Be careful here; the fat is extremely hot and can splatter. This is how I gave myself the worst oil burn of my life – truly a brisket to remember. Once the brisket is nicely browned on that side as well, transfer it to a large plate or sheet pan, leaving the fat behind. (This is a plea to use stainless steel–tipped tongs. Rubber tongs will never afford you the sort of grip you need to safely flip a piece of meat this large and heavy.)

6   Add the garlic and shallots, cut-side down, to the fat in the pot. Season with salt and pepper and cook, without moving, until nicely browned, 3–5 minutes.

7   Return the brisket (plus any juices that have accumulated) to the pot and add whatever broth you're using, the vinegar, Worcestershire sauce, horseradish and bay leaves.

8   Bring to a simmer and place the lid on. Transfer to the oven and let it gently braise for 3–3½ hours. Remove from the oven and make sure it's done by inserting the tip of a knife into the thickest part: It should meet no resistance, the whole slab jiggling like jelly.

9   To serve, transfer the brisket to a cutting board. Slice against the grain (easy to locate on a brisket – the grain is very apparent), as thick or thin as you like, and place on a large serving platter. Give the juices a taste – they should be tangy, salty and very beefy, with a bit of heat from the horseradish. Adjust with more Worcestershire, vinegar or horseradish as needed. Spoon the jammy shallots and garlic over the brisket, along with the juices from the pot. Serve with more horseradish on the side, along with some flaky salt and parsley (if using).

GOODBYE MEATBALLS

SERVES 6–8

FOR THE MEATBALLS
—
225 g (8 oz/1 cup) whole-milk ricotta

30 g (1 oz/½ cup) finely chopped parsley

30 g (1 oz/½ cup) grated Parmesan cheese

20 g (¾ oz/⅓ cup) panko breadcrumbs

2 large eggs

2 or 3 garlic cloves, finely grated or chopped

½ medium yellow or red onion, very finely chopped (you'll use the other half of the onion for the sauce)

2 teaspoons kosher salt, plus more to taste

freshly ground black pepper and/or chilli flakes

450 g (1 lb) minced (ground) beef

450 g (1 lb) minced (ground) pork (or more beef if you don't eat pork)

2 tablespoons olive oil

FOR THE SAUCE
—
1½ medium yellow or red onions, finely chopped

6 garlic cloves, thinly sliced

kosher salt and freshly ground black pepper

2 tablespoons tomato purée (paste)

a few anchovies or couple of dashes of fish sauce (optional)

4 × 400 g (14 oz) tins crushed tomatoes and/or whole peeled tomatoes, crushed by hand

I am proud of all my recipes, but especially of the canonically classic ones. It's not that I've reinvented them (as I said, they remain canon), but rather that I've configured each one to suit my platonic ideal, tailored to my specific criteria, tweaked to meet my often ridiculously high standards. Buttermilk biscuits. Matzo ball soup. Pie crust. Meatballs. I am particular, and so are these recipes.

Perhaps more than other classics, meatball recipes tend to have a lot of 'secrets': The bread for the crumbs has to be from a five-day-old loaf, the crumbs must be soaked in whole milk, there should be a scant teaspoon of Top Secret Thing, they should be seared first or, wait, no, dropped straight into the sauce ... so on and so forth. If you're interested in making wonderful meatballs, I'm sure you've heard one or more of these things before. Through trial and error, eating many subpar and excellent meatballs, and texting my Aunt Liz in New Jersey, I arrived at my own recipe, though tragically devoid of 'secrets'.

These are your basic, very good meatballs in the style of Italian American red-sauce joints, and to me, they are perfect: a mixture of beef and pork, with panko breadcrumbs (I love an all-purpose crumb) that are softened in ricotta with eggs to bind. There are plenty of alliums (raw onion and garlic), lots of fresh parsley and a good amount of hard, salty Parmesan. They're seared in the pot before building the sauce because I do not think a meatball browned in the oven is brown enough. It's admittedly more work to do them stovetop, sure, but you reap the rewards in the form of rendered fat, toasted bits and browned, delicious meat that flavours your sauce.

1 Make the meatballs: Mix the ricotta, parsley, Parmesan, breadcrumbs, eggs, garlic and onion in a medium bowl. Season with salt, pepper and chilli flakes (if you like), and let sit for 10 minutes or so. (This hydrates the breadcrumbs, which leads to very juicy meatballs – do not skip or rush this step.)

2 Add the beef, pork and remaining 2 teaspoons (Diamond Crystal) kosher salt (1 teaspoon if using Morton salt). Using your hands (I have never had good luck using a spoon), mix everything together well – it should look like sausage, evenly flecked with bits here and there, but not paste-like. Once it is well mixed, roll one tiny sacrificial meatball to cook.

NOTE

I first made these meatballs after a not-so-tragic breakup. For better or for worse, the name stuck.

DO AHEAD

The raw meatball mixture freezes well, so you could always make half and freeze the rest for later.

EAT WITH

Meatballs really need no suggestions, but I will say that beyond the bowl of spaghetti or platter of rigatoni, they are excellent over soft, cheesy polenta (page 189) or simply on their own with some garlic bread with which to dunk.

3 Heat the olive oil in a large pot over a medium heat. Add the sacrificial meatball and cook until it's well browned on all sides and cooked through. Take it out of the pot and eat it. Does it taste amazing? Salty? Meaty? Tender and juicy without falling apart? Do you want it spicier? Go ahead and adjust the seasoning as needed.

4 Roll the rest of the mixture into balls 3–5 cm (1½–2 inches) in diameter. This is my preference, so if you enjoy a LARGER meatball, then be my beautiful guest. I get roughly 24 meatballs from this mixture, more or less.

5 Working in batches, brown the meatballs on all sides, 4–6 minutes per batch. They will not be cooked through – that's fine; they will finish cooking in the sauce. It's important to remember that this isn't a round meatball contest; it's a brown meatball contest (not the time or place to sacrifice deliciousness for aesthetics).

6 Once the meatballs are properly browned, transfer them to a large plate or bowl and continue with the rest of the meat. Once they are all browned, congratulate yourself on a job well done and let them hang out while you make the sauce.

7 Make the sauce: Without wiping out the pot, add the onions and garlic and season with salt and pepper. Cook, stirring occasionally, until they're translucent and tender but not yet browned, 8–10 minutes. Add the tomato purée and anchovies (if using) and stir until the anchovies are melted and the tomato purée has begun to caramelise and turn a darker shade of red, 2–3 minutes.

8 Add the tinned tomatoes. Fill one of the empty tins halfway with water and swirl to get all the tomato bits out, then pour the liquid into the pot. Season with salt and pepper.

9 Bring to a simmer and adjust for salt, knowing the sauce will reduce and become a bit saltier while it cooks with the meatballs. Add your meatballs and all the juices that have collected at the bottom of the plate.

10 Reduce the heat to low and simmer the meatballs in the sauce, uncovered, until the sauce is thickened and impossibly delicious and the meatballs are cooked through and perfectly tender, 30–40 minutes.

MEATS & FISHES

STEAK LIKE TARTARE

SERVES 4

675–900 g (1½–2 lb) hanger steak (or any steak, such as ribeye, boneless short rib, sirloin, etc.)

kosher salt and freshly ground black pepper

2–3 tablespoons neutral oil (grapeseed or rapeseed/canola)

1 medium shallot, finely chopped

4 anchovy fillets, finely chopped, plus more for serving

2 tablespoons capers, drained, finely chopped

2 tablespoons red wine vinegar or white wine vinegar, plus more as needed

½ teaspoon Worcestershire sauce, plus more to taste

25 g (1 oz/½ cup) finely chopped chives

10 g (½ oz/¼ cup) parsley, tender leaves and stems, chopped, plus more to serve

120 ml (4 fl oz/½ cup) olive oil, plus more as needed

some sort of bread, halved lengthways or sliced

NOTE

If you don't do beef, I can confidently say this staple sauce is also great with pork or lamb chops or any sort of chicken.

DO AHEAD

The sauce can be made a day or two ahead, stored refrigerated.

EAT WITH

I must confess I've always fantasised about ordering some McDonald's french fries and serving them next to this steak, if I could time it right.

This is everything I love about steak tartare, except the steak is . . . cooked (but, yes, on the rare side). The components stay classic – shallot, capers, chives, Worcestershire, anchovies – lending an unmistakable bistro vibe to your domicile, made possible with ingredients you likely already have on hand. Just like with a tableside tartare, when seasoning the salsa-verde-ish sauce, you should adjust it as you see fit based on your preferences and what you have in your pantry, adding hot sauce or horseradish if you want, more or less vinegar, and so on. Also, much like tableside tartare, you should eat this with a crunchy baguette or tiny toasts over a long, late lunch or gloriously early dinner with a glass of something fabulous.

1 Season the steak with salt and pepper.

2 Heat the oil in a large skillet, preferably cast iron, over a medium-high heat, swirling to coat the surface. Once the oil starts to shimmer, add the steak. (If using hanger steak, set it flat-side down. Work in batches if needed to avoid crowding the pan.) Press it a bit with tongs to ensure good contact with the skillet – this is how you get even browning. For hanger steak, cook until deeply browned, 4–5 minutes. (Thicker pieces of meat will take closer to 5–6 minutes.) Using tongs, flip and cook until browned on that side as well, another 3–4 minutes.

3 Transfer the steak to a plate to rest, leaving any meaty bits or rendered fat behind in the skillet.

4 While the steak rests, make the sauce. In a medium bowl, combine the shallot, anchovies, capers, vinegar, Worcestershire sauce, chives and parsley. Stir in the olive oil along with any meat juices from the plate. Taste the sauce and season with more vinegar, Worcestershire, salt and pepper as needed. The seasoning (like tartare itself) is deeply personal and should be adjusted to suit you and your loved ones.

5 If you like, use the skillet with all the meaty bits to toast your bread over medium heat until golden brown and crisp, 2–4 minutes, adding a little olive oil to the skillet if it needs it.

6 To serve, slice the steak against the grain. Arrange the steak on a large serving plate and spoon the sauce over it. Scatter with more parsley and serve with toast and, if you've got them, more anchovies alongside.

PANKO BREADCRUMBS

ARE THE PERFECT BREADCRUMBS

There once was a time I was saving old bread and grinding my own breadcrumbs in a food processor. Those breadcrumbs were great, and I'll still go that route for special occasions, but I'm sure I speak for all of us when I say I'm glad that time has passed. Now, for pretty much any reason I'd need breadcrumbs, I use panko (small, light, Japanese-style breadcrumbs). They're already perfectly dried and crunchy as is, but toasted or lightly fried in olive oil, they become golden brown and almost permanently crunchy, withstanding the sauciness of an aubergine (eggplant) Parmesan (page 240) or a skillet of buttered radishes (see page 296). I use them as a highly seasoned topping for salads (like Caesar, page 150), to take the place of white bread as the binding agent for meatballs (page 288), and as a crispy coating for cutlets like the ones that follow. As with most things, my preference is to avoid the seasoned kind so you can control the salt and add your own flavours as you wish.

CRISPY SCHNITZEL with BROWNED BUTTER RADISHES

SERVES 2

2 bone-in or boneless pork chops (rib or loin), cut about 1 cm (½ inch) thick (approximately 175 g/6 oz each)

kosher salt and freshly ground black pepper

90 g (3¼ oz/1½ cups) panko or fresh, coarse breadcrumbs

60 ml (2 fl oz/¼ cup) neutral oil, such as grapeseed or rapeseed (canola), plus more as needed

4 tablespoons unsalted butter

2 tablespoons capers, drained

1 bunch radishes, with tops on if you like, cut into quarters

flaky sea salt

1 lemon, cut into wedges

NOTE

Most prepackaged pork chops are, in my opinion, cut too thin, which is bad news for anyone looking for a giant, juicy chop but excellent news for anyone looking to make this crispy, breadcrumb-coated number. About 1 cm (½ inch) thick, these thin chops require no further pounding, making them ideal for a casual crispy pork cutlet.

EAT WITH

Salty Celery Salad with Anchovy (page 134), Browned Butter Potato Salad (page 140).

Call it schnitzel, tonkatsu or Milanese: A crispy pork cutlet is one of life's greatest pleasures. Fatty pork chops coated in crunchy breadcrumbs and fried in your largest skillet need little more than a dusting of flaky salt and finishing squeeze of lemon to be one of the shiniest examples of 'something from nothing'. Because I live to simplify, this version is decidedly casual and requires little to no technique or fuss. The chops don't need to be pounded (although they can be if you're feeling moved) and I won't ask you to engage in a multistep dredging process (just press your seasoned pork into a pile of breadcrumbs – they'll stick, I promise). While boneless or bone-in pork chops both work, I prefer bone-in because I find nibbling on the crumb-coated bone to be extremely delightful, an experience not to be missed.

1. Season the pork with salt and pepper. Place the panko in a shallow baking dish or tray and season it with salt and pepper. Working one at a time, firmly press both sides of each pork chop into the seasoned panko until the chops are evenly and well coated.

2. Heat the oil in a large skillet over a medium-high heat; it should evenly coat the bottom of the skillet. If it doesn't, add a bit more oil. Place the pork chops in the skillet and cook, pressing lightly to make contact with the skillet, until deeply golden brown, like the colour of a well-baked croissant, 3–4 minutes.

3. Using tongs or a spatula, flip the pork and continue to cook until it's well browned on the other side, another 2–3 minutes. Transfer the pork to a plate, platter or cutting board lined with paper towels and season with salt.

4. Wipe out the skillet and return it to the stove over a medium-high heat. Add the butter, letting it sizzle, brown and foam. Add the capers and half of the radishes, seasoning them with salt and pepper. Toss a few times, just to wilt the radish greens, if they're still on, and to evenly coat the radishes with the browned butter and capers.

5. Divide the pork chops among plates and nestle in the butter-tossed radishes and capers, along with the remaining raw radishes. Sprinkle with a bit of flaky salt and serve with lemon wedges alongside for squeezing over.

CRUNCHY CHICKEN PARMESAN with BURST TOMATOES

SERVES 2

60 g (2 oz/1 cup) panko breadcrumbs
30 g (1 oz/½ cup) finely grated Parmesan cheese, plus more as needed
kosher salt and freshly ground black pepper
1 large egg
1 × 280–350 g (10–12 oz) boneless, skinless chicken breast
6 tablespoons olive oil, plus more as needed
2 garlic cloves, thinly sliced
350 g (12 oz) fresh tomatoes, halved if small, chopped if large
1 teaspoon sherry vinegar, red wine vinegar or white wine vinegar
flaky sea salt
1 handful basil or parsley, coarsely chopped or torn (optional)

NOTE

For anyone wondering why the cutlet on page 296 doesn't require egg but this one does, it's because chicken breast is so lean, it doesn't really give the breadcrumbs anything to stick to. The egg also gives a more 'breaded' texture.

DO AHEAD

The cutlets can be breaded (but not cooked) 2 days ahead, each separated with baking paper, wrapped and refrigerated, or frozen for up to 1 month (good advice if you are, in fact, planning on doing this for a crowd).

EAT WITH

A plate of buttered angel hair pasta and a big glass of Chianti like you're at Dan Tana's on a Friday night.

There is almost nothing I like more than eating a crunchy cutlet alone, frying one piece of breaded meat to a golden-brown crisp for just me, myself and I. Cutlets are quite annoying to cook more than one at a time, which is why this is my most honest answer to someone asking, 'What should I make if I'm cooking for one?' That said, I am generous, so this recipe – a cheeky homage to chicken Parm – serves two.

1. Combine the panko and Parmesan in a shallow baking dish or tray and season with salt and pepper; set aside.

2. Whisk the egg with 1 teaspoon water in a medium bowl (one with enough room to dunk a chicken breast into). Season with salt and pepper; set aside.

3. Slice the chicken breast in half from top to bottom into two thin pieces. Place each thin piece between a folded piece of baking paper or two sheets of cling film (plastic wrap). Using a meat pounder or small heavy skillet, pound each piece to 5 mm (¼ inch) thick. (Better to be thicker than thin here.)

4. Season the chicken with salt and pepper, then dip it into the egg mixture. Using your hands (or tongs), pick up the cutlet, letting any excess egg run off. Firmly press the cutlet into the breadcrumb mixture, covering it so that the chicken is well coated. Shake off any excess crumbs and set aside. Repeat with the remaining cutlet.

5. Heat 4 tablespoons of the olive oil in a large skillet over a medium-high heat. Working one at a time, place a chicken cutlet in the skillet and cook, pressing lightly to make contact with the skillet, until deeply golden brown, 3–4 minutes. Using tongs, flip the chicken and continue to cook until it's well browned on the other side, 2–3 minutes. Transfer to a plate and season with flaky salt. Repeat with the remaining cutlet.

6. Wipe out the skillet and return it to the stove over a medium-high heat. Add the remaining 2 tablespoons olive oil and the garlic. Cook, stirring occasionally, until the garlic starts to brown, 2–3 minutes. Add the tomatoes and season with salt and pepper. Cook, tossing occasionally, until the tomatoes burst, 3–5 minutes. Add the vinegar and season again with salt and pepper.

7. Spoon the tomatoes around and over the cutlets. Finish with a little flaky salt, some torn basil (if using) and another good dusting of Parmesan.

CRISPY FISH WITH DILL & FRIED CAPERS

SERVES 4

90 g (3¼ oz/1½ cups) panko breadcrumbs
20 g (¾ oz/½ cup) finely chopped dill, plus more as needed
kosher salt and freshly ground black pepper
1 large egg
4 fillets thin white fish, such as flounder, tilapia or basa
8 tablespoons olive oil, plus more as needed
8 garlic cloves, 7 thinly sliced, 1 finely grated
40 g (1½ oz/¼ cup) capers, drained
250 g (9 oz/1 cup) full-fat Greek yoghurt
10 g (½ oz/¼ cup) finely chopped parsley or chives
Aleppo pepper or gochugaru (optional)
2 lemons, quartered, for serving

EAT WITH
—
Vinegar-Braised Greens (page 106), cucumber salad (page 132).

If these remind you of fish fingers (fish sticks), well, yes. However, I have tried to make crispy fish in the oven (like a fish finger) and have been disappointed every time. Sadly, it's the pan-frying on the stovetop that will please you the most and make this worth your while. The skillet of hot oil keeps the breadcrumbs stuck to the fish, evenly browning and properly crisping without overcooking what's underneath. Anyway, the best part of this recipe is the dill in the breadcrumb mixture, which, coupled with the yoghurt sauce, invites a sort of Greek feel to the whole thing (if they had fish fingers in Greece).

1 In a shallow baking dish or bowl, combine the panko and finely chopped dill and season with salt and pepper. Set aside.

2 In a medium bowl, whisk the egg with 1 teaspoon of water. Season with salt and pepper and set aside.

3 Season the fish with salt and pepper on both sides, then dip into the egg mixture. Using your hands (or tongs), pick up the fish, letting any excess egg run off. Firmly press the fish into the panko mixture and cover it with crumbs, packing them on until the fish is well coated. Shake off any excess crumbs and set aside. Repeat with the remaining fish.

4 In a large skillet, heat 6 tablespoons of the olive oil over a medium-high heat. Working two at a time, place the fillets into the skillet and cook, pressing lightly to make contact with the skillet, until nicely golden brown, 3–4 minutes. Using tongs or a spatula, flip the fish and continue to cook until well browned on the other side, 2–3 minutes. Transfer to a paper towel-lined plate and repeat with the remaining fish.

5 Wipe out the skillet and return it to the stove over a medium-high heat. Add the remaining 2 tablespoons olive oil and add the sliced garlic and capers. Cook, stirring or swirling occasionally, until the garlic and capers are starting to brown and crisp, 5–8 minutes.

6 Meanwhile, combine the yoghurt and the finely grated garlic in a small bowl and season with salt and pepper.

7 To serve, spoon some garlicky yoghurt onto a plate, top with crispy fish, and spoon over the crispy garlic and capers. Top with parsley, Aleppo pepper, if you like, and more dill. Serve with the lemon wedges.

SLOW-ROASTED SALMON with PRESERVED LEMON & SESAME

SERVES 4

1 × 675–900 g (1½–2 lb) skin-on salmon fillet
kosher salt and freshly ground black pepper
150 ml (5 fl oz/⅔ cup) olive oil
1 preserved lemon, seeds removed, finely chopped
3 tablespoons fresh lemon juice, white wine vinegar or sherry vinegar, plus more to taste
1 garlic clove, finely grated
2 tablespoons toasted sesame oil
2 tablespoons white sesame seeds
1 large handful of coriander (cilantro) and/or dill, tender leaves and stems, coarsely chopped

NOTE
—
Alternatively, you can grill the whole piece of salmon, or cut it into four individual pieces and sear skin-side down until crispy and cooked through.

DO AHEAD
—
The preserved lemon dressing can be made 5 days ahead, stored sealed and refrigerated. For what it's worth, this salmon is excellent cold the next day, so even if you're only cooking for two, it's nice to make the full recipe.

EAT WITH
—
Toasted Rice Pilaf (page 191), a bowl of simple orzo or pearl couscous, Olive Oil-Fried Lentils with Harissa (page 180).

While the salmon in this recipe could easily be grilled or seared, I still believe it's the slow roast that is the finest way to cook a large piece of fish, especially salmon. That said, it's the salty, lemony, sesame-forward dressing that we are here for and, frankly, could be spooned on any number of things – fish, yes, but also chicken, rare steak, pork chops, a pile of roasted cauliflower. Truly, it might be the best reason to keep preserved lemons on hand. For more on them, see page 182.

1 Preheat the oven to 150°C/140°C/300°F.

2 Place the salmon in a large baking dish (if you don't have one that will accommodate the size of the salmon, cut it into two pieces) and season with salt and pepper. Pour half of the olive oil over everything and roast, without moving, until the salmon is mostly cooked through but still nicely medium-rare in the centre, 20–25 minutes (some will always prefer their salmon well done – if this is you, cook another 8–10 minutes or so).

3 Combine the preserved lemon, lemon juice and garlic in a small bowl. Season with salt and plenty of black pepper. Add the remaining olive oil and the sesame oil and season with salt, pepper and more lemon juice or vinegar if you want it. Set aside.

4 Toast the sesame seeds in a large (preferably non-stick) skillet over a medium-high heat, shaking the skillet frequently until the seeds are nicely toasted and smelling like popcorn, 3–4 minutes. Transfer to a small bowl and set aside.

5 Transfer the salmon to individual plates or one large platter (for family-style) and spoon half of the dressing over the salmon. Top with the toasted sesame seeds and coriander and serve the remaining dressing alongside for more . . . dressing.

A SKILLET OF PRAWNS IN ANCHOVY BUTTER (WITH A BAGUETTE)

SERVES 4

2 tablespoons olive oil

6–8 garlic cloves, thinly sliced

1 lemon, half thinly sliced, half for squeezing over

kosher salt and freshly ground black pepper

8–10 anchovy fillets (about one 55 g/2 oz tin)

6 tablespoons unsalted butter, softened

675–900 g (1½–2 lb) shell-on prawns (shrimp), preferably head-on

1 baguette, sliced, torn and/or toasted, for serving

EAT WITH
—
A bowl of barely cooked greens (page 129) or ears of grilled corn.
A Leafy, Herby Salad (page 148).
Very cold beer.

At the risk of using the words 'haunt' and 'shrimp' together in the same sentence, there is, incidentally, a shrimp dish that haunts me. It came from a little place in Lambertville, New Jersey, called Hamilton's Grill Room (now sadly closed), a perfectly lit restaurant with superlative food and exquisite, personal service. I can't tell you what the menu looked like other than that they always had a plate of large, head-on prawns smothered in anchovy butter on offer. If I had to guess, these were my first exposure to head-on prawns (and likely anchovy butter), and I fell deeply in love with everything about them: the way they looked and tasted and the effort it took to remove the shell and suck the heads, double-dipping into the salty, almost-browned butter that mingled with the juices from the bodies. A wonderful way to spend a Saturday night, eating a plate of head-on prawns remains one of my favourite pastimes, no matter the day of the week.

Anchovy butter will make anything feel special (a roast chicken, soft-boiled eggs, a skillet of sautéed broccoli, a salted cracker), so yes, of course you can make this with regular prawns (shell-on preferred but not required).

1 Heat the olive oil in a large skillet over a medium heat. Add the garlic and cook, stirring occasionally, until nicely golden (but not too dark), 2–3 minutes. Add the lemon slices and season with salt and pepper. Cook, stirring occasionally, until they've also started to turn a nice golden brown and frizzle at the edges, 3–4 minutes.

2 Add the anchovies, letting them melt into the oil (they will break down without much encouragement, but you can give them a stir with a wooden spoon or something). Once they've started to brown and break down, add the butter, letting it melt and bubble up, almost starting to brown. It'll look like a lot of sauce in the skillet, but the prawns need it to properly bathe!

3 Add the prawns, season with salt and pepper, and cook, tossing until the prawns are nicely coated in the lemon and garlic slices, have turned a deep, bright pink and are noticeably firmer, 4–6 minutes. Remove from the heat, squeeze the other lemon half over everything, and toss to combine. Transfer the prawns to a platter, serving with the baguette to sop up all the sauce.

SLOW-COOKED TUNA with WHITE BEANS & AIOLI

SERVES 4–6

675 g (1½ lb) tuna or swordfish, preferably 2.5–3 cm (1–1½ inches) thick
kosher salt and freshly ground black pepper
1 large red onion, unpeeled, sliced into wedges
4 garlic cloves, crushed
1 lemon, half thinly sliced, half for squeezing over
sprigs of thyme, marjoram, rosemary or oregano
2–3 dried chillies or 1 teaspoon chilli flakes (optional)
480 ml (16 fl oz/2 cups) olive oil, possibly more
1 × 400 g (14 oz) tin white beans or chickpeas (garbanzos), drained and rinsed
Aioli (page 45) or mayonnaise spruced up with some finely grated garlic (optional)
2 handfuls of parsley, tender leaves and stems

DO AHEAD
—
This tuna keeps about a week in the fridge, submerged in as much olive oil as you can spare. Use that oil for your next batch.

You can find a nice tin or jar of fancy tuna pretty much anywhere these days, the kind that's good for things like turning into salad (page 138) or snacking on next to chilli-crushed olives (page 38). But this tuna is more meant to be eaten like, well, a nice piece of fish: for dinner, with candles on the table and 'the cloth napkins'. A thick slab of raw tuna, slow-cooked in a pot of oil, is a thing of elegance: meaty and tender, with a rosy blush of pink in the centre. Sometimes I'll add a lemony aioli (made with the leftover oil); other times I'll turn it into something nicoise-y, served over lightly dressed lettuces, blanched green beans, boiled potatoes and crushed olives.

1 Season the fish with salt and pepper and place in a medium pot. Scatter the onion, garlic, lemon slices, herbs and chillies, if you like, into the pot. Add the oil – it should come up almost over the top of the tuna (depending on the thickness, you may need more oil).

2 Turn the heat to medium-low and keep an eye on it, making sure the oil doesn't get too hot too fast. Maintain a gentle, steady heat; you shouldn't see more than the occasional bubble. Cook until the fish is firm and has turned white and opaque, 12–20 minutes. For me, it's better to undercook this fish than overcook it. Remove from the heat and let the fish cool in the oil.

3 Transfer the tuna to a large serving platter or shallow bowl and spoon some of the cooking oil over it. Transfer all but 60 ml (2 fl oz/¼ cup) of the oil to a glass jar or other container for later use.

4 Add the beans to the oil in the pot and season with salt and pepper. Cook over a medium heat until they're sizzling at the edges, 10–15 minutes. Taste one! Cook longer if needed to taste as good as possible.

5 To serve, spoon a little aioli (if using) onto the bottom of a plate or bowl and top with those beans. Using a spoon or fork, break off large pieces of fish and place on top of the beans, followed by the parsley and a squeeze of lemon.

TOMATO-POACHED FISH with CRISPY CHILLI OIL

SERVES 4

60 ml (2 fl oz/¼ cup) olive oil, plus more for drizzling
4 garlic cloves, thinly sliced
1 small shallot, thinly sliced into rings
1 teaspoon chilli flakes
450 g (1 lb) small, sweet tomatoes, halved (or one 400g/14 oz tin whole, peeled tomatoes, drained, then crushed by hand)
kosher salt and freshly ground black pepper
1 teaspoon fish sauce
575 g (1¼ lb) skinless cod, basa or flounder, cut into 4 equal pieces
1 handful of coriander (cilantro), tender leaves and stems
limes or lemons, halved, for serving (optional)

EAT WITH
—
A bowl of perfectly cooked rice, orzo or pearl couscous. Warmed corn tortillas or toasted sourdough. Crunchy Green Beans Dressed in Chilli Oil (page 125). A very cold glass of white wine.

Poaching boneless, skinless, mild fish fillets in a flavourful, brothy sauce is not just my favourite way to cook fish but also the easiest method with the highest success rate among those who say 'I'm afraid to cook fish.' A 'flavourful, brothy sauce' can mean any number of things, but I find the best, most crowd-pleasing one is a bright, spicy, sweet tomato number. It starts with the beginnings of a very basic chilli oil (for something more complex, see page 127), fresh or tinned tomatoes and a very healthy splash of fish sauce for added depth. The broth should be bold enough to season the fish as it gently cooks but not so punchy that you can't drink it by the spoonful afterwards. While this could be turned into a sort of fish stew (cut your fish into bite-size pieces before cooking, and add prawns (shrimp), clams or mussels), I would take advantage of this moment to just enjoy some fish on its own in a lovely little sauce.

1 Heat the olive oil in a large skillet over a medium-high heat. Add the garlic and shallot and cook, swirling the skillet constantly, until they start to toast and turn light golden brown, 2 minutes or so. Add the chilli flakes and swirl to toast for a few seconds. Remove from the heat and transfer the crispy garlic and shallots and all but 1 tablespoon of the oil to a small bowl (the garlic and shallots can sit in the oil – that's fine).

2 Add the tomatoes to the skillet (if using tinned tomatoes, add them) and season with salt and pepper. Cook, tossing occasionally, until they burst and start to become saucy and jammy, 5–8 minutes. (Give tinned tomatoes closer to 10–12 minutes to take the tinned edge off.) Add the fish sauce and 360 ml (12 fl oz/1½ cups) water, swirling to release any of the bits stuck on the bottom of the skillet.

3 Cook until the sauce is slightly thickened but still nice and brothy, 3–5 minutes. Season with salt and pepper.

4 Season the fish with salt and pepper and gently lay the pieces in the brothy tomatoes. Cover the skillet (if your skillet has a lid, use that – if not, use a baking tray) and cook until the fish is opaque and just cooked through, 4–6 minutes (slightly longer for a thicker piece of fish, like halibut).

5 To serve, transfer the fish and brothy tomatoes to a large shallow bowl or divide among four bowls. Drizzle with more olive oil and the crispy shallots and garlic. Top with coriander and serve with limes for squeezing.

THANK YOU

Making a book is such a wild process, one of my greatest joys, and something that can only be pulled off with the help of many people.

In no particular order of importance, I want to thank the team at Clarkson Potter – every copy editor and production editor who looked at, read and proofed this book to make it read and look so gorgeous; every person on the marketing and publicity team who made sure this book got into as many hands as possible: Stephanie Huntwork, Jana Branson, Kate Tyler, Joey Lozada, Allison Renzulli, Joyce Wong, Terry Deal, Kim Tyner, Alex Noya and Darian Keels. Thanks, especially, to my editor, Francis Lam, whose great patience, kindness and understanding really came in handy when my baby arrived a month early. He knew then and there that the book would definitely *not* be turned in on time.

To Britt Cobb, who will go to the ends of the earth to make a beautiful book, thank you for your keen eye and most collaborative, open mind. Chris Bernabeo, who made the most of those rainy days (so many rainy days), thanks for making lemonade from lemons and always saying yes to all the ideas (and thank you for bringing Clay and Jimmy into our lives!). To Rebecca Bartoshesky, whose chic taste and elegant style made me look like I was constantly living the dream, thank you for embracing the chaos. To Rosie McGuinness, for your gorgeous illustrations that really brought this book to life. To Lauren Stanek, Jane Morgan and Alivia Bloch, thank you for being on set, cooking, schlepping, organising, keeping the jars full of water and our spirits high, and for picking up my slack when I was too tired or nauseous to be my best self.

Thank you to all the farmers in Delaware County who kept us in good produce and beautiful meats to photograph. To Dylan Hartung, for all your help with the shoot and keeping First Bloom running, well stocked and gorgeous through the whole thing.

To Narni Summerall, for keeping the wheels on, literally, emotionally and metaphorically through it all; I could not have done any of this without you.

To Kim, who was here in Charlie's early days to let me sleep so I could wake up and (try to) write.

To Julia Kramer, 'No one will know how much gratitude I have for you' (verbatim).

To my husband, Max, for literally everything, every day. Cooking for you is my greatest joy; thank you for being my biggest fan despite your aversion to olives and anchovies.

To my son, Charlie, thank you for being born. I can't wait to feed you something other than milk.

INDEX

A

Aioli for Everything, 44, 45
ANCHOVY(IES)
  Butter, 37
  Butter, A Skillet of Prawns with, 304, 305
  Caramelised Shallot Pasta, 212, 213
  Green Bagna Cauda, 20, 21
  & Parmesan, Artichoke Hearts with, 18, 19
  Salted Celery Salad with, 134, 135
  Steak Like Tartare, 292, 293
  Tiny White Beans in Green Bagna Cauda, 172, 173
  Weeknight Lamb Ragù with, 244, 245
  Wine-Braised Romano Beans with, 96, 97
APPLE(S)
  Celery, & Tahini, Beetroot with, 130, 131
  Fruit Salad with Chives & Sticky Walnuts, 136, 137
ARTICHOKE
  Dip, Herbed, 30
  Hearts with Anchovies & Parmesan, 18, 19
AUBERGINE
  Parm, A Little, 240–41, 243
  Pasta, Saucy Roasted, 202, 203

B

BACON
  Almost Cassoulet, 166–67, 168
  Carbonara for Two, 210, 211
  Very Classic Split Pea Soup, 62, 63
BAGNA CAUDA
  Green, 20, 21
  Green, Tiny White Beans in, 172, 173
BEAN(S)
  Almost Cassoulet, 166–67, 168
  Caramelised, with Tomato & Cabbage, 160, 161
  Chilli, 162, 163
  A Chilli, Because You Asked, 178, 179
  Crispy Baked, with Mushrooms & Parmesan, 174, 175
  Crunchy Green, Dressed in Chilli Oil, 124, 125
  & Greens, French Onion, 176, 177
  Long-Cooked Brothy Chickpeas with Shallot & Chilli, 158, 159
  Lupin, with Garlic & Parsley, 22, 23
  Olive Oil-Roasted Chicken & Chickpeas, 256, 257
  Spiced Chickpeas & Greens, 164, 165
  Stew, Dilly, with Cabbage & Frizzled Onions, 64, 65
  Tiny White, in Green Bagna Cauda, 172, 173
  Wax, Vinegar'd, with Dill & Cheddar, 108, 109
  White, & Aioli, Slow-Cooked Tuna with, 306, 307
  Wine-Braised Romano, with Anchovy, 96, 97
BEEF
  Bolognese with Fennel, 246–47, 249
  A Chilli, Because You Asked, 178, 179
  Goodbye Meatballs, 288–89, 290
  Spicy Braised Short Ribs with Garlic & Lemon, 278–79, 281
  Steak Like Tartare, 292, 293
  Tangy Braised Brisket with Shallots & Horseradish, 284–85, 286
BEETROOT
  with Celery, Apple & Tahini, 130, 131
  Cold Borscht, 86, 87
Bolognese with Fennel, 246–47, 249
Borscht, Cold, 86, 87
Broth, Chicken, The Long Way, 51
BUTTER
  Anchovy, 37
  Calabrian Chilli, 37
  Snail, 35, 36

C

CABBAGE
  & Frizzled Onions, Dilly Bean Stew with, 64, 65
  Olives, & Lemon, Braised Pork Stew with, 282, 283
  & Tomato, Caramelised Beans with, 160, 161
CAPERS
  Braised Chicken Piccata, 260, 261
  Browned Butter Potato Salad, 140, 141
  Crispy Schnitzel with Browned Butter Radishes, 296, 297
  & Fennel, Deeply Roasted, 94, 95
  Fried, & Dill, Crispy Fish with, 300, 301
  Fried, & Toasted Garlic, Savoury Tomatoes with, 121, 123
  Pasta Salad with Courgette, Lemon & Walnuts, 218, 219
  Steak Like Tartare, 292, 293
Carbonara for Two, 210, 211
Carrots, Butter Roasted Spiced, with Walnuts, 100, 101
Cassoulet, Almost, 166–67, 168
Cauliflower Pasta, Creamy, with Pecorino Breadcrumbs, 204, 205
CELERY
  Apple, & Tahini, Beetroot with, 130, 131
  Creamy Clam Chowder with, 84, 85
  Matzo Ball Soup, 77, 78
  Salad, Salted, with Anchovy, 134, 135
CHEESE
  Artichoke Hearts with Anchovies & Parmesan, 18, 19
  Baked (But Not Stuffed) Shells, 238, 239
  A Caesar for All Occasions, 150, 151
  Carbonara for Two, 210, 211
  Creamy Cauliflower Pasta with Pecorino Breadcrumbs, 204, 205
  Crispy Baked Beans with Mushrooms & Parmesan, 174, 175

CHEESE (cont'd)
  Crunchy Chicken Parmesan with Burst Tomatoes, 298, 299
  Goodbye Meatballs, 288–89, 290
  Lemon Pepper Pasta with Browned Butter, 198, 199
  A Little Aubergine Parm, 240–41, 243
  Spicy Pork Soup with Pasta & Parmesan, 80, 81
  Vinegar'd Wax Beans with Dill & Cheddar, 108, 109
CHICKEN
  Broth, The Long Way, 51
  & Chickpeas, Olive Oil-Roasted, 256, 257
  Crisp, Hot Roast, with Leeks, 262–63, 264
  Crushed-Olive, with Turmeric, 266, 267
  Noodle Salad with Spicy Lime Dressing, 224, 225
  Noodle Soup with Lots of Lemon, 52, 53
  Parmesan, Crunchy, with Burst Tomatoes, 298, 299
  Piccata, Braised, 260, 261
  Pot Pie (A Real Classic), 270–71, 272
  Saucy, Wine-Roasted, with Mushrooms, 268, 269
  Soup for Summer Colds, 56, 57
  Spicy Vinegar, over Tomatoes, 258, 259
CHICKPEA(S)
  & Chicken, Olive Oil-Roasted, 256, 257
  Long-Cooked Brothy, with Shallot & Chilli, 158, 159
  Spiced, & Greens, 164, 165
CHILLI(ES). See also Chilli Oil
  Calabrian, Butter, 37
  Calabrian, & Garlic, Barely Cooked Cime di rapa with, 128, 129
  Chilli Beans, 162, 163
  & Shallot, Long-Cooked Brothy Chickpeas with, 158, 159
  & Toasted Garlic, Winter Squash Pasta with, 208, 209
  Chilli, Because You Asked, 178, 179
CHILLI OIL
  Crispy, Tomato-Poached Fish with, 308, 309
  Crunchy Green Beans Dressed in, 124, 125
  Quick, 126, 127
CHIVES
  Herbed Artichoke Dip, 30
  Leafy, Herby Salad with Sherry Vinegar, 148
  Snail Butter, 35, 36
  & Sticky Walnuts, Fruit Salad with, 136, 137
  Walnut Pesto Pasta, 196, 197

CIME DI RAPA
  Barely Cooked, with Calabrian Chilli & Garlic, 128, 129
  Spicy Pork Soup with Pasta & Parmesan, 80, 811
CLAM(S)
  Chowder, Creamy, with Celery, 84, 85
  & Linguine with Spicy Breadcrumbs, 228–29, 230
CORIANDER
  Ginger & Greens Noodle Soup, 54, 55
  Leafy, Herby Salad with Sherry Vinegar, 148
  Olive Oil-Fried Lentils with Harissa & Herbs, 180, 181
  Pork Noodle Soup with Toasted Garlic & Greens, 66, 67
CORN
  Fresh, Buttered Polenta with, 188, 189
  Summer Vegetable Soup with Hominy & Lime, 68, 69
COURGETTE(S)
  Lemon, & Walnuts, Pasta Salad with, 218, 219
  Summer Vegetable Soup with Hominy & Lime, 68, 69
CUCUMBER(S)
  Cold Borscht, 86, 87
  & Fennel, Picnic Salad with, 132, 133

D

DATES
  Browned Butter, Forever-Roasted Squash with, 104, 105
  & Crushed Walnuts, Toasted Rice Pilaf with, 190, 191
DILL
  Browned Butter Potato Salad, 140, 141
  & Cheddar, Vinegar'd Wax Beans with, 108, 109
  Cold Borscht, 86, 87
  Dilly Bean Stew with Cabbage & Frizzled Onions, 64, 65
  & Fried Capers, Crispy Fish with, 300, 301
  Herbed Artichoke Dip, 30
  Potato Leek Soup with Dark Leafy Greens, 72, 73
DIPS
  Aioli for Everything, 44, 45
  Green Bagna Cauda, 20, 21

Herbed Artichoke, 30
Labneh with Caramelised Harissa, 28, 29
Lentil, with Toasted Garlic & Crispy Herbs, 26, 27
Dressing, An Excellent Mustard, 149

E

EGG(S)
  Carbonara for Two, 210, 211
  Jammy, Salad, 142, 143
  A Soft, & Rice, Kimchi-Tomato Soup with, 60, 61
  Spanish Tortilla & Friends, 40–41, 43

F

FENNEL
  Bolognese with, 246–47, 249
  & Capers, Deeply Roasted, 94, 95
  & Cucumbers, Picnic Salad with, 132, 133
  & Lentils, Buttered Tomato Soup with, 82, 83
FISH. See also Anchovy(ies)
  Crispy, with Dill & Fried Capers, 300, 301
  Slow-Cooked Tuna with White Beans & Aioli, 306, 307
  Slow-Roasted Salmon with Preserved Lemon & Sesame, 302, 303
  Tomato-Poached, with Crispy Chilli Oil, 308, 309
  Tuna Salad Salad, 138, 139
FRUIT. See also specific fruits
  Salad with Chives & Sticky Walnuts, 136, 137

G

GARLIC
  Aioli for Everything, 44, 45
  & Calabrian Chilli, Barely Cooked Cime di rapa with, 128, 129
  Green Bagna Cauda, 20, 21
  & Lemon, Spicy Braised Short Ribs with, 278–79, 281
  & Parsley, Lupin Beans with, 22, 23
  Potatoes, & Lemon, Long-Cooked, 98, 99

Shrimp Scampi, 226, 227
Snail Butter, 35, 36
Snail Butter Pasta (Snails Optional), 232, 233
Tiny White Beans in Green Bagna Cauda, 172, 173
Toasted, & Chilli, Winter Squash Pasta with, 208, 209
Toasted, & Crispy Herbs, Lentil Dip with, 26, 27
Toasted, & Fried Capers, Savory Tomatoes with, 121, 123
Toasted, & Greens, Pork Noodle Soup with, 66, 67
Ginger & Greens Noodle Soup, 54, 55
Grains. *See Spelt; Polenta; Rice*
Green Beans, Crunchy, Dressed in Chilli Oil, 124, 125

GREENS
  & Beans, French Onion, 176, 177
  A Caesar for All Occasions, 150, 151
  Chicken Soup for Summer Colds, 56, 57
  Dark Leafy, Potato Leek Soup with, 72, 73
  Fruit Salad with Chives & Sticky Walnuts, 136, 137
  & Ginger Noodle Soup, 54, 55
  Leafy, Herby Salad with Sherry Vinegar, 148
  & Spiced Chickpeas, 164, 165
  & Toasted Garlic, Pork Noodle Soup with, 66, 67
  Tuna Salad Salad, 138, 139
  Vinegar-Braised, 106, 107

H

HARISSA
  Caramelised, Labneh with, 28, 29
  & Herbs, Olive Oil-Fried Lentils with, 180, 181
HERBS. *See specific herbs*
Hominy & Lime, Summer Vegetable Soup with, 68, 69
Horseradish & Shallots, Tangy Braised Brisket with, 284–85, 286

K

Kimchi-Tomato Soup with Rice & a Soft Egg, 60, 61

L

Labneh with Caramelised Harissa, 28, 29
LAMB
  & Potatoes in White Wine, Overnight, 276, 277
  Ragù, Weeknight, with Anchovy, 244, 245
LEEK(S)
  Crisp, Hot Roast Chicken with, 262–63, 264
  Frizzled, Mushrooms, & Sour Cream, Spelt with, 184, 185
  Potato Soup with Dark Leafy Greens, 72, 73
LEMON
  Braised Chicken Piccata, 260, 261
  Cabbage, & Olives, Braised Pork Stew with, 282, 283
  Courgette, & Walnuts, Pasta Salad with, 218, 219
  & Garlic, Spicy Braised Short Ribs with, 278–79, 281
  Lots of, Chicken Noodle Soup with, 52, 53
  Pepper Pasta with Browned Butter, 198, 199
  Potatoes, & Garlic, Long-Cooked, 98, 99
  Preserved, Spelt & Pea Salad with, 186, 187
  Preserved, & Sesame, Slow-Roasted Salmon with, 302, 303
LENTIL(S)
  Dip with Toasted Garlic & Crispy Herbs, 26, 27
  & Fennel, Buttered Tomato Soup with, 82, 83
  Olive Oil-Fried, with Harissa & Herbs, 180, 181
  & Spiced Squash Soup with Fried Shallots, 74, 75

M

Matzo Ball Soup, 77, 78
Meatballs, Goodbye, 288–89, 290
MUSHROOM(S)
  Frizzled Leeks, & Sour Cream, Spelt with, 184, 185
  & Parmesan, Crispy Baked Beans with, 174, 175
  Saucy Wine-Roasted Chicken with, 268, 269
  & Sesame, Brothy Vinegar Noodles with, 220, 221
  Soup, Golden, with Orzo & a Pat of Butter, 88, 89
Mustard Dressing, An Excellent, 149

N

NOODLE(S)
  Brothy Vinegar, with Mushrooms & Sesame, 220, 221
  Chicken, Salad with Spicy Lime Dressing, 224, 225
  Chicken Soup with Lots of Lemon, 52, 53
  Pork Soup with Toasted Garlic & Greens, 66, 67
  Soup, Ginger & Greens, 54, 55

O

OIL, CHILLI
  Crispy, Tomato-Poached Fish with, 308, 309
  Crunchy Green Beans Dressed in, 124, 125
  Quick, 126, 127
OLIVE(S)
  Cabbage, & Lemon, Braised Pork Stew with, 282, 283
  Cracked Spiced, 38, 39
  Crushed-, Chicken with Turmeric, 266, 267
ONION(S)
  French, Beans & Greens, 176, 177
  Frizzled, & Cabbage, Dilly Bean Stew with, 64, 65
  & Pickled Peppers, Spicy Tomatoes with, 120, 122

P

PARSLEY
Ginger & Greens Noodle Soup, 54, 55
Green Bagna Cauda, 20, 21
Leafy, Herby Salad with Sherry Vinegar, 148
Olive Oil-Fried Lentils with Harissa & Herbs, 180, 181
Snail Butter, 35, 36
Snail Butter Pasta (Snails Optional), 232, 233
Walnut Pesto Pasta, 196, 197

PASTA. *See also Noodle(s)*
Baked (But Not Stuffed) Shells, 238, 239
Bolognese with Fennel, 246–47, 249
Caramelised Shallot, 212, 213
Carbonara for Two, 210, 211
Creamy Cauliflower, with Pecorino Breadcrumbs, 204, 205
Ginger & Greens Noodle Soup, 54, 55
Golden Mushroom Soup with Orzo & a Pat of Butter, 88, 89
Lemon Pepper, with Browned Butter, 198, 199
Linguine & Clams with Spicy Breadcrumbs, 228–29, 230
& Parmesan, Spicy Pork Soup with, 80, 81
Salad, Secret Ingredient, 216, 217
Salad with Courgette, Lemon & Walnuts, 218, 219
Saucy Roasted Aubergine, 202, 203
Shrimp Scampi, 226, 227
Snail Butter (Snails Optional), 232, 233
Spicy Vinegar Chicken over Tomatoes, 258, 259
Walnut Pesto, 196, 197
Weeknight Lamb Ragù with Anchovy, 244, 245
Winter Squash with Chilli & Toasted Garlic, 208, 209

PEA
& Spelt Salad with Preserved Lemon, 186, 187
Split, Soup, Very Classic, 62, 63

PEPPERS. *See also Chillie(s)*
Pickled, & Onions, Spicy Tomatoes with, 120, 122
Picnic Salad with Cucumbers & Fennel, 132, 133

Pesto, Walnut, Pasta, 196, 197
Polenta, Buttered, with Fresh Corn, 188, 189

PORK. *See also Bacon*
Almost Cassoulet, 166–67, 168
Bolognese with Fennel, 246–47, 249
Carbonara for Two, 210, 211
Crispy Schnitzel with Browned Butter Radishes, 296, 297
French Onion Beans & Greens, 176, 177
Goodbye Meatballs, 288–89, 290
Noodle Soup with Toasted Garlic & Greens, 66, 67
Soup, Spicy, with Pasta & Parmesan, 80, 81
Stew, Braised, with Cabbage, Olives & Lemon, 282, 283

POTATO(ES)
Browned Butter, Salad, 140, 141
Creamy Clam Chowder with Celery, 84, 85
Garlic, & Lemon, Long-Cooked, 98, 99
& Lamb in White Wine, Overnight, 276, 277
Leek Soup with Dark Leafy Greens, 72, 73
Spanish Tortilla & Friends, 40–41, 43
Pot Pie, Chicken (A Real Classic), 270–71, 272

PRAWN(S)
Scampi, 226, 227
A Skillet of, in Anchovy Butter (with a Baguette), 304, 305

R

Radishes, Browned Butter, Crispy Schnitzel with, 296, 297
Ragù, Weeknight Lamb, with Anchovy, 244, 245

RICE
& a Soft Egg, Kimchi-Tomato Soup with, 60, 61
Toasted, Pilaf with Crushed Walnuts & Dates, 190, 191

S

SALADS
Beetroot with Celery, Apple & Tahini, 130, 131
Browned Butter Potato, 140, 141
A Caesar for All Occasions, 150, 151

Celery, Salted, with Anchovy, 134, 135
Chicken Noodle, with Spicy Lime Dressing, 224, 225
Spelt & Pea, with Preserved Lemon, 186, 187
Fruit, with Chives & Sticky Walnuts, 136, 137
Jammy Egg, 142, 143
Leafy, Herby, with Sherry Vinegar, 148
Pasta, Secret Ingredient, 216, 217
Pasta, with Courgette, Lemon & Walnuts, 218, 219
Picnic, with Cucumbers & Fennel, 132, 133
Salty Sungolds with Sesame & Soy, 120, 122
Savoury Tomatoes with Toasted Garlic & Fried Capers, 121, 123
Spicy Tomatoes with Pickled Peppers & Onions, 120, 122
Tuna Salad, 138, 139
Salmon, Slow-Roasted, with Preserved Lemon & Sesame, 302, 303

SAUCES
Aioli for Everything, 44, 45
Tomato, A Very Good, 236, 237

SAUSAGES
Almost Cassoulet, 166–67, 168
Braised Pork Stew with Cabbage, Olives & Lemon, 282, 283

SESAME
& Mushrooms, Brothy Vinegar Noodles with, 220, 221
& Preserved Lemon, Slow-Roasted Salmon with, 302, 303
& Soy, Salty Sungolds with, 120, 122

SHALLOT(S)
& Chilli, Long-Cooked Brothy Chickpeas with, 158, 159
Fried, Spiced Squash & Lentil Soup with, 74, 75
& Horseradish, Tangy Braised Brisket with, 284–85, 286
Pasta, Caramelised, 212, 213

SHELLFISH. *See Clam(s); Prawn(s)*
Snail Butter Pasta (Snails Optional), 232, 233

SOUPS
Buttered Tomato, with Lentils & Fennel, 82, 83
Chicken, for Summer Colds, 56, 57
Chicken Noodle, with Lots of Lemon, 52, 53

Cold Borscht, 86, 87
Creamy Clam Chowder with Celery, 84, 85
Ginger & Greens Noodle, 54, 55
Golden Mushroom, with Orzo & a Pat of Butter, 88, 89
Kimchi-Tomato, with Rice & a Soft Egg, 60, 61
Matzo Ball, 77, 78
Pork Noodle, with Toasted Garlic & Greens, 66, 67
Potato Leek, with Dark Leafy Greens, 72, 73
Spiced Squash & Lentil, with Fried Shallots, 74, 75
Spicy Pork, with Pasta & Parmesan, 80, 81
Split Pea, Very Classic, 62, 63
Summer Vegetable, with Hominy & Lime, 68, 69

SOUR CREAM
Herbed Artichoke Dip, 30
Mushrooms, & Frizzled Leeks, Spelt with, 184, 185

SOY (SAUCE)
Brothy Vinegar Noodles with Mushrooms & Sesame, 220, 221
Crunchy Green Beans Dressed in Chilli Oil, 124, 125
& Sesame, Salty Sungolds with, 120, 122
Spanish Tortilla & Friends, 40–41, 43

SPELT
with Mushrooms, Frizzled Leeks & Sour Cream, 184, 185
& Pea Salad with Preserved Lemon, 186, 187
Split Pea Soup, Very Classic, 62, 63

SQUASH
Forever-Roasted, with Browned Butter Dates, 104, 105
Pasta Salad with Courgette, Lemon & Walnuts, 218, 219
Spiced, & Lentil Soup with Fried Shallots, 74, 75
Summer Vegetable Soup with Hominy & Lime, 68, 69
Winter, Pasta with Chilli & Toasted Garlic, 208, 209

STEWS
Braised Pork, with Cabbage, Olives & Lemon, 282, 283
A Chilli, Because You Asked, 178, 179
Dilly Bean, with Cabbage & Frizzled Onions, 64, 65

SWEDE
Very Classic Split Pea Soup, 62, 63

T

Tahini, Celery, & Apple, Beetroot with, 130, 131
Tartare, Steak Like, 292, 293

TOMATILLOS
Chicken Soup for Summer Colds, 56, 57

TOMATO(ES)
Baked (But Not Stuffed) Shells, 238, 239
Bolognese with Fennel, 246–47, 249
Burst, Crunchy Chicken Parmesan with, 298, 299
& Cabbage, Caramelised Beans with, 160, 161
Caramelised Shallot Pasta, 212, 213
A Chilli, Because You Asked, 178, 179
Goodbye Meatballs, 288–89, 290
Kimchi Soup with Rice & a Soft Egg, 60, 61
A Little Aubergine Parm, 240–41, 243
Oil-Roasted, Perfect, 113, 114–15
Poached Fish with Crispy Chilli Oil, 308, 309
Salty Sungolds with Sesame & Soy, 120, 122
Sauce, A Very Good, 236, 237
Saucy Roasted Aubergine Pasta, 202, 203
Savory, with Toasted Garlic & Fried Capers, 121, 123
Secret Ingredient Pasta Salad, 216, 217
Soup, Buttered, with Lentils & Fennel, 82, 83
Spicy, with Pickled Peppers & Onions, 120, 122
Spicy Vinegar Chicken over, 258, 259
Weeknight Lamb Ragù with Anchovy, 244, 245
Tortilla, Spanish, & Friends, 40–41, 43

TUNA
Salad Salad, 138, 139
Slow-Cooked, with White Beans & Aioli, 306, 307

V

VEGETABLE(S). *See also specific vegetables*
Summer, Soup with Hominy & Lime, 68, 69

VINEGAR
Braised Greens, 106, 107
Chicken, Spicy, over Tomatoes, 258, 259
Noodles, Brothy, with Mushrooms & Sesame, 220, 221
Vinegar'd Wax Beans with Dill & Cheddar, 108, 109

W

WALNUT(S)
Courgette, & Lemon, Pasta Salad with, 218, 219
Crushed, & Dates, Toasted Rice Pilaf with, 190, 191
Pesto Pasta, 196, 197
Spiced, Butter Roasted Carrots with, 100, 101
Sticky, & Chives, Fruit Salad with, 136, 137

Y

YOGHURT
Crispy Fish with Dill & Fried Capers, 300, 301
Spelt & Pea Salad with Preserved Lemon, 186, 187
Herbed Artichoke Dip, 30
Labneh with Caramelised Harissa, 28, 29
Spiced Chickpeas & Greens, 164, 165